9

KODANSHA
ENCYCLOPEDIA OF
JAPAN

Supplement

KODANSHA

Distributors
JAPAN: KODANSHA LTD., Tokyo.
OVERSEAS: KODANSHA INTERNATIONAL LTD., Tokyo.
　U.S.A., Mexico, Central America, and South America: KODANSHA INTERNATIONAL/USA LTD.
　　through HARPER & ROW, PUBLISHERS, INC., New York.
　Canada: FITZHENRY & WHITESIDE LTD., Ontario.
　U.K.: HARPER & ROW LTD., PUBLISHERS, London
　Continental Europe: HARPER & ROW, PUBLISHERS, Hilversum, The Netherlands
　Australia and New Zealand: HARPER & ROW (AUSTRALASIA) PTY. LTD., Artarmon, N.S.W.
　Asia: TOPPAN COMPANY (S) PTE. LTD., Singapore.

Published by Kodansha Ltd., 12-21, Otowa 2-chome, Bunkyo-ku, Tokyo 112 and Kodansha
International/USA Ltd., 10 East 53rd Street, New York, New York 10022.
Supplement, first edition, 1986.

LCC 83-80778
ISBN 0-87011-814-5 (Supplement)
ISBN 0-87011-620-7 (Set)
ISBN 4-06-144540-5 (0) (in Japan)

Library of Congress Cataloging in Publication Data
Main entry under title:

Kodansha encyclopedia of Japan.

　Includes index.
　1. Japan—Dictionaries and encyclopedias. I. Title:
Encyclopedia of Japan.
DS805.K633 1983　　　952′. 003′21　　　83-80778

Action Program for Improving Market Access

The name of a package of policies adopted by the Japanese government in July 1985 in response to demands from the United States and other nations that the Japanese domestic market be made more open to international trade. The policies called for access to the Japanese market to be improved by the relaxation of various regulations under the slogan, "Free as a rule and limited as an exception." The policies, to be implemented within three years, would reduce or abolish customs duties on 1,853 items, make changes in the nation's system for product standards and certification, simplify import procedures and government procurement procedures, liberalize and internationalize Japan's financial systems and capital markets, improve the area of services for foreign businesses in Japan (e.g., by allowing foreigners to be covered by NATIONAL HEALTH INSURANCE and by allowing foreign attorneys to practice in Japan), and promote the importation of goods. The package included such features as unilateral tariff reductions by Japan and foreign participation in the deliberative council on standards and certification.

NISHIKAWA Masao

advanced ceramics

A general term for exotic materials resulting from a sophisticated reaction-bonding calcination of chemically synthesized inorganic compounds. Also called high-performance ceramics and, in Japan, "fine ceramics." The term is used to refer to high-grade ceramics used for electronics and structural and medical materials as distinguished from traditional ceramic products such as cement, glass, pottery, and china. Thanks to Japan's long tradition of ceramics, the nation has achieved outstanding results in the field of advanced ceramics. Almina-ceramic, used for forming integrated circuit boards, is a good example of an advanced ceramic. Other examples are silicon carbide, silicon nitride, and partially stabilized zirconia. Since these advanced ceramics have excellent heat resistance, good impact resistance, and high strength, they are expected to lead to innovations in engineering technology. Also expected is the development of ceramic parts for automobile engines.

NISHIMATA Souhei

age of capital equipment

The age of capital equipment is sometimes used as a point of reference to indicate the degree of modernity of industrial technology. If equipment investments are continually sluggish, the age of capital stock increases. According to estimates made by the Ministry of International Trade and Industry, the average age of equipment in the United States in 1984 was less than that in Japan. Equipment used for manufacturing industries in Japan had an average age of 6.65 years in 1973, but after the oil crisis of that year, this figure increased. In 1980 the average age of capital equipment in Japan was 8.06 years; in 1984 it was 8.35 years. In the United States, however, the average age of capital equipment was 9.5 years in 1979, but only 8.2 years in 1984. Simple comparisons of the average age of capital equipment are dangerous because of differences in the method of estimation, industrial structure, and the composition of capital goods. Nevertheless, such figures are often used as one index of an economy's capacity for growth. ŌMORI Takashi

Age of Local Government

(Chihō no Jidai; literally, "The Age of the Local"). A slogan that was first used as the theme of a symposium on the issues of local government held in Yokohama in July 1978. In a speech that concluded the symposium, Nagasu Kazuji (b 1919), the governor of Kanagawa Prefecture, criticized the Japanese tendency toward centralization in politics, economics, and cultural affairs and insisted that "the local" had a unique meaning and value which should not be ignored. The slogan was afterwards taken up by local governments throughout Japan and used on occasions when they were about to implement independent policies.

One way of achieving the ideal behind this slogan would be to carry out administrative and financial reforms designed to move Japan as a whole in the direction of greater local autonomy and decentralization, giving more political authority and financial resources to local governments. As of late 1985, however, there was little movement in that direction. What progress was being made was either in demonstrating local creativity and inventiveness, as in the One Village, One Product Movement (Isson Ippin Undō) of Ōita Prefecture, or in the field of what is referred to in Japan as "cultural administration," one example being the efforts at preserving local historic cultural properties that were being carried out in many areas. In this sense, the slogan was still little more than a fundamental rallying cry addressing the question of the direction in which Japanese local governments should proceed in the future.

NAKAMURA Kiichi

aging population

One of the most important social issues faced by Japan during the first half of the 1980s was the problem of an aging population. Government, business, and ordinary citizens were hard pressed to find an appropriate response to this problem and the host of associated problems spawned by the emergence of an aging society.

A Growing Average Life Expectancy——The average life expectancy of the Japanese people had become one of the world's highest. According to a survey, by country, of such statistics as average life expectancy at birth and cause of death that was published by the World Health Organization (WHO) in December 1985, the average life expectancy for Japanese males was 74.8 years, the highest in the world, and that for Japanese females was 80.7 years, the world's second highest. The nation that ranked second to Japan in life expectancy for males was Switzerland, with 73.8 years, followed by Iceland, with 73.4 years, and Israel, with 73.1 years. The world's highest average life expectancy for females was Switzerland's 80.8 years. Japan was followed by Iceland, with 80.6 years, and the Netherlands and Norway, each of which had 79.8 years.

A year and a half before this WHO survey, in June 1984, Japan's Ministry of Health and Welfare had already announced that Japan now had the world's highest average life expectancy for both males and females and that the Japanese were thus the longest-lived people on earth. According to that announcement, the life expectancy of Japanese males was 74.2 years, and that of females was 79.8 years. The ministry's statement went on to give the following figures for changes in Japanese life expectancy. In the period 1891–98 it had been 42.8 years for males and 44.3 years for females. The figure for both sexes finally exceeded 50 years in 1947. It first exceeded 60 years in 1952 and 70 years in 1971. Before World War II the saying in Japan had been "the 50 years of human life." Now it was possible to say "the 80 years of human life."

The factors most commonly cited to explain this rapid rise in the life expectancy of the Japanese people were a succession of peaceful decades in which Japan was involved in no wars, an improved diet, and advances in medical treatment and drugs.

The Emergence of an Aging Society——The most obvious consequence of an extended life expectancy was an overall aging of the Japanese population. According to an estimate of the elderly population that was drawn up by the government's Management and Coordination Agency and dated 14 September 1985, the number of the elderly—those aged 65 years and over—was 12,455,000 people, an increase of 470,000 people over the year before. The proportion of people 65 and over in the total population had increased from 9.9 percent in 1984 to 10.3 percent in 1985, the first time this figure had reached the 10 percent range. The agency estimated that the proportion of people 65 or older within the total population would continue to rise, reaching the 15 percent level by the year 2000 and exceeding 20 percent by 2015.

In the same decade, the percentage of the total population of some Western nations represented by people 65 or over was higher than that of Japan. In Sweden it was 16.6 percent (1981 data), in the United Kingdom 14.9 percent (1983), and in the United States 11.6 percent (1982). However the Management and Coordination Agency estimated that by about 1995 the percentage of people aged 65 or over in Japan would become greater than that in the United States and that by the year 2010 it would reach the level of Sweden.

As an aging society emerged, it was already being accompanied by a variety of new problems, and both government and business were being driven to find an appropriate response to them.

Extension of the Mandatory Retirement Age——One such problem was the problem of guaranteeing employment for the elderly. After World War II it became an accepted idea in Japanese society that in private business corporations the mandatory age for retirement was 55 at the latest. Workers who reached the age of 55 had no choice but to retire. However, as the average life expectancy of employees continued to rise, there were more and more corporations that extended the mandatory retirement age. According to a survey of 7,000 companies in 9 types of business conducted by the Ministry of Labor in January 1985, 70 percent of the companies surveyed had a uniform retirement age. Of these, 55.4 percent had a retirement age of 60 or above. In the survey for the previous year, this figure had been 52.0 percent. In the 1985 survey, a particularly high percentage—72.8 percent—of the large corporations of 5,000 or more employees had retirement ages of 60 or above. This represented a sharp 15 percent increase over the corresponding figure for 1984.

The government, for its part, was planning to introduce legislation in the 1986 regular Diet that was intended to systematically establish the 60-year retirement age in Japanese society. This legislation would obligate corporations to make an effort to set a retirement age of 60 or above, and in the case of corporations that failed to implement such a policy in the absence of special circumstances, it would empower the government to take strong administrative action. The government could, for example, order the corporation in question to draw up a plan for raising its retirement age.

However, most of the corporations that had already raised their retirement age had compensated for the resulting increases in personnel costs and staff size by imposing salary reductions and other decreases in worker benefits on those workers who took advantage of the opportunity for delayed retirement. For the majority of white-collar workers, extension of the retirement age—at least as it was being carried out so far—was not necessarily a completely good thing.

Revised Welfare Benefits: Medical Expenses —— Another problem that accompanied the emergence of an aging population was the necessity of revising welfare programs aimed at the elderly. In principle, as the number of older people increases, there ought to be a corresponding increase in welfare programs designed to aid them. However, with Japan's national finances already burdened by an enormous debt, such increases could not be continued. On the contrary, welfare programs were already being subjected to annual cutbacks.

One example of this problem is health care expenses for the aged. The problem is symbolized by the complete collapse, after February 1983, of the system of free health care for people aged 70 or over that the government had been carrying out since 1973. According to government statistics, expenditures for health care for the elderly gradually increased along with the greater number of older people in the population, and by 1981 the proportion of health care expenditures for the elderly to health care costs for the whole population was about 20 percent. In anticipation of an aging society on an even larger scale, and for the purpose of slowing down increasing health-care costs for the aged, the government introduced into the Diet a bill that would require elderly patients to bear a part of the expenses for their own health care. This bill was passed in 1982 as the Law concerning Health and Medical Services for the Aged and took effect in February 1983. It required people aged 60 or over to pay ¥400 (US $1.70 at 1983 exchange rates) per month of the costs of their own medical care in the case of outpatient care and ¥300 (US $1.30) per day in the case of hospitalization. However, the government maintained that even this did not stop the rapid rise in expenditures for elderly health care, and it decided to introduce in the 1986 regular Diet an amendment to the Law concerning Health and Medical Services for the Aged, which would further increase the share of costs borne by individual older people for their own health care.

Changes to the Pension System —— Still another problem was that the increase in the number of older people was being accompanied by an increase in the number of pension recipients, resulting in heavier burdens on the nation's pension system. In order to assure long-term stability for the public pension system, the government launched an effort to raise the starting age for some types of pensions with starting ages lower than 65 and to straighten out other inequalities in the system. In April 1986, a new, more unified pension system was put into effect, based on revisions of the National Pension Law, the Employees' Pension Insurance Law, and the laws affecting the other types of public pensions (see PENSIONS). The new system combined the National Pension—for which all categories of citizen were eligible and which was now referred to as the Basic Pension—with the other types in a way designed to assure equal benefit levels for equal conditions, and it also corrected an earlier inequality by guaranteeing the pension rights of women. At the same time, 65 was made the uniform starting age for public pensions.

Whatever the effects of the new pension system, it was obvious

that an increasingly aging society would continue to bring with it newer and deeper problems for the Japanese people. Nevertheless, when the Ministry of Health and Welfare sponsored a contest for "the most appropriate name for the 50s and 60s as we enter the age of 'the 80 years of human life,'" the name chosen from among 300,000 entries was "the age of fruition." IWADARE Hiroshi

AIDS

The first confirmed case of AIDS in Japan was reported in May 1985. As of February 1986 the Ministry of Health and Welfare had officially confirmed the existence of 14 AIDS victims in Japan, 9 of whom had died. Of these victims, 7 had been hemophiliacs and 7 had been male homosexuals. The number of victims in Japan was less than one-thousandth of that in the United States; however, it was assumed that there were many others who had been infected by the virus but had remained latent carriers of the disease. Most of the hemophiliacs had been infected by blood preparations that had been imported from the United States for the treatment of hemophilia. The Ministry of Health and Welfare began pushing for development of blood preparations that could be guaranteed to be free of the AIDS virus. NISHIMATA Souhei

Akihabara

A district in the northeastern part of Chiyoda Ward, Tōkyō, specifically the area around the Akihabara Station of the Japanese National Railways. Akihabara is the home of over 200 discount and wholesale dealers in electric and electronic products (the number was 234 as of 1982). The area developed its character as a district of electric stores after World War II. Also located near Akihabara Station is the Kanda Market of the Tōkyō Central Wholesale Market, a market for fruit and vegetables that was established in 1928. The name of the district derives from that of the Akiba Shrine, which was founded there in 1870.

amorphous metals

In the mid-1980s, a dozen Japanese firms, including the Nippon Steel Corporation and Hitachi Metals, Ltd, were concentrating on the development of advanced amorphous metal alloys. Amorphous metals are formed when hot melted metals are instantly frozen. This process provides metals with high strength as well as excellent resistance against corrosion. The other notable feature of amorphous metals is their magnetic sensitivity, which is ideal for the high-performance magnetic heads used for video tape recorders and computer disk drives. An important goal of amorphous-metal development was to improve transformers by replacing their silicon steel cores with amorphous-metal cores, making the devices more energy-efficient. Loss of electricity in the process of transforming voltage was costing Japanese power industries up to ¥100 billion (US $420 million, based on 1985 exchange rates) each year, and it was anticipated that a considerable amount of energy could be conserved through the use of amorphous metals. NISHIMATA Souhei

anti-nuclear-weapons movement

In the first years of the 1980s, the anti-nuclear-weapons movement in Japan was in the midst of a period of newly heightened activity which had begun in 1977 and which reached a peak in 1982 before declining in 1983. The reason that 1977 represented a new starting point for the movement was that in this year the movement, which had long been divided into factions, was reunited. In 1977 the groups associated with the JAPAN SOCIALIST PARTY and the opposing groups associated with the JAPAN COMMUNIST PARTY, which up until that point had been engaging in disputes with each other, united to sponsor the World Conference against A- and H-Bombs. This realization of unity in the movement brought about the return to the movement of various independent citizens' groups, including youth groups, women's groups, and cooperative associations, which had been disassociating themselves from it. This gave the movement a new breadth, and it again began to take on the character of a movement that represented a cross-section of the population.

Such was the situation in Japan at the advent of the United Nations Second Special Session on Disarmament (SSD II) in 1982. The Japanese groups associated with the antinuclear movement saw this as an excellent opportunity to make the voices of Japanese people who were opposed to nuclear weapons heard by the

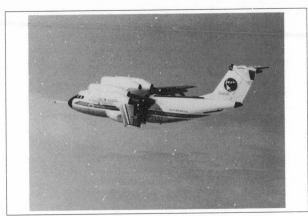

Asuka

The Asuka during a test flight in October 1985. Attached to the nose is a sensor used for research.

governments of the world's nations. They cooperated in forming the SSD II Japanese Liaison Committee for Nuclear and General Disarmament and launched a campaign to gather signatures for a petition addressed to the United Nations. The result was that the signatures of 28,860,000 people were gathered, and in June 1982 a delegation of 1,200 people carried them to United Nations Headquarters in New York and presented them to the secretary general while SSD II was in session. Similar but separate petition campaigns were conducted by other Japanese organizations. The KŌMEITŌ (Clean Government Party), the DEMOCRATIC SOCIALIST PARTY, the NEW LIBERAL CLUB, the UNITED SOCIAL DEMOCRATIC PARTY, and DŌMEI (the Japanese Confederation of Labor) collected a total of 16,180,000 signatures, and the UNION OF NEW RELIGIOUS ORGANIZATIONS OF JAPAN, led by the RISSHŌ KŌSEIKAI, collected a total of 36,740,000. These signatures too were delivered to the United Nations. There were also successive antinuclear appeals issued by literary figures, musicians, and other cultural leaders, which awakened a great public response.

After these events the SSD II Japanese Liaison Committee disbanded. In 1983 and after, factionalism reasserted itself, and the movement remained in a slump. _IWADARE Hiroshi_

Aoki Isao (1942–)

Professional golfer. Born in Chiba Prefecture. Aoki became a caddy at the Abiko Golf Club in the city of Abiko, Chiba Prefecture, after graduating from middle school, and he entered the ranks of pro golf in 1964. He won the Kantō Pro Golf Championship in 1971, the Japan Pro Golf Championship in 1973 and 1981, and the Japan Open Golf Championship in 1983. As of March 1986, he had won a total of 42 Japanese tournaments. As for overseas tournaments, he won the World Match Play in England in 1978, was runner-up to Jack Nicklaus in the US Open in 1980, and won both the Hawaii Open and European Open (England) in 1983. He acquired an American tour license beginning in 1981. Aoki is known particularly for his ability in approach shots.

Arakawa Shūsaku (1936–)

Western-style painter. A pioneer of conceptual art. Born in Aichi Prefecture. Arakawa attended Musashino Art School (now Musashino Art University) but withdrew before graduating. He exhibited works at the Yomiuri Salon des Artistes Indépendants between 1958 and 1961. From around 1960 he became active in the antiart movement, producing works consisting of masses of cement and fabric and organizing a group called the "Neo-DADA Organizers." In 1961 he moved to New York City, where he began producing diagram-like paintings in which diagrammatic lines and symbols and English words appear in precise detail on a milk-white background. His works in this style include his "Diagram" series and his "Mechanism of Meaning" series. In 1979 Arakawa published a book entitled _The Mechanism of Meaning_ with his wife, the poet Madeline H. Gins, as coauthor.

Asakusa

A district in the eastern part of Taitō Ward, Tōkyō, on the western shore of the river Sumidagawa. The district grew up during the Edo period (1600–1868) as a temple town (MONZEN MACHI) surrounding the temple Sensōji, which is popularly called the Asakusa Kannon from the name of the deity enshrined there. (The name Sensōji uses an alternate pronunciation of the Chinese characters used to write the name Asakusa.) Asakusa has been famous as a pleasure district since the Genroku era (1688–1704). It is made up of a number of thriving subdistricts, each of which has a distinctive character. Nakamise and Shin Nakamise are shopping arcades with many stores specializing in traditional Japanese goods (bags, shawls, and ornaments for use with the _kimono_, as well as dolls and traditional confections). Rokku is a popular entertainment district containing movie theaters and halls for RAKUGO (oral storytelling) and other traditional popular performing arts. Large crowds are attracted by the district's annual festivals. These are the SANJA FESTIVAL of the Asakusa Shrine in May, the HŌZUKI ICHI of the temple Sensōji in July, the TORI NO ICHI of the Ōtori Shrine in November, and the HAGOITA ICHI of the Asakusa Shrine in December.

Asari Keita (1933–)

Theatrical producer. Leader of the theatrical group Shiki. Born in Tōkyō. Asari attended Keiō University, but withdrew without graduating. He formed the Shiki group in 1953 while still at the university. Asari has been active in the staging of a repertory of modern French plays in the orthodox style known as the "new classicism." He began staging musicals in 1971 and was responsible for the Japanese productions of a succession of Broadway hits, including _Applause_, _Chorus Line_, and _Cats_. His production of _Madam Butterfly_ for La Scala in Milan in December 1985 was a great success.

Asuka

Japan's first short-takeoff-and-landing (STOL) aircraft. Specially designed to provide quiet takeoffs and landings, the _Asuka_ was developed by the National Aerospace Laboratory (NAL) of the Science and Technology Agency, and had its maiden flight on 28 October 1985. Its length and wingspan are both about 30 meters (98.4 ft), and its weight is roughly 39 metric tons (42.9 short tons). The fuselage, from a domestically made C-1 transport plane of the Air Self Defense Force, has four FJR 710–600S turbo fan engines mounted on its wings; these engines were developed by NAL in 1984. Employing an upper surface blowing (USB) system to direct the exhaust jet downward from the engines, the _Asuka_'s goal is a STOL performance with a 596-meter (1,955 ft) takeoff and a 512-meter (1,679 ft) landing. _NISHIMATA Souhei_

attainment-level grouping in the schools

The issue of whether classes in the nation's schools should be grouped within grades by attainment level (or scholastic ability) was the subject of considerable discussion in Japan in the mid-1980s. It was evident that, whereas the promotion rate in Japan's high schools was 94 percent (1985), there were disparities in scholastic ability. The Ministry of Education, in a revision of its SCHOOL COURSE GUIDELINES for high schools dated August 1978 (effective from 1982), stipulated that scholastic attainment levels should be taken into consideration in determining class groupings. By 1984 attainment-level grouping had been implemented in 43 percent of all daytime academic public high schools. In 74 percent of those schools, the new grouping had been implemented only in certain specified subjects. One reason for the low rate of implementation of the new policy was that there was much public opposition to it, based on fears that it would foster elitism in the public schools.

balance of payments in the 1980s

Japan's merchandise trade balance (see BALANCE OF PAYMENTS) increased tremendously in the first half of the 1980s, reaching US $45.6 billion in 1984. This increase is attributable to a sharp rise in Japan's exports (with the exception of 1982), primarily to the United States, and a simultaneous decrease in its imports due to lowered consumption of raw materials and energy per unit of production.

Until the late 1970s, Japanese payments abroad for freight and travel expenses caused the invisible trade deficit to increase annually; however, beginning in 1980 this deficit declined, and in 1984 it was US $7.7 billion. The investment-income balance also improved remarkably after 1980 as a result of expanded external net assets. Thus, the surplus in the current-balance account, which is principally the sum of the trade, transfer-payment, and invisible balances, increased steadily, except during the two oil crises, following the adoption of a floating exchange rate for the yen in 1973.

The massive current-balance surplus in 1977 and 1978 was checked by the rising value of the yen and the second oil crisis; from 1981 on, the surplus increased again, reaching US $37 billion in 1984. However, the large surplus was not followed by an appreciation of the yen because residents of Japan, where interest rates were relatively low, continued to invest in dollar assets in response to the high interest rates prevailing in the United States. In 1984 and 1985 the deficit of long-term capital accounts exceeded the current-balance surplus so that the overall balance of payments showed a US $14.5 billion deficit. Through this current-balance surplus and capital-account deficit, Japan's external assets grew to rival Great Britain's. In the meantime, the 1981 revision of the Foreign Exchange and Foreign Trade Control Law accelerated capital outflow from Japan by facilitating cash flow. NISHIKAWA Masao

biotechnology

When the Japanese boom in biotechnology began in 1981, the country relied on the cooperation of European and American ventures for information in fields such as genetic engineering and monoclonal antibodies. Since that time, Japanese expertise has developed greatly. A report entitled "Commercial Biotechnology," prepared in January 1984 by the United States Office of Technology Assessment, stated that Japan was a keen competitor in the industrialization of biotechnology and that it would soon be a strong rival of the United States.

One reason for Japan's rapid advancement is the country's long history in fermentation technology, which plays a significant role in biotechnology. Through fermentation industries, such as the manufacturing of *sake*, *miso*, soy sauce, and other products, Japan has accumulated a broad knowledge of fermentation and of breeding and stocking the microorganisms necessary for the fermentation process. This knowledge has enabled Japan to dominate the field of manufacturing amino acids by the fermentation method. Indeed, the amino acid market is virtually monopolized by Japanese firms.

In 1986, more than 200 Japanese companies in various fields such as pharmaceuticals, chemicals, food, and fiber electronics were engaged in biotechnological research and development. However, new business ventures like those in the United States that focus strictly on biotechnology had few counterparts in Japan, where research and development in areas such as medicine (both therapeutic and diagnostic), chemical products, foods, agricultural chemicals, livestock, bioelectronics, and research equipment tended to be carried out by existing enterprises using their own funds.

The Japanese government was also taking an interest in biotechnology. The Ministry of International Trade and Industry, the Ministry of Health and Welfare, the Ministry of Agriculture, Forestry, and Fisheries, the Science and Technology Agency, and the Ministry of Education were all playing major roles in research and development in biotechnology. The Environment Agency, the Ministry of Construction, and the Ministry of Labor had also shown an interest by appropriating funds for biotechnological development in their budgets. The estimated combined allocation for biotechnology for fiscal year 1986 was about ¥42 billion (US $17.6 million). The biotechnological boom was affecting local governments, too. Japan's 47 prefectures (including Tōkyō and Hokkaidō) were encouraging biotechnological research and development by offering research seminars and by cooperating with local industries.

bird sanctuaries

A number of bird sanctuaries have been established in Japan as a result of advocacy by the Wild Bird Society of Japan and other groups. It was felt that Japan's existing wildlife protection areas were little more than areas where hunting was prohibited and that there was a need for areas in which wildlife would be protected as an integral part of its natural environment. The first such area was established in 1981 on the shores of Lake Utonai near the city of Tomakomai in Hokkaidō as a result of independent efforts by the

Wild Bird Society of Japan. The second was the Fukushima City Kotori no Mori Sanctuary, which was established by the city of Fukushima in 1982. The movement to set aside similar bird sanctuaries throughout Japan continued to grow, and as of March 1986 there were six such sanctuaries.

bond dependency

The relative dependence on bonds of the Japanese government's General Account Budget is expressed as the ratio of the value of new national bonds issued to total revenue. The relative dependence on public borrowing in Japan was 39.6 percent in fiscal year 1979. Although the ratio decreased thereafter, it was still 22.2 percent in fiscal year 1985. The Japanese government's economic plan developed in 1983 called for the elimination of deficit-financing national bonds and the reduction of the budget's dependence on bonds. ŌMORI Takashi

brain death

In Japan, controversy still surrounds the definition of brain death, a concept that allows a person to be declared dead when the overall brain functions stop, even if the heart is still beating. Brain death has an important bearing on organ transplants, since brain dead patients are potential donors of hearts, lungs, livers, kidneys, and other organs necessary for the survival of the recipients. In 1985 a medical advisory committee on brain death presented Japan's Ministry of Health and Welfare with new guidelines for certifying a patient as brain dead. The guidelines include five necessary conditions that must be evident before a person can be diagnosed as brain dead. They are deep coma, disappearance of spontaneous respiration, fixation of pupils, disappearance of brain stem response, and a period of six hours after the first four conditions have been established, during which it is confirmed that there is no change in the patient's condition. With the passage of time, the concept of brain death is slowly gaining acceptance in Japan. NISHIMATA Souhei

bullying

(ijime). Bullying among schoolchildren became a serious social problem in Japan in the 1970s and 1980s. Bullying, or *ijime*, as it is called in Japanese, is a concept for which there is no clear definition. In a survey conducted by the Tōkyō Metropolitan Board of Education it is defined as "behavior directed against someone weaker than oneself; objectionable behavior in which physical or psychological attacks are carried out repeatedly, causing deep suffering to the victim." However, the judgment of whether or not a particular behavior constitutes bullying depends much on the subjective point of view of the people concerned. Bullying as a problem among Japanese schoolchildren began to increase in the 1970s, and it increased more and more, becoming an insidious problem, in the 1980s. The spread of bullying among schoolchildren was seen as one of the symptoms—along with school violence, refusal to attend school (known in Japan as "school allergy"), and various forms of misconduct—of a so-called blight that seemed to be affecting the Japanese educational system, and it was recognized as the most difficult of these problems to solve. Some Japanese felt that bullying had also existed as a problem in Japanese schools before World War II, while others felt that it was a new phenomenon to be found only among the most recent generation of children.

Bullying was the cause of nine suicides among students in Japanese middle schools in 1985. According to a survey by the Ministry of Education, in the period from April to October 1985 there were 155,066 reported bullying incidents, affecting 21,899 public schools ranging from elementary to high school—55.6 percent of the nation's public schools. The incidents were most numerous in large cities. In Tōkyō bullying incidents had occurred in 90 percent of the middle schools and in 70 percent of the elementary schools.

There was no clear explanation for this frequent occurrence of bullying. According to one of the theories most often advanced, urbanization had led to a decrease in the amount of open space for children to play in, and the common practice of sending children to special classes after regular school had cut down on the time left for play. As a result, children were being deprived of the opportunity to play together in groups and hence were being deprived of an outlet needed for healthy emotional development. According to the theory, it was this deprivation that led to the outbreaks of bullying.

YAMAGISHI Shunsuke

bungakukan (literary museums)

The term *bungakukan* first came into general use after the founding of the MUSEUM OF MODERN JAPANESE LITERATURE in 1967. The rest of this article will briefly describe some of Japan's other literary museums.

Akiyama Korekushon (Akiyama Collection). Located within the Nishinomiya Municipal Library in the city of Nishinomiya, Hyōgo Prefecture. Opened in 1953. A collection of some 1,300 first issues of magazines gathered by the city official Akiyama Shigeharu (1908–53). The magazines in the collection, which cover all fields, range from 1888 to 1951. A catalog of the collection was published in 1974.

Arishima Kinenkan (Arishima Museum). Located in the town of Niseko, Hokkaidō. Opened in 1978. Niseko is known as the place where the novelist ARISHIMA TAKEO (1878–1923) distributed his agricultural lands among the tenant farmers in 1922. The museum was opened to commemorate the 100th anniversary of Arishima's birth, when the Arishima Memorial Association donated to the town the materials contained in an earlier museum there. The exhibits in the museum include materials on Arishima himself (autograph manuscripts, letters, and paintings) as well as materials on the Arishima agricultural lands (the register of tenant farmers, the distribution declaration, etc).

Chikamatsu Kinenkan (Chikamatsu Museum). Located in the city of Amagasaki, Hyōgo Prefecture. Opened in 1975. The museum contains an exhibit of some 60 items once belonging to the KABUKI playwright CHIKAMATSU MONZAEMON (1653–1724), which had been stored in Chikamatsu's family temple and never before exhibited to the public. The museum also has a theater where plays by Chikamatsu are performed.

Chōfu Shiritsu Mushanokōji Saneatsu Kinenkan (Mushanokōji Memorial Hall). Opened in 1985. After the death of the writer and painter MUSHANOKŌJI SANEATSU (1885–1976), a collection of his books and manuscripts, as well as works of art painted or collected by him, was given to the City of Chōfu, where he had lived. The city built this museum to contain the collection.

Dazai Osamu Shiryōshitsu (Dazai Osamu Room). Located in the town of Kanagi, Aomori Prefecture, within the Kanagi Municipal Museum of History and Folklore. Opened in 1978. The collection includes autograph materials by the novelist DAZAI OSAMU (1909–48), who was born in Kanagi, letters, and first editions of his works.

Hagiwara Sakutarō Bunko (Hagiwara Sakutarō Library). Located in the city of Maebashi, Gumma Prefecture, where the poet HAGIWARA SAKUTARŌ (1886–1942) was born. The library, which opened in 1953, is in one of a number of rooms in the Maebashi Municipal Library devoted to collections on writers who were born in the city. The Hagiwara collection consists of 5,000 items, including manuscripts, books containing handwritten annotations by Hagiwara, and other related materials. There is also a Hagiwara Sakutarō Museum in the city's Shikishima Park. Part of the house where Hagiwara was born was moved there and restored, and it is used to exhibit reproductions of original materials belonging to the library. This museum opened in 1975.

Hokkaidō Bungakukan (Hokkaidō Literary Museum). Located in the city of Sapporo, Hokkaidō, within the Sapporo City Document Museum. Opened in 1979. Contains exhibits of materials concerning writers who were born in Hokkaidō, such as ITŌ SEI (1905–69), KOBAYASHI TAKIJI (1903–33), and SHIMAKI KENSAKU (1903–45), as well as writers whose names are associated with Hokkaidō, such as ISHIKAWA TAKUBOKU (1886–1912), KUNIKIDA DOPPO (1871–1908), and ARISHIMA TAKEO (1878–1923). There is a room dedicated to the

Hokkaidō-born novelist Funayama Kaoru (1914–81), which contains the Funayama Kaoru Library.

Ichiyō Kinenkan (Higuchi Ichiyō Museum). Located in the Ryūsen district (formerly Ryūsenji district) of Taitō Ward, Tōkyō, near the former home of the novelist HIGUCHI ICHIYŌ (1872–96). Opened in 1961. The collection contains manuscripts of Higuchi Ichiyō's works, including an early draft of her novelette *Takekurabe*, the stock ledger for the store she kept for a time, her letters to her mentor Nakarai Tōsui (1861–1926), portraits of Ichiyō, and her combs and hair ornaments.

Ishikawa Kindai Bungakukan (Ishikawa Museum of Modern Literature). Located in the city of Kanazawa, Ishikawa Prefecture. Opened in 1968. A collection of manuscripts and calligraphy by IZUMI KYŌKA (1873–1939), TOKUDA SHŪSEI (1871–1943), MUROO SAISEI (1889–1962), and other writers who were born in Ishikawa Prefecture or whose names are associated with the prefecture.

Ishikawa Takuboku Kinenkan (Ishikawa Takuboku Museum). Located in the village of Tamayama, Iwate Prefecture. Opened in 1970. The museum is situated in the Shibutami district of Tamayama, where the poet ISHIKAWA TAKUBOKU (1886–1912) was raised. Exhibits include manuscripts of his free-verse poems and his TANKA as well as materials from his years as an elementary school teacher in Shibutami. A new museum, built to mark the 100th anniversary of the poet's birth, was opened in May 1986.

Issa Kinenkan (Issa Museum). Located in the Kashiwabara district of the town of Shinano, Nagano Prefecture. Opened in 1960. The museum, which is situated near the grave of the HAIKU poet ISSA (also known as Kobayashi Issa; 1763–1827), contains a collection of his calligraphy and personal articles as well as research materials about the poet and his works. There is also a wooden statue of Issa.

Iyo Haikai Bunko (Iyo Haikai Library). Located in the city of Matsuyama, Ehime Prefecture. Opened in 1969. In 1966, in commemoration of the approaching 100th anniversary of the poet MASAOKA SHIKI's (1867–1902) birth, a library of materials on *haikai* poetry (see HAIKU) that had been started in 1943 was given by the Haikai Library Association to the Ehime Prefectural Library. This was opened to the public as the Iyo Haikai Library in 1969, Iyo being the ancient provincial name for the prefecture.

Izu Kindai Bungaku Hakubutsukan (Izu Museum of Modern Literature). Located in the town of Amagi Yugashima on the Izu Peninsula, Shizuoka Prefecture. Opened in 1980. The museum, which is part of a facility known as the Shōwa no Mori Kaikan, contains materials on the authors of modern Japanese literary works with settings on the Izu Peninsula. Included are exhibits on KAWABATA YASUNARI (1899–1972) and INOUE YASUSHI (b 1907).

Kamakura Bungakukan (Kamakura Museum of Literature). A municipal museum located in the Hase district of the city of Kamakura, Kanagawa Prefecture. Opened in 1985. A collection of autograph manuscripts, letters, and first editions of works by KAWABATA YASUNARI (1899–1972), SATOMI TON (1888–1983), KUME MASAO (1891–1952), TACHIHARA MASAAKI (1926–80), and other writers who lived in the city of Kamakura. The collection, which also includes personal articles owned by these writers, is housed in a villa built by the MAEDA FAMILY, a former *daimyō* family, in 1935.

Kanagawa Kindai Bungakukan (Kanagawa Museum of Modern Literature). Located in the Yamate district of Naka Ward, Yokohama. Opened in 1984. A collection of materials on writers who were either born in or lived in Yokohama as well as writers whose names are associated with the MEIJI ENLIGHTENMENT. The total number of books and other items is 200,000.

Kindai Bunko (Modern Library). Located in Setagaya Ward, Tōkyō. Opened in 1958. A special collection within the library of Shōwa Women's University devoted to modern Japanese writers and thinkers. The 60,000 volumes in the collection include biographies and other works on the 800 authors represented, as well as works by them. The magazine collection includes 3,500 titles. A collection devoted to the poets YOSANO TEKKAN (1873–1935) and YOSANO AKIKO (1878–1942) contains autograph manuscripts and letters as well as personal articles.

Kitahara Hakushū Seika (Kitahara Hakushū Birthplace). Located in the city of Yanagawa, Fukuoka Prefecture. Opened in 1969. The house where the poet KITAHARA HAKUSHŪ (1885–1942) was born dates from the middle of the 19th century. It was purchased, restored, and opened to the public by the city of Yanagawa with funds raised by a drive for that purpose. The restorations include the main house, the grain storehouse, and the well. The main house and grain storehouse contain exhibits of Kitahara's personal articles, calligraphy, and literary works.

Koizumi Yakumo Kinenkan (Lafcadio Hearn Memorial Museum). Located in the city of Matsue, Shimane Prefecture. Opened in 1933. A collection that includes autograph manuscripts and letters of Lafcadio HEARN (1850–1904), the early interpreter of Japan to the West, who is known in Japan by his Japanese name, Koizumi Yakumo. There is also a library of related books. The museum was opened in 1933 on land adjoining Hearn's former home in Matsue by the Yakumo Memorial Association and given to the city the following year. The building eventually deteriorated, and it was rebuilt and reopened in 1984.

Kumamoto Kindai Bungakukan (Kumamoto Museum of Modern Literature). Located in the city of Kumamoto, Kumamoto Prefecture. Opened in 1985. The museum, an annex to the Kumamoto Prefectural Library, contains exhibits on writers who were born in or residents of the Kumamoto area, including TOKUTOMI SOHŌ (1863–1957), TOKUTOMI ROKA (1868–1927), TOKUNAGA SUNAO (1899–1958), TAKAMURE ITSUE (1894–1964), Nakamura Teijo (b 1900), Ishimure Michiko (b 1927), and TANEDA SANTŌKA (1882–1940). The exhibits include books, calligraphy, letters, and manuscripts.

Mita Bungaku Raiburarī (Mita Literary Library). Located in the Mita district of Minato Ward, Tōkyō. Opened in 1966. A collection of published works, manuscripts, calligraphy, and other materials by writers whose names are associated with Keiō University. Housed within the Keiō University Library and established with funds donated by the novelist and playwright KUBOTA MANTARŌ (1889–1963), the collection includes materials on SATŌ HARUO (1892–1964), HORIGUCHI DAIGAKU (1892–1981), and others. There is also a collection of literary magazines, including *Mita bungaku*, *Yamamayu*, and *Seidō jidai*.

Miyazawa Kenji Kinenkan (Miyazawa Kenji Museum). Located in the city of Hanamaki, Iwate Prefecture. Opened in 1982 in anticipation of the 50th anniversary of the death of the poet MIYAZAWA KENJI (1896–1933). The few manuscripts and other autograph writings that survived the air raids on Hanamaki during World War II are arranged under seven headings: environment, religious beliefs, science, art, agriculture, synthesis, and research. The museum also has a collection of Miyazawa's photographs and personal articles.

Ōgai Kinen Hongō Toshokan (Hongō Library for Mori Ōgai). Located in the Sendagi district (formerly part of the Hongō district) of Bunkyō Ward, Tōkyō. Opened in 1962. Built on the site of Kanchōrō, the former home of the novelist and man of letters, MORI ŌGAI (1862–1922). The collection of some 5,000 items includes manuscripts of Ōgai's novels and translations, letters, diaries, and scholarly writings. The library publishes *Ōgai*, a magazine of Ōgai research, twice a year. Most of Ōgai's own personal library of 20,000 volumes is housed in the nearby Tōkyō University Library.

Osaragi Jirō Kinenkan (Osaragi Jirō Memorial Museum). Located in the Yamate district of Naka Ward, Yokohama. Opened in 1978. A collection containing the novelist OSARAGI JIRŌ's (1897–1973) manuscripts, notes, diaries, and letters, as well as his personal library of 30,000 volumes and a collection of 13,000 magazines. Of special interest is Osaragi's collection of materials relating to the Paris Commune (some 2,000 items) and his collection of French political cartoons, which numbers some 2,600 items.

Roka Kōshun'en The house where the author TOKUTOMI ROKA (1868–1927) lived during the last half of his life. Located in the Kasuya district of Setagaya Ward, Tōkyō. The house, along with the surrounding land, was given to the city of Tōkyō by Roka's wife Aiko in 1936. Kōshun'en was the name of the estate. Within the grounds is a museum where Roka's manuscripts, books, letters, and personal articles are displayed.

Saitō Mokichi Kinenkan (Saitō Mokichi Memorial Hall). Located in the city of Kaminoyama, Yamagata Prefecture, where the TANKA poet SAITŌ MOKICHI (1882–1953) was born. Opened in 1968. The museum's collection includes manuscripts of Saitō's *tanka* and other writings, his calligraphic scrolls, and his letters. There are also other materials pertaining to modern *tanka*, particularly the work of Saitō's best-known contemporaries.

Shiki Kinen Hakubutsukan (Shiki Memorial Museum). Located in the city of Matsuyama, Ehime Prefecture. Opened in 1981. Exhibits on the life and work of the poet MASAOKA SHIKI (1867–1902), including autograph materials, reproductions of autograph materials, charts, and other visual aids. There are also materials on the modern TANKA and HAIKU movements, of which Shiki was a leader, and on the Matsuyama locality.

Shōchiku Ōtani Toshokan (Shōchiku Ōtani Library). Located in the Tsukiji district of Chūō Ward, Tōkyō. Opened in 1958. Established to commemorate the awarding of the Order of Culture to Ōtani Takejirō (1877–1969), former president of Shōchiku Co, Ltd, the theatrical and motion picture enterprise. The collection includes theatrical and movie scripts, programs, still photographs, newspaper movie reviews, and theatrical woodblock prints.

Takamura Kinenkan (Takamura Museum). Located in the city of Hanamaki, Iwate Prefecture. Opened in 1967. The museum is situated in a grove of trees near the mountain hut where the poet and sculptor TAKAMURA KŌTARŌ (1883–1956) spent his last years. Among the items displayed in the museum is a prototype for Takamura Kōtarō's nude figures on the shore of Lake Towada, autograph manuscripts and letters, cutout pictures by his wife Chieko, his fountain pen, and his glasses.

Tōson Kinenkan (Tōson Memorial Hall). Located in the Magome district of the village of Yamaguchi, Nagano Prefecture. Opened in 1947. Magome is the birthplace of the novelist and poet SHIMAZAKI TŌSON (1872–1943). The museum contains a collection of Tōson's manuscripts, notes, letters, and books of poetry.

Yoshikawa Eiji Kinenkan (Yoshikawa Eiji Museum). Located in the City of Ōme, Tōkyō Prefecture. Opened in 1977. The house where the novelist YOSHIKAWA EIJI (1892–1962) lived from 1944 was made into a museum where the manuscripts of his best-known works, including *Miyamoto Musashi*, are exhibited, along with biographical materials, his personal library of some 20,000 volumes, and scrolls written or painted by him. Yoshikawa's study is preserved as he left it.

ASAI Kiyoshi

butō

Japanese avant-garde dance form. *Butō* is an original Japanese dance form that differs from both the traditional Japanese dance and such Western forms as the ballet or modern dance. The founder of *butō* is said to be Hijikata Tatsumi (1928–86), who developed a unique form that he called *ankoku butō* in the late 1950s, seeking his inspiration from bodily attitudes and gestures associated with Japanese folk practices. Another important early *butō* figure is Ōno

Butō

A scene from Sankaijuku's performance of *Kinkan shōnen* at the 1980 Nancy Festival in France. (*Kinkan shōnen*, known in English as *The Kumquat Seed*, describes a young boy's dream of the origins of life and death.)

Kazuo (b 1906). In the 1970s, Kasai Akira (b 1943) and Maro Akaji (b 1943) were particularly active. The latter, who founded a troupe called Dai Rakudakan in 1972, introduced a strong element of spectacle into the performances. *Butō*, which was regarded as having spiritual associations with the traditional Japanese dramatic and dance form NŌ, attracted much attention in America and Europe. In the 1980s the most active troupe was Sankaijuku, which was founded in 1975 by Amagatsu Ushio (b 1949), who had been a member of Dai Rakudakan. The performers of this troupe, their heads shaved, their bodies painted white, created a sensation with their performances in various countries around the world.

CAD/CAM

(computer-aided design and computer-aided manufacturing). Initially developed in the United States by the General Motors Corporation in the mid-1960s, CAD/CAM systems, which use computer and graphic display systems to design and manufacture products, were introduced in Japan in the late 1960s by the shipbuilding, semiconductor, and automobile industries. Computer-controlled design data are converted to a programmed numerical control tape that controls the automatic machine tools used to manufacture products. The development of three-dimensional color display systems remarkably improved the capability of CAD/CAM. The biggest users of three-dimensional CAD systems in Japan are automobile manufacturers such as the Toyota Motor Corporation, the Nissan Motor Co, Ltd, and the Honda Motor Co, Ltd. Nissan introduced a CAD/CAM system consisting of several large central computers (the IBM-3081 and the IBM-3090) with 420 graphic terminals (the IBM-3258 and the IBM-5080) for basic research, body design, component design, body manufacturing, and other functions. The growing use of CAD/CAM systems by many industries led to yearly increases in the production of cathode-ray-tube displays, Japanese sales of which totaled about ¥250 billion (US $1.052 billion) in 1984. *NISHIMATA Souhei*

cancer

In 1981, cancer became the foremost killer in Japan, claiming even more lives than cerebral apoplexy, which had previously been the most common cause of death in the country. Cancer was responsible for 176,206 deaths in 1983, or 23.8 percent of all the deaths in the nation that year. Gastric cancer claimed the most lives in both sexes in Japan, although it was declining due to medical advances, changes in eating habits, and more accessible and frequent health examinations, among other factors. The numbers of deaths due to lung, liver, and colon cancers, however were increasing. Fewer women were dying of uterine cancer, but deaths caused by breast cancer were increasing in number.

As of 1986, there was still no definitive method of preventing or curing all forms of cancer, so the most urgent task was to develop a means of detecting and treating the disease as early as possible.

According to the Law concerning Health and Medical Services for the Aged (effective 1983), each municipality was required to offer annual examinations for gastric and uterine cancer to persons 40 years of age or older. Some municipalities were also offering annual examinations for lung and breast cancer, and some offered the examinations to all people 30 years of age or older. The X-ray computerized-tomography scanner and ultrasonic diagnostic devices were obtaining excellent results in detecting cancer deep within the body. Good progress was also being made in cancer research through the application of laser beams, the development of nuclear magnetic resonance devices, and diagnostic studies using monoclonal antibodies, which recognize only cancerous cells.

A national "Comprehensive Ten-Year Strategy for Cancer Control," which gave priority to subjects such as oncogenes (cancer causing genes), was adopted in 1983. Invitations were being issued to foreign scholars in the field of cancer research to join the study, and the program was also promoting the education and employment of young cancer researchers. *NISHIMATA Souhei*

carbon fiber

The Japanese firms of Tōray Industries, Inc, and Tōhō Rayon Co, Ltd, were the world's leading manufacturers of carbon fiber in 1986. Carbon fiber is a typical reinforced fiber and is promoted as being "lighter than aluminum, stronger than iron." One type of carbon fiber results from the calcination of acrylic fiber in a closed nitrogen environment. Another is made from pitch derived from natural fossil fuels. The former is called polyacrylonitrile carbon fiber, while the latter is known as pitch carbon fiber. Tōray Industries and Tōhō Rayon are known as manufacturers of polyacrylonitrile carbon fiber. Two large Japanese manufacturers of pitch carbon fiber are Mitsubishi Chemical Industries, Ltd, and Teijin, Ltd. Carbon fiber, with its high strength and elasticity, has been widely used in aerospace and automobile manufacturing, as well as in other industries. Carbon fiber has also been used for the shafts of golf clubs and for fishing rods. *NISHIMATA Souhei*

Children's Castle

(Kodomo no Shiro). An all-round facility for children in Shibuya Ward, Tōkyō. Established in 1985. The building, which has thirteen stories above ground and four below ground, was planned and constructed by the Ministry of Health and Welfare in commemoration of the United Nations International Year of the Child (1979). Individual facilities include an arts and crafts studio, two music studios, a personal computer room, a computer playroom, an audiovisual library, a pool, an exercise room, and two theaters. The audiovisual library has over 2,000 videocassettes, which can be viewed at will. There is also a video classroom, where the children can learn to shoot and edit their own video tapes. The Children's Castle is particularly rich in computers and other scientific facilities. In the computer playroom, for example, game programs are displayed on a large screen, and these can be played from four touch panels simultaneously. There are also lodging facilities and a restaurant.

Chiyo no Fuji (1955–   )

SUMŌ wrestler. Fifty-eighth *yokozuna* (grand champion). Born in Hokkaidō. Real name Akimoto Mitsugu. A member of the Kokonoe Stable. He fought his first match in the fall tournament of 1970 and achieved *makuuchi* ("within the curtain") status in the fall tournament of 1975. After this he suffered a decline because of dislocations of the left shoulder which became chronic; however, he overcame these by means of muscle strengthening and was elevated to *ōzeki* (champion) by a victory in the first tournament of 1981. He became *yokozuna* by achieving a second victory in a tournament in Nagoya in July of the same year. With a height of 183 centimeters (6 ft) and a weight of 118 kilograms (260 lb), he is a comparative lightweight, but his quick style of wrestling has won him a large following and the nickname of "the wolf" (*urufu*). His favorite technique is a double left-handed grapple (*hidariyotsu*) followed by a belt throw (*uwatenage*).

citizens' general identity number

A proposed system under which the government would assign a personal code number to every citizen of Japan for the sake of centralized management of various types of information relating to the individual and greater efficiency in government administration. As of 1985, the various kinds of information that the government gathers with regard to the individual citizen were being collected and managed separately by different government organizations. Resident registration information, for example, was being handled by the local governments, social security information by the Ministry of Health and Welfare, and tax information by the Ministry of Finance. If it were possible to coordinate the computerization of these various types of information by means of a single card for each citizen, government business could be conducted more efficiently. The Administrative Management Agency, the Ministry of Finance, and other government agencies had been studying the possibility of such a system since 1967. The Ministry of Finance had shown particular interest in the proposed system for the purpose of tax collection and the identification of tax evaders. However, there was strong public opposition to the proposal on the grounds that compilation of a government file on every individual represented an invasion of privacy. In 1973, FUKUDA TAKEO (b 1905), who was then chief of the Administrative Management Agency, recommended that "a conclusion should be reached after a study of the trends of the times and the drift of the popular consensus," after which the specific plan was shelved. *NAKAMURA Kiichi*

coalition government plans

The LIBERAL DEMOCRATIC PARTY failed to win a majority in the December 1983 election for the House of Representatives and was only able to maintain conservative rule by forming a union within the Diet with the NEW LIBERAL CLUB—the Liberal Democratic Party–New Liberal Club National Union (Jiyū Minshutō–Shin Jiyū Kokumin Rengō). This development led to a series of active discussions, beginning in 1984, between the government and opposition parties concerning various plans for possible coalition governments. A number of political factors lay behind these discussions. One was the likelihood that the Liberal Democratic Party would again in the future be unable to maintain a majority. Another was the fact that the leading opposition party, the JAPAN SOCIALIST PARTY, had long shown a tendency towards decline, and it had lost much of the magnetism needed to unify the other opposition parties. On the other hand, the long existence of a multiparty system with the same party in power had given the opposition parties a consciousness of the comparative leadership of the Liberal Democratic Party as unshakable. This made a movement from the traditional conservative-progressive standoff toward coalition with at least a part of the Liberal Democratic Party conceivable. Another factor was a shift of the Japanese people toward more conservative sentiments, which was beginning to influence the socialist parties to disassociate themselves from progressive ideologies and choose more practical policies.

As of the end of 1985, there were active overtures from both the KŌMEITŌ (Clean Government Party) and the DEMOCRATIC SOCIALIST PARTY regarding a possible conservative–middle-of-the-road coalition with the Liberal Democratic Party. Both parties aimed at becoming part of the government in order to implement party policies and fulfill their political responsibilities to their supporters, thus widening their base of popular support. However, the government and opposition parties were still divided by disagreement over such issues as revision of the constitution, increased national defenses, and the establishment of ethical standards for politicians in the wake of the LOCKHEED SCANDAL, and there was no way of predicting whether or not they would be able to come to an agreement. In the meantime, the Liberal Democratic Party had succeeded in stabilizing conservative control of the government by means of its coalition with the New Liberal Club. With the July 1986 elections, in which the Liberal Democratic Party once again won a majority, the Liberal Democratic Party's need to maintain a coalition government was eliminated. *NAKAMURA Kiichi*

combined elections of 1980

On 22 June 1980, the 12th election for the House of Councillors and the 36th election for the House of Representatives were held simultaneously. Interest in the election for the House of Councillors, in which half the members are elected every three years, centered on whether or not the LIBERAL DEMOCRATIC PARTY would be able to maintain its independent majority. The Liberal Democratic Party

was left with 66 members who were not up for election, and, since the membership of the house is 252, they would have to win 60 of the 126 seats that were up for election in order to maintain their majority. At the same time, in order to defeat the Liberal Democratic Party, the opposition parties were engaging in a wholehearted policy of cooperation in elections for one-member districts—one party agreeing to support another party's candidate in one district in exchange for similar support for its own candidate in another district.

As interest in this election mounted, the JAPAN SOCIALIST PARTY introduced a vote of no confidence against the cabinet of Prime Minister ŌHIRA MASAYOSHI (1910–80) in the plenary session of the House of Representatives on 16 May. Because members of antimainstream factions of the Liberal Democratic Party had absented themselves from their seats in large numbers, the motion passed with a vote of 243 for, 187 against. Prime Minister Ōhira dissolved the House of Representatives on 19 May. The election for the House of Councillors, which had been scheduled for 29 June, was moved up a week earlier to 22 June, and the first simultaneous elections for both houses in Japanese history were held on that day.

One of the reasons the government and the Liberal Democratic Party chose double elections was that all political parties would be running candidates in all districts for the House of Representatives election, and this would have a dampening effect on the opposition parties' plans for cooperation in certain districts for the House of Councillors election. Another reason was that the campaigning of Liberal Democratic candidates in the House of Representatives election would work towards resuscitating the Liberal Democratic vote in the election for the House of Councillors.

The Liberal Democratic strategy was successful. Moreover, Prime Minister Ōhira's sudden death in the midst of the campaign and the resulting transformation of the election into a "battle of vindication" also worked to the Liberal Democratic Party's advantage. The result was an overwhelming victory for the Liberal Democratic Party in both houses, and the party was able to ride out a crisis which had promised the possibility of a reversal of conservative and progressive fortunes. The interest of voters in the election was high. The percentage of the electorate voting in the election for the House of Councillors was the highest since World War II, and that for the House of Representatives was the fourth highest. *NAKAMURA Kiichi*

combined elections of 1986

On 6 July 1986, the 14th regular election for the House of Councillors (upper house) and the 38th general election for the House of Representatives (lower house) were held simultaneously. The combined elections were called for by the ruling LIBERAL DEMOCRATIC PARTY (LDP) in an attempt to duplicate their victory in the first-ever combined elections on 22 June 1980. Though the opposition parties came out against the combined elections and criticized them as "elections of, by, and for the LDP" and "elections of, by, and for Prime Minister NAKASONE YASUHIRO (b 1918)," their resistance proved futile. The elections resulted in a record-breaking victory for the LDP, which won 304 of 512 seats in the House of Representatives. The JAPAN SOCIALIST PARTY (JSP), the leading opposition party, suffered a crushing defeat, losing 26 of its 111 seats. Chairman Ishibashi Masashi (b 1924) assumed responsibility for the defeat and announced his intention to resign.

The LDP, which had failed to win a majority in the 1983 general election and had hastily formed a coalition government to bolster its position, assumed, with its rousing 1986 victory, complete leadership in state affairs. More important still, the Nakasone government strengthened its hold, and Prime Minister Nakasone's term of office as party president, which was due to expire in late October 1986, was extended by one year. The opposition parties suffered to various degrees. The NEW LIBERAL CLUB led by KŌNO YŌHEI (b 1937), which had been organized in 1976 by dissatisfied LDP members, was disbanded in August 1986, the overwhelming LDP victory and the lack of party strength being the foremost reasons for its downfall. Most of its members rejoined the LDP. The JSP's executive committee resigned en masse and Doi Takako (b 1928) was elected to succeed Chairman Ishibashi, with the aim of revitalizing the party. Further, as a result of the combined elections—which also saw the crushing defeat of the DEMOCRATIC SOCIALIST PARTY, a slight decrease in the number of KŌMEITŌ Diet members, and the status quo of the JAPAN COMMUNIST PARTY barely sustained—the opposition parties were compelled to rebuild their party strength and face a severe "time of winter." *KUNIMASA Takeshige*

commercial technology

In the first half of the 1980s, technological research and development in such fields as communications, new materials, semiconductors, and biotechnology, and the application of the new technologies to manufactured products continued to have a significant commercial value throughout the world, and Japanese firms were among the leaders in developing the new commercial fields.

New digital communications networks using computers and optical-fiber cables were being put into place throughout Japan, and information networks for use by businesses (referred to as value added networks in Japan) became available. The privatization of the Nippon Telegraph and Telephone Public Corporation, which occurred on 1 April 1985, in effect deregulated the use of communications circuits by private business and thus opened the way for private information and communications services. A number of private firms were also expressing an interest in using satellite technology for communications and broadcasting systems.

Research was also being conducted in the development and use of new materials such as shape-memory alloys (microcrystalline metals that change their shape when heated but return to their original form when cooled) and hydrogen-storage alloys (which absorb hydrogen as they cool or when they are put under pressure and expel it when the conditions are reversed). Practical applications were being found for the former in room-heating apparatus and for the latter in air conditioning and exhaust-heat recovery systems. Another new material that was being developed was gallium arsenide crystalline, which had important applications in the manufacture of semiconductors.

The Japanese semiconductor industry itself continued to make great progress in the 1980s. During 1984 and 1985, the market price of semiconductors dropped sharply, with the price of 64K dynamic RAMs going down to one-sixteenth and that of 256K dynamic RAMs dropping to one-tenth of their former prices, respectively. By the spring of 1986 the semiconductor market seemed to have bottomed out. Meanwhile, the lower prices encouraged the broad use of large-scale integrated circuits (LSIs) in various fields, which in turn led semiconductor manufacturers into a race to develop more highly integrated products for the newly expanded market. Some manufacturers were developing 1M and 4M dynamic RAMs, and one of them had already begun shipping 1M dynamic RAMs in the spring of 1986. The tempo of semiconductor integration was expected to continue increasing, and it was obvious that wafer-stepper technology would have to be revolutionized in order to keep up with this trend in the industry.

Large enterprises in such key industries as steel, shipbuilding, and chemicals were seeking to take advantage of the new developments and to develop their own new technologies. Some companies had already achieved rewarding results by applying advanced technology, especially in the field of electronics, to their traditional operations. For example, in 1975 Mitsubishi Heavy Industries, Ltd (MHI), whose major products are ships, aircraft, and power plants, used 110 tons of steel to achieve an output of ¥100 million (US $337,000). However, in 1985 the company achieved the same output using only 40 tons of steel. The startling difference resulted from a structural change from a conventional heavy industry providing customers with products assembled with steel as the raw material to a sophisticated industry producing complex integrated hardware and software necessary for modern manufacturing systems. During the same ten years MHI reduced its manpower by one-third, cutting the number of employees from 80,700 to 52,200. Similar tendencies could be seen in many other major industrial firms in Japan.

Biotechnology was also finding commercial applications in the early 1980s so that a report prepared in January 1984 by the United States Office of Technology Assessment recognized Japan as a formidable competitor in the industrialization of biotechnology. Effective methods of diagnosing and treating cancer were being sold to more than 500 hospitals in Japan, and progress in this field was expected to continue. In all, more than 200 Japanese companies in industries such as pharmaceuticals, food, chemicals, and fiber electronics were engaged in biotechnological research and development by 1986.

The Japanese government had long promoted technological development as part of an effort to establish an economy based on advanced technology. Top priority, however, had been given to applied, improved, and commercial technologies, with basic research being neglected, thus creating a great imbalance. The government recognized this imbalance, and in January 1985 the Science and Technology Agency published a fact-finding survey entitled "The Level of Japan's Science and Technology" in an effort to clarify the points at issue. The survey rated 83 technological areas in Japan in comparison with their American counterparts on a scale of 1 to 5. Japan was given the highest score of 5 in none of the areas, and in only 14 was it given a score of 4, topping the score of 3 for the same areas in the United States. In Japan, 30 of the areas received scores of 2 or below. To overcome such weaknesses in research and technological development, many Japanese corporations were beginning to emphasize basic research, and there was a strong movement to establish research institutes for the purpose of basic research in each of the major areas of technology. In the years remaining before the beginning of the 21st century, still further changes were expected in attitudes toward technological development in Japan.

UCHIHASHI Katsuto

compact discs

The compact disc (CD) for the recording of digitally encoded audio signals was jointly developed by the SONY CORPORATION and N. V. Philips, a major Dutch electronics firm, at the end of the 1970s. A standard 12 centimeter (4.7 in) compact disc has a three-mile-long spiral track of microscopic bumps on its bottom surface instead of ordinary record grooves. As the disc spins at a rate of up to 500 rpm, a readout laser beam is focused on a tiny point on the spiral track, and the flat mirrorlike surfaces between the bumps reflect the laser beam back to the photodetectors. These detectors convert the light into electronic signals, which a computer then translates into sound.

The compact disc has revolutionized the field of home audio equipment, and by 1986 dozens of firms were perfecting more elaborate laser-disc systems. Of the 4.133 million compact disc players that were manufactured in Japan in 1985, 3.054 million were exported to Europe and the United States. In 1985 the number of compact disc titles available in Japan was 4,546. Compact discs can also be used as read-only-memories in computer systems to store reference materials such as encyclopedias or dictionaries. In this application, a single disc can store up to 600 million bytes, or characters.

NISHIMATA Souhei

computer graphics

Japanese manufacturers of cathode-ray-tube displays for use in computer graphics (visual images drafted and processed by computers) achieved sales of ¥250 billion (US $1.052 billion) in 1984. Computer graphics play an important role in computer-aided design (CAD), industrial engineering, management information, scientific simulation, technical models, art for television commercials and movies, and many other fields. With the development of high-resolution color graphic displays and three-dimensional graphic displays, applications of computer graphics were becoming even wider in the 1980s. *NISHIMATA Souhei*

crash of Japan Airlines Flight 123

The crash and burning of a Japan Airlines Boeing 747 SR jumbo jet in mountains near the village of Ueno, Gumma Prefecture, at approximately 7 PM on 12 August 1985. Of the 524 people aboard the plane, 4 miraculously survived. The other 520 perished. This was the worst aviation disaster in Japanese history and the worst in the world involving a single airplane. The jet was Japan Airlines Flight 123 bound for Ōsaka from Tōkyō's Haneda Airport. It took off from Haneda at 6:12 PM, and at about 6:30, when it was over the Izu Peninsula, its flight suddenly became unstable, and it gradually veered to the right off its flight path and began to wander on a giant clockwise circular course, which ended with its crash on Osutakayama, a mountain in Gumma Prefecture. At the end of 1985, the Aircraft Accident Investigation Commission of the Ministry of Transport was still investigating the cause of the crash. However, in December the US National Transportation Safety Board issued a statement judging that maintenance of the cabin bulkheads had been inadequate, that there had been a rupture of a pressure bulkhead, that this had led to a rupture of the vertical stabilizer, leading in turn to a rupture of hydraulic lines within the tail, and that this rupture mechanism had made the plane uncontrollable and led to the crash. The crash cast doubt on the safety of jumbo jets, which up to that point had been thought to be among the safest of airplanes.   IWADARE Hiroshi

culture centers

These English words are used in Japan as a general term for commercially operated adult-education centers that offer courses on a wide variety of subjects for a fee. Many such centers, which are open both days and evenings, are operated by newspaper companies, department stores, and broadcasting companies. Culture centers offer an extremely rich variety of courses, including such subjects as languages, art, traditional Japanese accomplishments (tea ceremony, flower arrangement, calligraphy, etc), sports, musical instruments, personal computers, and word processing. The Asahi Culture Centers, the largest chain of such centers in the Tōkyō metropolitan area, are operated by the newspaper *Asahi shimbun*. The Shinjuku center, the largest of Asahi's three centers in the Tōkyō metropolitan area, offers 1,250 classes in 530 subjects (counting different levels of the same subject), and the total number of students at this center is around 50,000. Culture centers first became extremely popular in the late 1970s. Almost 80 percent of their students are women, an overwhelming number of them being in their forties. These centers play an important role in Japan in providing an opportunity for "lifelong education."

defense in the 1980s

These years saw military exchanges between the United States and China, a rapprochement between China and the Soviet Union, and some progress in talks between North and South on the Korean peninsula. The first US-Soviet summit conference in 6 years also brought some degree of relaxation of tensions between East and West. However, the basic structure of the military confrontation remained unchanged.

Military Conditions Surrounding Japan—— The buildup of Soviet military forces both in quality and quantity that had begun in the mid-1960s continued on into the 1980s, and at the end of 1985 from one-fourth to one-third of the combined strength of all forces was deployed in the Far East. In addition, there were thought to be over 135 of the INF (Intermediate Range Nuclear Force) SS 20 missiles that had begun being deployed at the end of the 1970s and approximately 85 medium-range Backfire bombers, and land forces in the Japanese Northern Territories (under Soviet occupation but claimed by Japan; see TERRITORY OF JAPAN) were thought to have been raised to the division level. Other conspicuous developments included the establishment of a theater headquarters near Lake Baikal, the posting of the carrier *Novorossijsk* on the heels of the *Minsk*, the deployment of approximately 30,000 special forces in Ussurisk, land exercises by marines near Haiphong in the Socialist Republic of Vietnam, the use of Cam-ranh Bay, the maintenance of the harbor at Petropavlovsk-Kamchatski, deployment of the newest large-scale nuclear submarines in the Sea of Okhotsk, and the first maneuvers of carrier forces in the central Pacific. All of these developments were seen as symptomatic of the growing Soviet emphasis on the Far East in recent years. In the meantime, although the United States, under the Reagan administration, had begun to emphasize military preparedness, its overall military strength in the Far East had remained at the same diminished levels since the 1970s. And the Soviet Union, which had already outstripped the United States in terms of quantity of strategic nuclear forces, was in the process of closing the gap in terms of quality also.

Japanese-American Relations—— As a means of dealing with the growth of Soviet military might and America's own retreat from power, from the mid-1970s, and particularly after the Afghanistan incident, the United States government began to make stronger demands on its allies for a cooperative strengthening of defenses. Japan was included in these demands. At the same time, in the 1980s, a number of resolutions containing demands aimed at Japan were introduced in the US Congress, and congressional hearings were held on the "Japan problem." At the beginning, the chief American concerns addressed to Japan had included such things as increased air defense and antisubmarine capabilities, maintaining US military bases in Japan, an increase in the Japanese share of the expense of American forces stationed there, and cooperation in

military technology. Gradually, however, the emphasis shifted to defense of sea lanes of communications (SLOC), the blockading, in time of emergency, of the Sōya Strait, the Tsugaru Strait, and the Tsushima Strait, abolition of the limit on Japan's defense expenditures to one percent of its gross national product (GNP) followed by an increase in defense spending, a review of Japan's Outline of the National Defense Program, an increase in the sustained defense capacity of Japan's SELF DEFENSE FORCES, and a clarification of the latter's military role. More immediate concerns that were turning out to be problems included provision of a training base to replace Atsugi for night landing practice (NLP) by carrier-based planes, construction of housing at Zushi for families of American military personnel, and the question of whether or not Japan would participate in the Reagan administration's Strategic Defense Initiatives (SDI). As of early 1986, the attitude of the American government, dictated by confidence in the administration of Prime Minister NAKASONE YASUHIRO (b 1918), lay in the direction of watching and waiting for signs of reliable effort from the Japanese. At the same time, the Americans took such measures as the stationing of special forces in Okinawa, equipping its 7th Fleet with Tomahawk cruise missiles, and the stationing of F-16 fighters at its base at Misawa. Existing agreements and joint exercises between Japan and the United States were expanded by the participation of Japan's Maritime Self Defense Forces in RIMPAC (the Rim of the Pacific Exercises) beginning in 1980, the initiation of joint exercises between the Ground Self Defense Force and American forces, the conclusion of an agreement for Japanese defense technological assistance to the United States, the signing of a joint operations plan involving the Self Defense Forces and US forces, and the conduct of a joint study on sea-lane defense. Relations between the two countries had become closer than ever.

Developments within Japan—— In December 1981, the Peace Problem Study Council, a private consultative group formed by Prime Minister Nakasone, issued a report calling for the abolition of the one-percent limit on defense spending and advocated reliance on civilian control and public opinion as a brake on excess spending by the military. The report also said that the Outline of the National Defense Program should be reviewed and that work should begin on a new defense plan. Following this, the National Security Inquiry Committee of the ruling Liberal Democratic Party issued a report containing the same proposals. In the meantime, important changes were taking place in the policies of the opposition parties. In December 1981 the Kōmeitō adopted a policy of recognizing the Self Defense Forces as constitutional as long as their equipment and duties were limited to the preservation of Japan's own territory. It further recognized that under present circumstances the United States–Japan Security Treaty was also unavoidable. In February 1984 the Japan Socialist Party incorporated into its campaign principles the statement that the Self Defense Forces were unconstitutional but that they existed legally. In its April 1984 outline of priority policies, the Democratic Socialist Party was not opposed to exceeding the one-percent limit if it could not be avoided. It also declared that the Outline of the National Defense Program should be reviewed. According to public opinion surveys conducted in the 1980s, the Self Defense Forces were accepted by a majority— more than 80 percent—of the Japanese people. The United States–Japan security system, too, had the support of 70 percent of the people. A large majority of the people were of the opinion that defense expenditures should be held within the limit of one percent of the GNP.   FUKUSHIMA Yasuto

deregulation of the Japanese financial and capital market

When President Ronald Reagan visited Japan in November 1983, an agreement was reached between the president and Prime Minister NAKASONE YASUHIRO (b 1918) to establish a Japan–United States Ad Hoc Group on the Yen-Dollar Exchange Rate and the Financial and Capital Market Issues, with the minister of finance of Japan and the secretary of the treasury of the United States as co-chairmen.

In May 1984 the group submitted its report. By September 1986, a number of measures had been implemented in line with the recommendations in the report, which played a key role in promoting the liberalization of the Japanese financial market. The main steps taken toward liberalization include the following.

Liberalization of interest rates. The minimum unit of the existing certificate of deposit (CD; with market interest rate) was reduced to ¥100 million (US $420,000) in April 1985. The money market certificate (MMC), the interest rate of which is linked to that of CDs, was introduced in March 1986, and its minimum unit was reduced to ¥30 million (US $200,000) as of September 1986. Ceilings on the interest rates of large-unit time deposits were removed beginning in October 1985, and the minimum unit was reduced to ¥300 million (US $2 million) in September 1986. A yen-denominated banker's acceptance (BA) market was established in October 1985.

Opening of the Japanese market. The limit on the maximum amount of foreign currency that could be converted into yen by foreign or Japanese banks was abolished, effective June 1984. The trading of Japanese national bonds by non-Japanese banks was allowed from October 1984. Foreign banks were granted permission to participate in trust banking activities as of June 1985. Select foreign securities firms were given memberships on the Tōkyō Stock Exchange in December 1985.

Removal of restrictions on the Euromarket. The issuance of Euroyen bonds and CDs by nonresidents was liberalized in December 1984. Euroyen lending by nonresidents was liberalized as of April 1985. The imposition of a withholding tax on interest earnings by nonresident bearers of Euroyen bonds was discontinued from April 1985.

Steps continued to be taken to liberalize the market. Developments expected in the near future included the reduction of the minimum denomination units on ceiling-free deposits, the liberalization of small unit deposits, and, toward the end of 1986, the establishment of the Tōkyō offshore market.   TANAKA Tsutomu

dioxin pollution

Dioxin, an organochloric compound that is developed as a byproduct in the manufacture of agricultural chemicals, is highly carcinogenic and can cause birth defects. Its dangers first became widely known from its use as one of the ingredients in 245T, a defoliant employed by the American military in the Vietnam War under the code name of Agent Orange. This herbicide was formerly used in Japan as an agricultural weed killer, but its use was halted in 1971. However, in November 1983, a university researcher discovered that ash from a garbage incinerator in Ehime Prefecture contained dioxin. It was thought that the dioxin had been produced in the burning of plastic articles made from vinyl chloride and other organochloric resins, which are used in great quantities in everyday life. A different form of dioxin is contained in some herbicides used as weedkillers in paddy fields, and there were reports that these were also dangerous. The Ministry of Health and Welfare established a committee of specialists to study the problem of dioxin pollution, and safety guidelines were announced in May 1984. However, the problem of how to prevent the production of dioxin by garbage incinerators remained unsolved.

disbanding of the New Liberal Club

On 15 August 1986, members of the NEW LIBERAL CLUB (NLC), a conservative political party led by KŌNO YŌHEI (b 1937), decided at a party caucus to disband the party and return to the ruling LIBERAL DEMOCRATIC PARTY (LDP), from which it had split ten years earlier in June 1976. The immediate cause of the NLC's breakup was the LDP's decisive victory in the combined elections for the upper and lower houses that had been held on 6 July. Especially decisive had been the LDP's victory in the House of Representatives, where it had won an unprecedented 304 seats, thus assuring itself of an extremely stable majority. The NLC, on the other hand, had been able to retain only 6 seats in the House of Representatives. In 1983, when the LDP had failed to win a majority in elections following the first trial of former Prime Minister TANAKA KAKUEI (b 1918) in connection with the LOCKHEED SCANDAL, the NLC had joined the larger party in forming a coalition cabinet led by NAKASONE YASUHIRO (b 1918), the leader of the LDP. However, the LDP's victory in the July 1986 elections meant the end of the coalition. The NLC had thus lost its ability, as part of the coalition, to cast the deciding vote in important decisions and could no longer exercise its function as a check on the LDP administration. This and the fact that there seemed little likelihood of enlarging the party's constituency in the future had led the leadership of the NLC to decide on its dissolution.

discipline of Japanese history 1980-1986

There were many new developments in the field of Japanese historical research during the first half of the 1980s. A gradual move was underway to develop a new view of Japanese history and to reevalu-

ate some of the results of existing studies that were based on Marxist or other historical theory. What follows is a summary, by period, of some of the more important new research.

Archaeology—— Examination of the excavations at the Babadan-A site in Miyagi Prefecture (excavated 1984) resulted in estimates dating its cultural phase as approximately 150,000 years before the present. This estimate placed the site in the early paleolithic period, a development that was certain to lead to major revisions in the views of those scholars who denied the existence of that period or who placed the origin of the Japanese people at about 100,000 years before the present. Pottery older than the linear-relief *(ryūsemmon)* pottery that had been said to be the oldest type of JŌMON POTTERY was discovered in Nagasaki Prefecture (where a pottery with a pebbled surface known as *tōryūmon* was found in excavations in 1972–82) and Kanagawa Prefecture (where an undecorated pottery was found in excavations in 1979). However, there were differing estimates as to the period to which these types of pottery belonged.

Ancient History (to 1185)—— Emphasis in the research for the ancient period was on such documentary materials as the *mokkan* (wooden tablets) that were excavated in 1985 in a palace site in Asuka, Nara Prefecture, and the inscriptions revealed in 1983 by X-ray studies done on the so-called Nukatabe no Omi sword (a sword that had been unearthed in 1915 in Shimane Prefecture). These discoveries were leading to a critical reexamination of such traditional historical materials as the *Kojiki* (Record of Ancient Matters) and *Nihon shoki* (Chronicle of Japan). Much progress was made in the excavation of the earlier Naniwa Palace site in Ōsaka Prefecture (see NANIWAKYŌ), and it was now thought that this was the site of the Nagara no Toyosaki Palace, which was constructed shortly after the TAIKA REFORM of 645. It was hard to believe that the political administration that built this large-scale and imposing palace could have been formed without the political changes associated with the Taika Reforms, and there would now be fewer adherents to the theory that those reforms were a fiction.

Since the late 1970s growing numbers of scholars were coming to believe that the inscriptions on two iron swords, one of which was excavated from the INARIYAMA TOMB in Saitama Prefecture and the other from the ETA FUNAYAMA TOMB in Kumamoto Prefecture, both identify the makers of the swords as servants of Waka Takeru, another name for the late 5th century Emperor Yūryaku. These inscriptions from such widely separated sites were thus being taken as proof that this emperor had achieved control over almost all of the country.

New excavations of historical materials for the ancient period were also having a stimulating effect on research in local history. Particularly important was the discovery, in a number of locations, of so-called lacquered-paper documents (fragmentary documents thought to have been preserved because the discarded paper had been used to cover lacquer containers and had thus become soaked with lacquer). These discoveries include the tax records found at the Kanoko C site in Ibaraki Prefecture in 1979–81, the requests for payment of tribute and other documents found at the Tagajō site in Miyagi Prefecture in 1970–77, and the documents found at the Akitajō site in Akita Prefecture in 1977–83 and the Isawajō site in Iwate Prefecture in 1976–86. All of these materials threw new light on the actual structure of local financial administration in ancient times, and they were the subject of much discussion among scholars.

Medieval History (1185-1568)—— One of the issues being debated in the field of medieval history was the character of the state during the latter part of the HEIAN PERIOD (794–1185). At the center of the debate was a new theory that described the period from the beginning of the 10th century to the establishment of the KAMAKURA SHOGUNATE (1192–1333) as the period of the "imperial state system" *(ōchō kokka taisei)*. According to this theory, the imperial-state period falls into two subperiods, with the decade of the 1140s as the dividing line. During the first subperiod, an individual form of rule based on the *ritsuryō* system became untenable and was replaced by a system of indirect rule through provincial governors *(kokushi)*. The provincial governors were required to make tribute payments to the state; otherwise the rule of the provinces under them was left entirely to them. During the second subperiod there was a change to direct rule by the state. It became the practice for the state to send official representatives directly for the purpose of cadastral surveys *(kenden)*. The state then gradually began to levy taxes uniformly in all areas of the country, without special treatment for the *shōen* (private estates), and in other ways became directly involved in the local administrations of the provincial governors. Such were the general outlines of the theory. There were many differences of opinion regarding the validity of the imperial-state concept and the question of whether or not the state described possessed a feudal character. Another new theory that attracted much attention was the "*kemmon system*" theory, a reference to the fact that during the KAMAKURA PERIOD (1185–1333) the shogunate did not have complete control of the nation and that the functions of the state were divided among the "three powers" (*sankemmon*) of the court nobles (*kuge*), the temples and shrines (*jisha*), and the shogunate (*bakufu*). As these reexaminations of the state system were being carried out, some scholars also turned their attention to the nonagricultural classes of the common people. The land tax (*nengu*) was collected not only in rice but also in iron and other manufactured products. People who were engaged in the manufacture and distribution of such nonagricultural products were put in a special class called *kugonin*. As *kugonin* they were given the right to pass freely through the barrier stations of the various provinces. The fact that *kugonin* were under the control of the Kurōdo-dokoro (Bureau of Archivists) of the imperial court means that artisans were directly under the emperor. Such facts demand a reexamination of the role of the emperor in the hierarchical society of the medieval period and of the nature of political administration by the shogunate. However, the relationship between the military class (*bushi*) and the artisans (*shokunin*), including the fact that some *gokenin* (housemen of the shogunate) were also *kugonin* and the fact that some *kugonin* were given *kyūden* (salary land), would have to be included in any future debate on this issue.

Early Modern History (1568–1868)——The most important development in the scholarship on the early modern period was the beginning of a reexamination of the existing theory of the *bakuhan* system. What was being advocated was a reexamination of the role played by the shogunate in the social order—not just a diagrammatic view of a social system in which the shogunate and the *han* united in suppressing the people by means of a system of classes. According to the new view, the shogunate placed *kuni bugyō* (provincial commissioners) in all provinces in which the entire province was not under the direct control of one *daimyō*. Through the *kuni bugyō* the shogunate collected provincial levies (*kuniyaku*) and maintained separate control of the artisans as distinct from the peasants. (What the *han* in these provinces controlled was the warrior class and the peasants.) According to this theory, the hierarchical society represented by the phrases *heinō bunri* (separation of warriors from peasants) and *shi-nō-kō-shō* (warrior-farmer-artisan-merchant) was an imposed order that resulted from the labor tax that the shogunate collected through the *kuni bugyō*. The social hierarchy other than the position of the peasants was something that was created and supported by the power of the shogunate, and it was valued highly by the shogunate as a means of ensuring the unity of the state. However, this view was being criticized by some as vastly exaggerating the role of the shogunate in the formation of society. The critics pointed out that local self-government by village communities had been deeply entrenched since the SENGOKU PERIOD (1467–1568) and that the *bakuhan* system was erected on top of a system of village rights and customs such as *iriaiken* (the right to enter communal property) and the village contract system of tax payment and was not something that was organized according to the ideas of those in control. Several of the basic concepts of the theory had not been sufficiently thought out, and the future directions taken by this line of research would be watched closely.

Modern History (1868 to present)——In the field of modern history there was no single issue that engaged the attention of all scholars in the field. However, a number of scholars were attempting to go beyond the traditional debate over whether the MEIJI RESTORATION represented absolutism or a bourgeois revolution to a more concrete, empirical examination of the restoration itself, in terms of both the domestic factors and the international turning points that affected it. There was a debate over whether the restoration represented a revolutionary national struggle for independence in the face of outside pressure or a reactionary suppression of a popular struggle because of outside pressure. Individual research was also being done on such topics as the FREEDOM AND PEOPLE'S RIGHTS MOVEMENT, TAISHŌ DEMOCRACY, and the process by which the militarist government of World War II came into power. There were also new forms of research vigorously being developed that combined such diverse fields as the history of women, the history of daily life, and social history. *MATSUO Hikaru*

displaced Japanese war orphans in China

At the end of World War II a number of orphan Japanese children, ranging from infancy to the age of ten, were left behind in China, particularly Northeast China—then known as Manchuria. At the end of the war, large numbers of Japanese were living in Manchuria as a result of Japan's victory in the Russo-Japanese War of 1904–1905 and its subsequent takeover of Manchuria and invasion of China in the 1930s. By the last years of the war, they numbered around 270,000. When Soviet forces entered Manchuria on 8 August 1945, the Japanese began an evacuation to Japan, but many of them died along the way from starvation, exhaustion, or illness. Some of those children who miraculously survived these conditions were left behind, far from their nearest relatives, to be brought up by Chinese foster parents. After normalization of diplomatic relations between Japan and China in 1972, many of these Japanese orphans began to search for their families in Japan. In 1981 the Japanese government began a program of inviting the orphans to visit Japan and carry on their search there. As of March 1986, 842 people had visited Japan for the purpose, and 348 of them had established their identities as a result of the visit. The total number of orphans who had asked the Japanese government for aid in establishing their identity was 2,135. Of these the total number who had succeeded in establishing their identities was 941. This number includes the 348 who had visited Japan, the remainder having used correspondence or other means. There were 272 people who had returned to live in Japan. *IWADARE Hiroshi*

Doi Takako (1928–)

Politician. Born in Hyōgo Prefecture, Doi graduated from Dōshisha University, where she taught constitutional law as a lecturer. In 1969, she won a seat in the House of Representatives, running as the JAPAN SOCIALIST PARTY candidate from Hyōgo Prefecture. Within the party, she was active as a specialist in social, international, and defense issues. From 1983, she served as vice-chairperson under Ishibashi Masashi (b 1924), and in September 1986 she became the tenth chairperson of the party. She is the first female party chairperson in the history of modern Japanese politics.
KUNIMASA Takeshige

Domon Ken (1909–)

Photographer. Noted for his advocacy of social criticism in photography and an extremely influential figure in Japanese photography after World War II. Born in Yamagata Prefecture, Domon attended Nihon University but withdrew before graduating. In 1933 he began studying photography under Miyauchi Kōtarō. From 1935 to 1939 he worked as a member of Nihon Kōbō, a group of photographers led by Natori Yōnosuke (1910–62). After World War II Domon became a free-lancer. His best-known collections include *Hiroshima* (1958), *Chikuhō no kodomotachi* (1960, Children of Chikuhō), and *Koji junrei* (5 vols, 1963–75, A Pilgrimage to Old Temples). In 1983 the Domon Ken Museum of Photography was opened in his home town of Sakata in Yamagata Prefecture. It contains over 70,000 of his photographs. His collected works were published in 13 volumes from 1983 to 1985.

economic friction with other nations

Japan experienced increased "economic friction" with its international trading partners during the periods of 1969–72, 1976–78, and 1981 and thereafter. The nation's balance of payments was largely current surplus, while that of its trading partners was mainly current deficit. The economic friction of the 1980s differed from that of the earlier periods in several ways. The focus in the 1980s was on the reduction or abolition not only of customs duties and import restrictions but also of nontariff barriers—in other words, the opening of the Japanese market and facilitating access to it by foreigners. Whereas earlier friction regarding Japanese exports related to fiber and steel products, there was now greater antagonism in the field of high technology. There were now also demands for the opening up of Japan's financial system and capital market and the availability of more services to foreign traders in Japan. Regionally, Japan's economic friction was now not only with the United States and European nations but also with members of the Association of Southeast Asian Nations (ASEAN). The Japanese government's Action Program for Improving Market Access, which was launched in July 1985, represented an official effort to give Japan an open market similar to those of Western nations.
NISHIKAWA Masao

economic policy in the 1980s

Between 1980 and 1985 there were several changes in the Japanese government's economic policy. The importance of price stabilization increased following the abnormal rise in prices after the first oil crisis, and the BANK OF JAPAN was more attentive to trends in the money supply. To restore fiscal balance, the former Keynesian-type policy was abandoned in favor of a tighter financial stance. As a result, the general account budget's dependence on government bonds decreased from its 1979 peak of 34.7 percent, and various plans to build social overhead capital fell behind schedule.

An increased recognition of the importance of supply-side economics, the relaxation of various regulations, and the introduction of private initiative into public activities also reflected the financial conditions of the first half of the 1980s. Some goals, such as the privatization of the NIPPON TELEGRAPH AND TELEPHONE PUBLIC CORPORATION, were achieved quickly.

In international trade, given the massive surplus in the current-balance account, further opening of the Japanese market demanded extremely high priority. In 1985 the government's Action Program for Improving Market Access was developed to cope with this situaton.

It also became necessary to monitor the effect on increases of the surplus in the current-balance account caused by easy money and a tight financial policy through yen depreciation and excess domestic saving, respectively.

There was increased international cooperation in matters of economic policy. In addition to Japan's market-opening endeavors and stimulation of domestic demand, Japan also intervened in the currency exchange market in the autumn of 1985 in an attempt to achieve a reasonable exchange rate for the yen.   *Ōmori Takashi*

economy in the 1980s

Economic Trends —— The Japanese economy maintained an upward trend for about a year after the beginning of the oil crisis in 1978. Successive increases in the price of oil and restrictive monetary policies that were implemented in April 1979 resulted in a Japanese recession early in 1980. According to the business-cycle indicators used by the ECONOMIC PLANNING AGENCY, the 28-month expansionary phase that the economy had entered in October 1977 had peaked in February 1980 and finally yielded to a recessionary phase that lasted 36 months until February 1983, the longest recorded recession since World War II (the average length of a recession is 16 months). Whereas the growth rate of the gross national product (GNP) had exceeded 5 percent in fiscal years (FY) 1977–79, in FY 1980 the growth rate dropped to 4 percent and further slowed down to less than 4 percent for the three years from FY 1981 through FY 1983. (The Japanese fiscal year is calculated from April through March.)

The recession started with inventory adjustments that particularly affected the intermediary industries. Private consumption stagnated during FY 1980 and FY 1981 due to the adverse effect on real income of the price increases stemming from the increase in oil prices. Private fixed investment slowed down gradually, reaching a level in FY 1982 that was not more than 2 percent higher than that of the previous year. In contrast to the stagnant domestic demand, exports continued to increase. Of the 4 percent growth of the GNP in FY 1980, 3 percent was the result of net exports, and of the 3.3 percent growth of the GNP in FY 1981, only 1.2 percent, was attributable to the contribution of net exports. In FY 1982, private consumption recovered due to stabilized prices, but exports decreased due to the slowing US economy. Net exports contributed only 0.5 percent to the 3.2 percent growth of the GNP in FY 1982.

A business recovery began in February 1983, three months after the recovery of the US economy became evident. Exports recovered first, and then private fixed investment started accelerating in the middle of 1983. Private fixed investment in FY 1984 increased by 11 percent in real terms over the previous year, stimulated not only by exports, but also by technological innovations in microelectronics and other fields. Contrary to the expectations of many observers, private consumption decelerated with a stabilized wage increase. The policy of fiscal reconstruction being pursued rather strictly, government fixed investment was reduced. The economy grew in FY 1983 by 4.3 percent in real terms. The growth was led by foreign demand, and net exports contributed 1.5 percent to the overall growth. In contrast, the growth of the economy during and after FY 1984 was led by domestic demand. In 1984 the economy

grew by 5 percent, with only 1.5 percent being contributed by foreign demand. In 1985 the growth rate of the economy slowed to 4.2 percent, due chiefly to the decreased volume of exports. Per capita GNP in (calendar) 1984 stood at slightly more than US $11,000, ranking sixth among the countries of the Organization for Economic Cooperation and Development (OECD).

The business expansion which started in February 1983 reached the average 32-month length of expansionary phases by October 1985. However, in February of 1985 the value of the dollar dropped slightly, causing a corresponding decrease in exports, and some signs of slowdown were evident that summer. After the Group of Five (the finance ministers of the five advanced nations of the United States, Japan, France, West Germany, and the United Kingdom) met on 22 September 1985, the yen appreciated even more. Under the deflating influence of the yen appreciation, the growth rate of the Japanese economy decelerated sharply from the beginning of 1986.

Prices, Wages, and Unemployment —— Price increases after the oil crisis of 1978–79 were much smaller than those that had followed the 1973 oil crisis. The difference resulted from the absence of the worldwide overheating of economies that had prevailed before the first oil crisis, milder increases in the price of oil itself, and more modest wage increases following the increased price of oil. Wholesale prices increased by 13 percent in both FY 1979 and FY 1980 (as compared to 23 percent in FY 1974 after the first oil crisis), but from FY 1981 on they seemed to stabilize. Consumer prices also rose moderately, peaking at an increase of 7.8 percent in FY 1980 and followed by a 4.0 percent rise in the next fiscal year. Subsequently, price increases stabilized at a rate of approximately 2 percent. The yen appreciation after October 1985 and the simultaneous decrease in worldwide oil prices contributed further to the stabilization of prices. In 1985 wholesale prices dropped by 2.4 percent from the previous year's prices while consumer prices increased by 1.9 percent. It was expected that prices would become even more stable in 1986, and the figures for June 1986 onwards confirmed these expectations.

Although after the 1973 oil crisis the spring round of wage negotiations in FY 1974 resulted in a record-high 32.9 percent increase in wages, after the second oil crisis, which occurred in 1978–79, the wage increase was only 7.7 percent in FY 1981. In FY 1983 wages increased by only 4.4 percent, the lowest in the postwar period. In 1985 wages increased by a little over 5 percent, and in 1986 wage increases were reduced to 4.5 percent. The increases in the compensation of employees per capita had become smaller than increases in productivity (in terms of national accounts), creating decreases in wage costs and labor's share.

The unemployment ratio rose from 2.1 percent in FY 1980 to 2.7 percent in FY 1984 and 2.6 percent in FY 1985, due mainly to the fact that more women were entering the job market. After the autumn of 1985, what was seen as a tendency toward increasing unemployment was attributed to the slackening business situation.

National Economic Policies —— The importance of government bonds stepped up in FY 1975 and continued to increase until FY 1980, when issues reached the record height of ¥14 trillion (US $61.7 billion) in approximately equal amounts of construction bonds and deficit bonds. Under the circumstances, the government decided to reduce bond issuance in FY 1981 and bring it to zero by FY 1984. This policy, however, proved impossible, and in 1983 a new target of emerging from the dependence on deficit bonds and reducing bond dependency in general by FY 1990 was adopted. Bond issuance was reduced to ¥11.7 trillion (US $49.15 billion) by FY 1985, and the ratio of revenues from bonds to the total revenue of the central government's general account budget was reduced from the record high of 34.7 percent in FY 1979 to 22.2 percent in FY 1980. Expenditures for public works were reduced accordingly, which had a restrictive impact on the economy. With regard to the investment-saving balance, the general government excess investment decreased from 4.0 percent in FY 1980 to 1.9 percent in FY 1984 in terms of the GNP.

The BANK OF JAPAN raised its official discount rate in five stages between April 1979 and 1980 from 4.25 percent to 9 percent, a rate equivalent to the record high reached during the period after the first oil crisis. The Bank of Japan also emphasized control of the money supply, the rate of increase of which declined from the beginning of 1979 and decelerated below 7 percent of the previous year in FY 1980. Under the restrictive monetary policies, prices started stabilizing in the middle of 1980, and the general business situation turned sluggish. The Bank of Japan responded to these developments by reducing its discount rate several times between August

1980 and December 1981, when the discount rate reached 5.5 percent. The official discount rate was reduced further to 5 percent in October 1983, and remained at the same level until the end of 1985, 26 months later. At the end of January 1986 the rate dropped to 4.5 percent and both March and April saw a further 0.5 percent reduction in the official discount rate until it reached 3.5 percent, where it remained throughout the summer of 1986. The money supply increased only slightly, with an average annual growth rate of 8.7 percent.

In the meantime, after the latter part of 1984, Japanese financial markets were rapidly liberalized and opened up to foreigners. The propelling factors behind these changes were the fact that the restrictions on transactions in the markets of accumulated public bonds had been progressively abolished and the fact that US authorities had voiced strong appeals through the Yen-Dollar Committee established by the two governments. The liberalization and internationalization of Japanese financial markets were expected to progress further at a rapid pace.

Exchange Rate, Balance of Payments, and Trade Friction with the United States —— The value of the yen declined after the second oil crisis until April 1980, when it bottomed out at a monthly average exchange rate of 252 yen to the dollar. The subsequent appreciation brought the yen rate up to above 200 yen in early January 1981. However, the yen depreciated again after the inauguration of US President Ronald Reagan in the same month, until the rate reached 271 yen to the dollar in October 1982. Responding to the economic situation in the United States, where interest rates had been falling since the summer of 1982, the yen rose until April 1984, when the official discount rate in the United States was raised to 9.0 percent. The ensuing decline in the yen-dollar exchange rate was reversed by February 1985.

Then, on 22 September 1985, the Group of Five agreed upon a collective intervention in the exchange markets. The yen, which stood at 242 yen to the dollar immediately before the meeting, climbed to 202 yen to the dollar on 21 November, immediately after the Geneva summit meeting between the United States and the Soviet Union. The yen thus appreciated by 40 yen to the dollar in the space of two months. From November until the end of the year, the exchange rate remained between 200 and 204 yen to the dollar, supported partly by the Bank of Japan's policy of maintaining domestic interest rates at a reasonably high level.

In 1986 the yen continued to grow stronger. On 12 May 1986, after the Tōkyō Summit had taken place earlier that month, the yen-dollar exchange rate was 160 yen to the dollar. The strength of the yen was maintained throughout the spring. Forecasts for a weaker US economy, combined with the lowering of the US discount rate from 6.5 percent to 6 percent on 11 July, helped support the high value of the yen. By 21 July the yen had reached an exchange rate of 155 yen to the dollar. The average value of the yen, which had been exchanged at a rate of 260 yen to the dollar in Feburary 1985, had appreciated by 55 percent by June 1986, when the monthly average exchange rate was 168 yen to the dollar.

The balance of payments on current account showed a large deficit due to the increased oil bills in FY 1979 and FY 1980, but it returned to a surplus in FY 1981 owing both to the increase in exports and the decrease in imports. Except for FY 1982, when exports decreased under the influence of negative growth (minus 2.5 percent) in the United States, exports continued to increase and imports stagnated after reaching a peak level in FY 1980, partly due to the fall in oil prices, especially in March 1983 when the price dropped by five dollars per barrel. The surplus in the current account balance thus increased rapidly, reaching US $37 billion (or 3 percent of the GNP) in FY 1984. The surplus in FY 1985 was US $55 billion.

Another factor affecting Japan's balance of payments was the sharp decrease in oil prices that occurred in the early 1980s. By June 1986 the CIF import price of a barrel of oil was US $12.35. (In contrast, one barrel of oil had cost $27.31 in 1985.) This price reduction had a significant effect on the Japanese economy, since for every $10 decrease in oil prices the country would save $12.3 billion, increasing the trade surplus by 8.5 percent.

Japanese trade vis-à-vis the United States also increased a great deal, rekindling trade friction between the two countries. In FY 1984 Japan had a trade surplus with the United States of US $33.8 billion; by FY 1985 this figure had increased to $43.3 billion. Responding to requests from the United States, the Japanese introduced a number of measures intended to redress the trade imbalance, including restrictions on the exportation of Japanese passenger

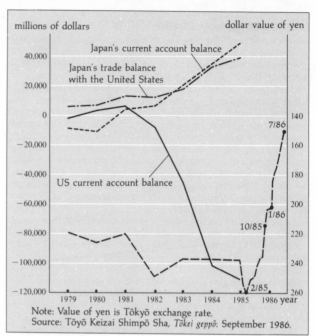

Note: Value of yen is Tōkyō exchange rate.
Source: Tōyō Keizai Shimpō Sha, *Tōkei geppō*: September 1986.

Economy in the 1980s —— Figure 1: Balance of trade between Japan and the United States and Yen-Dollar exchange rate

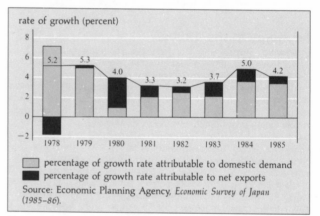

Source: Economic Planning Agency, *Economic Survey of Japan* (1985–86).

Economy in the 1980s —— Figure 2: Real rate of growth and contribution of domestic demand and net exports

cars to the United States, modification of Japan's system of standards and certification, liberalization of Japanese financial markets, increases in the tariff cuts agreed upon in the Tōkyō Round of GATT (General Agreement on Tariffs and Trade) discussions, and the reduction or abolition of tariffs on a number of items. Between December 1981 and July 1985, eight packages of economic measures incorporating such tactics as those mentioned above were introduced in order to open up the Japanese markets and thus improve the balance of trade.

On 7 April 1986 the Advisory Group on Economic Structural Adjustment for International Harmony, a private advisory group reporting to Prime Minister NAKASONE YASUHIRO (b 1918), submitted its recommendations in the Maekawa Report. In August 1986 the prime minister required each ministry affected by the report to begin working toward the implementation of the measures prescribed by the group. The measures, designed to increase domestic demand, called for the growth of public enterprises, increases in housing construction, which was to be encouraged by reducing related taxes, and the reduction of utility rates. These measures, when combined with the drastic appreciation of the yen, were anticipated to have beneficial results on Japan's controversial balance of trade. However, lower oil prices and the increased value of dollar-based exports would counteract the benefits. It was thought that any significant reduction in the dollar-based trade surplus would require time.

TANAKA Tsutomu

education in the 1980s

The event that had the greatest political impact on Japanese educational circles in the first half of the 1980s was a controversy surrounding government approval of school textbooks, which became an international issue.

The Textbook Issue—— In the years since World War II, conservative and progressive forces in Japan have confronted each other repeatedly over the issue of governmental approval of textbooks. As part of the educational reforms that were instituted after the war, the system of government-compiled textbooks that had existed up until that time was abolished and replaced by a system in which all textbooks were produced by private textbook companies and then subjected to approval by the Ministry of Education before being adopted by the schools. The system is the same for elementary, middle, and high schools.

One result of this system is that, depending on the ideology of the scholars who write the textbooks and the posture assumed by the Ministry of Education, conflicts of opinion surrounding textbook approval are unavoidable. Such confrontations have been particularly marked in the fields of social studies (especially government, economics, and history) and the Japanese language. There is a high degree of public interest in the content of school textbooks, and the process of government approval has been a favorite target of politicians who question its validity. The resulting controversies have often become major political and social issues.

The textbook controversy that dominated the years 1980–85 began with a series of articles published between January and August 1980 in *Jiyū shimpō*, the party organ of the ruling Liberal Democratic Party, under the general title "What Kind of Textbooks Are Being Used in Our Schools: Suggestions for the Normalization of Education." The main thrust of the articles was that the textbooks currently in use were dominated by an extreme left-wing bias that made them tools of the Japan Teachers' Union (NIKKYŌSO) and the Japan Communist Party in their fight against the establishment. The articles blamed a faulty attitude toward textbook approval on the part of the Ministry of Education and urged the ministry to reconsider its policies. Leaving aside the question of whether or not these articles were based on distortion or misunderstanding of the facts, they were evidence of a strong feeling of dissatisfaction within a segment of the Liberal Democratic Party toward the textbooks that were being used in Japan. In July 1980, Okuno Seisuke (b 1913), minister of justice and former minister of education, said, "There are many problems in our present textbooks. For example, they avoid the words 'love of country.'" At the bottom of this issue was a feeling that the existing textbooks with their strong peace consciousness stood in the way of an effort to strengthen Japan's defenses— an effort that would require an increased defense consciousness and a change in public attitudes towards such issues as war, the SELF DEFENSE FORCES, and nuclear weapons.

In the summer of 1982, in the midst of a growing public controversy over the validity of the textbook-approval system and the treatment in textbooks of such issues as patriotism, the Self Defense Forces, the Northern Territories (see TERRITORY OF JAPAN), and nuclear power plants, Japan received strong official protests from two other Asian nations concerning its textbook approval system.

These protests were seen as the culmination of an outcry that had arisen after completion of the approval process for high-school social-studies textbooks in June of that year. In order to get their books approved, the authors and publishers of certain Japanese history and other social studies textbooks had been forced to weaken considerably their descriptions of Japan's aggressive actions prior to World War II (for example, the word "invade" had been weakened to "attack" or "advance").

On 26 July the Chinese Ministry of Foreign Affairs delivered to the Japanese embassy a formal protest addressed to the Japanese government concerning the history textbook approval incident. And China was not alone. Newspaper editorials in such nations as North and South Korea, Thailand, Hong Kong, and the Philippines protested Japan's aggressive wartime actions and its attempt to camouflage them by means of its textbook-approval policies. In Korea the foreign minister handed the Japanese ambassador a note demanding that the revisions be reversed, and China rejected a visit by Ogawa Heiji (b 1910), the Japanese minister of education.

Within Japan there were nationwide expressions of concern, and on 26 August, in an informal talk given by the chief cabinet secretary, the government promised to take responsibility for correcting the offending passages in the textbooks. The Ministry of Education also added to its set of standards for the approval process a clause specifying that, in the future, international understanding and harmony with other Asian nations would be taken into consideration in the approval of history textbooks. Specifically, the word "invade" would no longer be changed to "attack" or "advance."

The international issue created by the Ministry of Education's textbook approval system was thus settled for the time being. However there were those who asked what was wrong with beautifying the history of one's own country, and there were complaints over the way the government had been forced to change decisions made in its approval process because of pressure from outside the country. It was evident that the political content of public school education would continue to be an important issue for the future.

High Academic Achievement—— The school enrollment rate in Japan's compulsory education is close to 100 percent, and achievement levels are also high. According to nationwide middle-school achievement-test results made public by the Ministry of Education on 27 December 1985, the lowest average score among the subjects of Japanese, social studies, mathematics, science, and English was 56.8 points out of 100 for second year English. The highest average score was 73 points for first year English. Almost all the other averages were in the range of 60 to 70 points.

These achievement tests were strong on the kind of questions that test memorized knowledge and weak in testing ability to express ideas logically in writing or ability in using the kind of structured thinking that is necessary for science or mathematics. Nevertheless, they show an overall rise in achievement levels compared to the similar study that was conducted 17 years before. Judging from such figures, Japanese primary and secondary education was at a high level, even when viewed on an international scale.

The Blight in the Schools—— The sore spot in Japanese school education was the situation being referred to as "the blight in the schools." According to police statistics for the year 1984, the number of young people under the age of 20 who had been put under police guidance because of criminal offenses was 248,540. Of these, 21 percent were 14 years old and 20.6 percent 15—in either case, of middle-school age. In 63.9 percent of the cases, the offense was bicycle theft or shoplifting. Nevertheless, the problem was not a small one.

At the beginning of the decade, child suicide had been prominent among the social problems being discussed in the newspapers and other mass news media. This topic was followed a little later by the subject of household violence. In 1982–83, the problem of school violence was given detailed coverage. As of the end of 1985, bullying, which had been responsible for nine suicides in the space of one year, was being discussed as a serious problem. The changes in community and family life that accompany urbanization and the development of an industrial society were being cited as factors that have had a great effect on Japanese children. However, an effective prescription for the so-called blight among young people of school age had not yet been found, and the discussion in the media continued without results.

Prime Minister NAKASONE YASUHIRO (b 1918) expressed a strong determination to find solutions to the problem, and one of the most important responsibilities of the Provisional Council on Educational Reform, which was established in 1984, was to investigate what kind of measures could be taken against the blight in the schools. The council released reports in 1985 and 1986, but these contained no recommendations for an adequate response to the school blight. Considering the difficulty of the problem, this was no doubt to be expected. However, the problem was already being used as political campaign material, along with the subject of entrance-examination reform. Education continued to be a favorite target for statements by politicians at election time, as well as a point of contention between the government and the opposition parties.

Entrance Examinations—— School and college entrance examinations have always been one of the greatest causes of emotional suffering among the modern Japanese. Every year in March, when entrance examinations are taken and the results announced, a number of young people are certain to commit suicide.

The Joint First-Stage Achievement Test, which was inaugurated in 1979 by Japanese national and other public colleges and universities on the model of the American SAT college entrance testing system, was implemented in a rigidly standardized way that differed sharply from the use of the SAT in the United States. As a result, there was loud opposition from the very beginning, and to all intents and purposes the test was scheduled to be abolished in its original form after 1988. In 1986, the Ministry of Education was conducting studies for a new joint test system to be implemented in 1989. This new test system would include private as well as public colleges and universities and would be so designed that it could be used more flexibly, as the SAT system is.

However, Prime Minister Nakasone criticized the proposed test on the grounds that multiple-choice tests like the ones being used cannot measure true scholastic ability, and there were many other people who agreed that essay-style tests should be used for college entrance testing. It seemed certain that Japan's college-entrance testing system would have to undergo a period of upheaval and trial-and-error experimentation before the issue could be resolved.

YAMAGISHI Shunsuke

energy conservation

Because Japan is largely dependent on other nations for its sources of energy, energy conservation is of particular importance to the nation. The 1979 Law concerning the Rational Use of Energy was designed to encourage a 17 percent reduction of energy consumption by 1985. Measures called for by the law include reduction of the energy consumed per unit of production through the development of pertinent technology or other means, energy conservation in automobiles and household electrical appliances, reductions in large, energy-consuming industries, and promotion of industries that were more energy-efficient.

The practice of energy conservation had remarkable results in many instances, notably in household electrical appliances. In 1985, new Japanese electric refrigerators used approximately 39 percent of the energy per month that they used in 1979. The figure for color television sets was 92 percent, air conditioners 84.6 percent, and vacuum cleaners 86 percent. Japan's crude oil imports in 1985 were less than 200 million kiloliters (1,680 million barrels) for the first time in 15 years. *IKEDA Minoru*

environmental impact assessment

A term that is used loosely to refer not only to prior assessment of the influence that development operations are likely to have on the immediate environment but also to the taking of steps to prevent pollution and environmental disruption. The US National Environmental Policy Act of 1970 is the first example of this concept being made into a law. From the standpoint of government administration of the environment, the concept stands for a movement away from measures taken after the fact toward measures taken before the fact and from individual regulation toward comprehensive regulation. In April 1981 the Japanese government introduced an Environmental Impact Assessment Bill in the Diet, but the opposition parties were strongly against the bill because electric power plants were excluded from the types of operations that it affected, and it did not pass. In the ordinary Diet of 1983 the opposition parties softened their attitude, and there seemed to be prospects of the bill's passage. However, this time there was strong opposition from industry and part of the LIBERAL DEMOCRATIC PARTY. It was asserted that environmental impact assessment itself was necessary but that making it into a law would give groups opposed to development a legal basis for their attacks and that such a law would thus prove an obstacle to development and diminish the willingness of businesses to make such investments. The bill was withdrawn when the House of Representatives was dissolved in November 1983. In August 1984 the government abandoned attempts at passage of a law and decided to handle environmental impact assessment as an administrative matter.

On the local-government level, environmental impact assessment laws had already been enacted in the form of local ordinances in the city of Kawasaki in 1976 and in Hokkaidō in 1978. As of March 1986 there were six local governments that had enacted such ordinances, including the metropolitan prefecture of Tōkyō.

IWADARE Hiroshi

environmental pollution

Japan's period of extremely high economic growth rate in the 1960s and 1970s was accompanied by such a succession of different forms of pollution that the situation in Japan became world famous, and Japan was even referred to as "one of the advanced nations of the world in pollution." Every region of the country was affected by some combination of such forms of pollution as air pollution, water

pollution, noise pollution, vibration pollution, mine pollution, pollution by agricultural chemicals, and food poisoning. POLLUTION-RELATED DISEASES became a matter of public concern, and in the cases of the so-called Minamata disease, Niigata Minamata disease, *itai-itai* disease, and Yokkaichi asthma, the lawsuits instituted by affected residents in an attempt to collect damages became known as the "four major pollution lawsuits."

However, after the oil crisis of 1973, Japan entered a period of lower economic growth rate. Protest movements organized by the residents of affected areas became more influential. Both the national and local governments made progress in imposing regulations, and business enterprises themselves promoted antipollution measures. As a result of all these factors, environmental conditions in Japan improved considerably. In the 1980s the cries of discontent from residents were less audible than they had been in the 1960s and 1970s, and some people in government circles began to say that pollution was no longer a problem and that the issue in the future was going to be other improvements in the quality of life. Nevertheless, it was not true that pollution no longer existed in Japan. According to figures released by the Environmental Disputes Coordination Commission of the Prime Minister's Office, the number of complaints from residents relating to pollution received by local governments throughout Japan during the 1984 fiscal year was 67,754. This was 5.9 percent more than the previous year. Of these complaints, 21,536 involved noise pollution, 12,998 were for offensive odors, and 9,403 involved air pollution. As for the sources of the pollution, 25 percent of the cases involved manufacturing, 12 percent construction, and 11 percent stores and food-service establishments. There was a notable increase in complaints concerning industrial waste disposal. There were 1,902 of these, which was an 11 percent increase over the previous fiscal year of 1983.

IWADARE Hiroshi

Equal Employment Opportunity Law for Men and Women

(Danjo Koyō Kikai Kintō Hō). A law intended to eliminate discrimination against women in the workplace. The law was passed in May 1985 (effective April 1986) to enable ratification of the United Nations Convention for Eliminating All Forms of Discrimination against Women, which Japan had signed in 1980.

The chief provisions of the law are as follows. 1. It is made mandatory for businesses to provide equal opportunities to women in terms of recruiting, hiring, work assignments, and advancement. 2. The protections established for women by the LABOR STANDARDS LAW of 1947 with regard to such issues as overtime work and work on holidays are modified with the exception of protections for women in certain types of heavy industry such as manufacturing, construction, and transportation. 3. Restrictions on late night work are eliminated for managerial, specialist, and similar types of work.

This new law was greeted in the Japanese workplace with a mixture of high expectations and puzzlement. Though the intentions of the law were clear, there was still no clear public consensus on how the law should be responded to, either by employers and employees or by Japanese society as a whole. *NOMURA Jirō*

ethical standards for the mass media

In the mid-1980s there was much criticism in Japan of excesses in news reporting by the mass media, particularly television, and the definition of ethical standards for the mass media had become an important issue. Public indignation was particularly aroused by two events that occurred in the summer of 1985. In June, journalists who happened to be on the scene when the president of a business firm was murdered were so enthusiastic about reporting the murder as it occurred that they made no attempt to stop it. In the second event, which occurred in August, the producers of an afternoon television show staged a mock lynching among middle-school girls and reported the incident as news in an attempt to give the show a more sensational content. The incident had a frightening effect on those girls who were not aware that it was staged. The father of one of the girls reported the incident to the police, and the director of the show was arrested for inciting violence. Events such as these raised serious doubts about the existence of ethical standards in television news reporting, and there was wide criticism of broadcasting companies for ignoring human rights when planning their programs.

Invasion of privacy by photojournalism also became an important issue, as some weekly photo magazines that capitalized on scan-

Flexible manufacturing system

A section of FANUC, Ltd's electric motor manufacturing plant, where robots are used to build robots.

dalous photographs boasted circulations in excess of 1.5 million.

Issues such as these were in the background when the 29th meeting of the All-Japan Conference of the Council for Ethics in the Mass Media was held in September 1985. The conference resolved to promote self-imposed ethical standards for the media, including more consideration for human rights, as a means of restoring public confidence. *Matsumoto Katsumi*

family in the 1980s

In the first half of the 1980s, the number of nuclear families in Japan increased rapidly. The annual survey on citizen welfare conducted by the Ministry of Health and Welfare showed that, in 1985, 18 percent of Japanese households were single-person households, 61 percent were nuclear families, and 15 percent were three-generation families living together. This was in contrast to the 1970 figures of 19 percent, 57 percent, and 19 percent, respectively. The national census taken in October 1985 counted 38.1 million households, 2.1 million more than in the 1980 census. The average number of persons per household was 3.18, less than the 3.25 of 1980.

Several factors contributed to the growing trend in Japan of establishing nuclear families. As young people who were born and raised in rural areas found few opportunities in their hometowns, they began seeking employment in cities, leaving their families behind. After marrying and settling down independently in their new urban locations, the young people often left their parents to live alone in the rural area. Young people born in urban areas also showed a preference for living apart from their parents after marriage, further accelerating the tendency to create nuclear families.

Another factor was the increase of single parents with children, a result of the higher divorce rate. The Ministry of Health and Welfare revealed that the number of divorces had increased annually since 1963, with 181,791 divorces reported in 1983. In 1984 this number decreased slightly to 181,337. In 1970, the greatest number of divorces was occurring in couples in which both partners were between 25 and 29; in 1982 those marriages most affected involved partners who were slightly older, between 30 and 34. By 1985, forty-one percent of all divorces were occurring after 10 years or more of married life, reflecting an increase in the number of individuals of middle or advanced age who were divorcing after longer periods of marriage. One contributing factor might have been the greater number of working women and their subsequent economic independence. In 1985, the number of divorced women was 352,000, greater than the number of those widowed and representing 49.1 percent of the total 718,000 single mothers in the country (Ministry of Health and Welfare, 1983).

The increasing number of nuclear families was causing various problems in the 1980s, one being the greater population of elderly people living alone. Of the 12.1 million individuals 65 years of age and older estimated by the Ministry of Health and Welfare in 1985, 1.1 million (9.3 percent) lived alone. The number of these elderly dying with no one attending them was growing in urban areas, and in Tōkyō's 23 wards there were 332 such deaths in 1985. *Iwadare Hiroshi*

fast-food restaurants

The opening up of the Japanese food-service industry to participation by foreign capital in 1969 was followed by the entrance of a succession of American fast-food chains (Kentucky Fried Chicken in 1970 and Mister Donut and McDonald's in 1971), an event that was to cause great changes in Japanese eating habits as well as in the domestic food-service industry. The top seller among the fast-food chains was McDonald's, which by January 1986 had 531 shops in Japan. The service and menus in these were essentially the same as in their American counterparts, aside from a few concessions to local tastes, and they became a part of the Japanese lifestyle, particularly among the younger generation. The imported food-service technology (centralized kitchens, standardized menus, the development of large-scale chains) was soon applied to such Japanese-style foods as sushi, *soba* (buckwheat noodles), and *gyūdon* (beef and rice in a bowl), leading to the development of Japanese-style fast-food chains.

fifth-generation computer

A Japanese project to develop a revolutionary type of computer that would process information more rapidly than any existing computer and that would possess an ability to learn and draw inferences in a way that resembles human intelligence. This fifth-generation computer was being developed during the 1980s by the Institute for New Generation Computer Technology (ICOT) under the guidance of the Ministry of International Trade and Industry (MITI). The national project was begun in 1982 and was scheduled for completion in 1992. The planned computer was being called a fifth-generation computer because it was seen as following the first (vacuum tube), the second (transistor), the third (integrated circuit, or IC, including the large-scale integrated circuit, or LSI), and the fourth (very-large-scale integrated circuit, or VLSI) generations of computers. While computers up through the fourth generation were von Neumann computers, which operated in a serial fashion, the fifth-generation machine was to be characterized by the parallel processing of information and the drawing of inferences from such information. Since it was to be capable of input and output by voice, graphs, and other images, and since it was to be capable of solving problems by its inferential function, the new computer would bear some similarity to human beings. Software was being written in the logic-programming language PROLOG. The basic experimental system of conversation comprehension, DUALS, developed by ICOT in 1984, was to enable the computer to answer test questions on the third-grade level. *Nishimata Souhei*

five-day workweek

As of the mid-1980s, Japan lagged considerably behind Europe and the United States in implementing a five-day workweek. As recently as 1970, only 17.9 percent of Japanese workers were on such a schedule, even including those working a five-day week on a partial basis (i.e., by getting every other Saturday or one Saturday a month off). Only 4.5 percent of Japanese workers worked a five-day week on a regular full-time basis. By 1975, however, these figures had climbed to 69.9 percent and 21.4 percent, respectively. After 1975 the adoption of the five-day workweek slowed down somewhat because Japan's declining economic growth hampered the introduction of the labor-saving investments that make a five-day schedule possible. In 1984, 77.3 percent of Japanese workers worked a five-day workweek on either a full or partial basis, and 27.0 percent of the workers worked such a schedule on a regular full-time basis. In 1985, 32.6 percent of businesses with 1,000 or more employees were on a full five-day workweek. National government workers got one Saturday off per month, as did employees of many local governments. The Ministry of Labor's "Outlook and Guidelines for Reduction of Working Hours," issued in June 1985, called for wider adoption of the five-day workweek as part of a broader campaign for the reduction of working hours. The average number of working hours per worker had been 2,116 in 1984, and the Ministry of Labor aimed at reducing this to 2,000 by the year 1990. The major Japanese labor organizations were also pushing strongly for overall adoption of the five-day workweek. *Yasuhara Norikazu*

flexible manufacturing system

(FMS). An automated manufacturing system designed to produce a variety of products in small quantities and with efficiency. Originating in the United States and introduced to Japanese industries in the early 1980s, the flexible manufacturing system consists of numerical-control-type machine tools, industrial robots, computerized control systems, and related components. Combined with computer-aided design (CAD) and computer-aided manufacturing (CAM), FMS results in an almost completely automated factory. Several such plants have been built in Japan, the most noted being FANUC, Ltd.'s plant at the base of Mount Fuji, where robots are used to build robots. In the mid-1980s, the Ministry of International Trade and Industry's Agency of Industrial Science and Technology was encouraging research into FMS aimed at developing an automatic sewing system for the Japanese clothing industry that would cut the production time in half for certain clothing items.

NISHIMATA Souhei

forestry in the 1980s

Beginning in 1980, there was a decrease in the number of new houses being built in Japan, and the proportion of wooden houses among newly constructed dwellings was also decreasing annually. The resultant slackening in demand for lumber combined with competition from imported lumber to produce a drop in lumber prices on the Japanese market. This slump in lumber prices dealt a serious blow not only to the Japanese lumber industry proper but also to forest management operations in the nation's forests, leading as it did to a slowdown in reforestation activities. The area being planted with trees annually, which had been around 400,000 hectares (988,000 acres) in 1960, was only 150,000 hectares (370,500 acres) in 1982 and after. During the same period, forest maintenance operations such as weeding and pruning also tended to fall behind. The result was a marked increase in damage to forests. Particularly serious was a pine-forest blight caused by the pine-wood nematode that is borne by the Japanese pine sawyer. This blight, which affected forests in all prefectures except Aomori Prefecture and Hokkaidō, reached a peak in the years 1979–81.

Thirty-one percent of Japan's total forest area is occupied by national forests (prefectural and other local forests account for another ten percent, the remainder being private). The national forests are managed under a special account called National Forest Operations, which has accumulated huge deficits. Efforts at rationalization, including personnel cuts and the sale of property, were instituted in response to recommendations contained in the 1983 report of the Provisional Commission for Administrative Reform. However, there was increasing public concern that these cuts would lead to a serious diminution of the public benefits derived from the maintenance of national lands, and in 1984 a number of programs were launched for "reviving green resources" with citizen participation. In one type of such program, the public is invited to invest in planted forests that are already under development, with the understanding that when the timber is cut down profits will be divided among investors and developers at an established ratio. These programs are known by such names as "home-town forest" and "white-collar workers' planted forest."

FURUNO Masami

Forty-seventh International P.E.N. Congress in Tōkyō

In May 1984 the 47th International P.E.N. Congress was held in Tōkyō under the sponsorship of the JAPAN P.E.N. CLUB. The congress was attended by 2,000 writers from 45 P.E.N. organizations around the world, and there were 600 Japanese participants. The central theme of the congress was "Literature in the Nuclear Age— Why Do We Write?" There were discussions of the role of the writer under the nuclear threat, and a resolution was passed calling for abolition of nuclear weapons. There were also discussions on such topics as "Literary Relations between East and West," "Writers and Human Rights," and "Literature and the Visual Media." In view of the fact that the congress was held in Tōkyō and that representatives from Chinese P.E.N. organizations attended, there was surprisingly little discussion of Asian literature, and a uniting of voices from all regions of Asia was something that would have to wait until some future occasion. Among the more prominent foreign participants in the congress were Kurt Vonnegut, Alain Robbe-Grillet, Ba Jin, and Alan Sillitoe. The Japanese authors who were most active in the congress included ENDŌ SHŪSAKU (b 1923), ETŌ JUN (b 1933), ŌE KENZABURŌ (b 1935), Nakano Kōji (b 1925), and NOMA HIROSHI (b 1915).

KONAKA Yōtarō

Fourth Comprehensive National Land Development Plan

(Daiyoji Zenkoku Sōgō Kaihatsu Keikaku; abbreviated as Yonzensō). Japan's fourth COMPREHENSIVE NATIONAL LAND DEVELOPMENT PLAN, which was being drawn up in 1986 by the National Land Agency as a national land plan that would take Japan into the 21st century. The plan was to cover the 15 years from 1986 to 2000. It was expected to carry forward the concept of "Established Zones for Habitation" (a government scheme to encourage population growth and development in certain regions), which was a feature of the 1972 Third Plan. Other goals of the fourth plan included social and economic planning in anticipation of the further "aging" of the Japanese population, increased regional autonomy, with emphasis on the role of the core cities of Japan's various regions, the construction of a high-speed transportation network, the establishment of a communications network capable of handling a large volume of information of many types, and a wider distribution, away from Tōkyō, of gateway cities to the outside world. A final overall goal of the plan was to achieve an ideal balance between regional autonomy and regional cooperation with the central government.

NAKAMURA Kiichi

freedom of information

One of the basic rights of the people in a democracy is freedom of access, upon demand, to the various types of information accumulated by government agencies. In Japan a strong movement seeking open access to government information grew up, starting around 1982. The aim of the movement was to establish a system for guaranteeing the public's right to possess such information and for imposing on government agencies the obligation to make the information available. As of September 1985, ordinances guaranteeing freedom of information had been established by 28 local governments, including those of the urban prefectures of Tōkyō and Ōsaka, three other prefectures, nine cities, four of the wards of Tōkyō, and ten towns. Some of these local ordinances exempted certain types of information from disclosure in order to protect the privacy rights of individuals and businesses. There were some local governments that established oversight committees composed of private citizens in order to assure the proper functioning of the system. The types of information being managed by these various types of local government organizations differed widely, and there were corresponding differences in the ordinances themselves. A citizens' movement to promote the passage of a national "freedom of information law" also sprang up. Progress was thus being made towards a guarantee of freedom of information; however, Japan still remained behind the United States and many of the nations of Europe.

NOMURA Jirō

Fujima Kanjūrō VI (1900–   )

Head of the Fujima school of the Japanese-style dance. Kabuki-dance choreographer. Real name Fujima Hideo. Born in Tōkyō. Fujima originally took the professional name of Onoe Umeo, but he was later adopted into the Fujima family, and in 1927 he became Fujima Kanjūrō VI. The same year he was made a choreographer for the Kabukiza after designing dances for the KABUKI actor Onoe Kikugorō VI (1885–1949). He is highly regarded both for his delicate yet highly orthodox choreography for classical dance pieces and for his novel designs for modern-style pieces. He is also known as a master of suodori, dances performed without costume or masks. He was designated as a Living National Treasure in 1960. In 1963 he received the Japan Art Academy Prize for his choreography for Makurajishi, and in 1967 he became a member of the academy. In 1982 he was awarded the Order of Culture.

Fujinoki tomb

A round tomb mound, dating from the latter half of the 6th century, in the town of Ikaruga, Nara Prefecture. The mound has a diameter of 40 meters (131.20 ft) and a height of 8 meters (26.24 ft). Enormous burial facilities and sumptuous funerary articles were discovered there in September 1985. The tomb's horizontal-hole stone chamber, which is the 10th largest in Japan, was found to contain a stone coffin in the shape of a house, painted cinnabar red, and 3,500 horse trappings (bagu). The designs on the splendid metal saddle fittings are unique. They include phoenix, tiger, dragon, lion, elephant, and honeysuckle-arabesque motifs. The elephant motif is

Gateball

A gateball match in progress.

the oldest example to be found in Japan. There are also incised demon and tortoise designs. The influence of Buddhism and the belief in the guardian gods of the four directions can be seen, providing fresh evidence of the unity of the cultures of Central Asia, China, India, and Korea. The horse trappings are thought to have been imported from the Asian continent. Since the tomb is situated close to the temple HŌRYŪJI, the person buried there is thought to have been a member of a powerful local family that later invited Prince SHŌTOKU (574–622) to Ikaruga. *Matsuo Hikaru*

Fuwa Tetsuzō (1930–   )

Politician. Real name Ueda Kenjirō (Fuwa Tetsuzō is a pen name). Born in Tōkyō. While a student at the First Higher School, Fuwa joined the JAPAN COMMUNIST PARTY (1947). He graduated from Tōkyō University in 1953. After working as secretary of the Japanese Federation of Iron and Steel Workers' Unions, he served from 1964 in the Communist Party headquarters. He was elected to the House of Representatives in 1969 as a Communist Party candidate from Tōkyō. In 1970, at the age of 40, he became the youngest member of the party's central leadership and at the same time assumed the office of secretary-general. In 1982 he was elected to succeed MIYAMOTO KENJI (b 1908) as the party chairman. He is known as the party's leading theorist, and is the author of many books and articles. His brother, Ueda Kōichirō (b 1927), is also a member of the party leadership.

gateball

An outdoor game, modeled on croquet, which was developed in Japan shortly after World War II. ("Gateball," the name of the game, is a Japanese coinage.) Synthetic-resin balls 7 to 7.5 centimeters (2.8 to 3 in) in diameter are hit with wooden mallets and driven through a series of three metal gates (arches) to strike a goalpost in the center of the court. The game is played by two competing five-person teams, each person having one ball. The winner is the first team whose members all reach the goalpost within a 30 minute time limit (or the team that comes the closest to doing so). The game became popular as a sport for the elderly from around 1975 and was spread throughout Japan by old people's clubs. A national tournament is held, and there are numerous district meets. The number of players nationwide ranges from 4.5 to 6 million people.

Gotō Noboru (1916–   )

Businessman. Born in Tōkyō. The eldest son of GOTŌ KEITA, founder of the TŌKYŪ CORPORATION, Gotō graduated from the Faculty of Law of Tōkyō University in 1940, worked for the Toshiba Corporation, and then moved to the Tōkyū Corporation, of which he became president in 1954. Using the Tōkyū Express Railway Company as a base, Gotō diversified into the fields of distribution, real estate, and tourism to build what became the Tōkyū Group. In May 1984 he was elected the 14th president of the JAPAN CHAMBER OF COMMERCE AND INDUSTRY.

Green Energy Project

A research project being carried out in the 1970s and 1980s by Japan's Ministry of Agriculture, Forestry, and Fisheries. The program was begun in 1978 as a ten-year project with the official name of "Comprehensive Research for Effective Utilization of Natural Energy in Agriculture and Fishery." The project's aims were to reduce the amount of oil used to heat the forcing houses (hothouses) in which many varieties of vegetables are raised in Japan. In an attempt to exploit alternative natural resources, the project intended to investigate the use of solar power, geothermal power, windmill power, and hydropower. At the same time, scientists began to explore new technological developments such as the possibility of developing techniques for controlling productive environments for vegetation, enhancing the photosynthesis capacity of vegetation, and working with the process of nitrogen fixation, which is vital to plant growth. *Nishimata Souhei*

Hattori Takaaki (1912–   )

Ninth chief justice of the Japanese Supreme Court. Born in Aichi Prefecture. Hattori graduated from the Faculty of Law at Tōkyō University. He served as chief judge of the Tsu District Court, the Tsu Family Court, the Tōkyō Family Court, the Fukuoka High Court, and the Ōsaka High Court. He became an associate justice of the Supreme Court in 1975 and was chief justice from 1979 to 1982. A specialist in civil law, he was internationalist in outlook, having studied at Harvard University. In the trial resulting from a lawsuit over noise at the Ōsaka airport, he recognized the right to damages of the residents who had brought the suit but refused to impose a ban on flights. *Nomura Jirō*

health care

Changes in the Health-Care Environment in Japan——One major change in the health-care environment in Japan in the first half of the 1980s was in the structure of diseases. Infectious and other acute diseases were on the decrease, and chronic diseases, especially the so-called adult diseases, were showing great increases. Cancer was the major cause of death from 1981, followed by cerebral apoplexy. Another change was in the structure of the Japanese population. The overall population was aging at a rapid rate, with a correspondingly rapid increase in demand for health and medical care. The proportion of national health-care expenditures accounted for by health care for the aged was increasing greatly, and, as a result, the system of free government health care for the aged that had been in effect since 1973 was abolished in 1983, when the Law concerning Health and Medical Services for the Aged went into effect. A third change was that health care was becoming more intensive and specialized owing to the remarkable advances that had been made in the field of medicine. A fourth change was that the Japanese people were becoming more conscious of the importance of health, and health-care needs were both increasing and becoming more diverse. A fifth type of change involved economic conditions. With little prospect of large-scale economic growth for the immediate future, there was a need to control the growing increases in health-care expenditures. One response to this need was a revision of the nation's health-insurance system in 1984.

Measures Taken to Meet Future Health-Care Needs——With 1985 as the target date, the Japanese government planned and put into effect a number of measures to provide better for the nation's overall health-care needs. These included measures to provide health care in remote areas, adjustments in the system for emergency health care, and measures to improve the network of specialized health-care facilities for certain serious diseases. The Law concerning Regional Health and Medical Care Planning was also passed in 1985. This law divided the nation's prefectures into health-care zones in order to provide more fully balanced health care in all regions of Japan, and it specified the number of hospital beds that were to be available in each zone. As for the demand for doctors, dentists, and other health-care professionals, in 1983 the goal of 150 doctors for every 100,000 people in the population was realized (in 1984 the figure reached 158 doctors for every 100,000 people). It was obvious that Japan would have to begin to worry about a future surplus of doctors, and in 1984 the Ministry of Health and Welfare set up a special commission to study future needs. The commission proposed that the number of new entrants into the medical profession be reduced by 10 percent by 1995. The question of how to implement this control measure was a problem that remained to be solved.

Facilities for an Aging Population —— The increasing burden borne by many Japanese families for the care of elderly family members who were bedridden or afflicted with senile dementia was becoming a serious social problem. The government was giving high priority both to the development of an overall policy on health, medical, and welfare services to meet the diverse needs of elderly people who require custodial care and to the setting up of a system of facilities. The Ministry of Health and Welfare was studying proposals for "intermediate facilities" that would combine the functions of hospitals and old-people's homes by providing both medical and welfare services.

The Need for a System of Family Medicine —— It was obviously unavoidable that medical care would continue to become even more intensive and specialized in the future. At the same time, it was essential to insure the availability of primary health care in order to provide full overall health-maintenance and medical services on a continuing basis. For this reason the Ministry of Health and Welfare in 1985 began studying specific proposals for developing a system of family medicine, including physicians trained to provide primary care. This system would be modeled in part on the primary health-care system that was already being developed in the United States.

NOSE Takayuki

health food

A growing public consciousness of health issues in Japan during the early years of the 1980s was accompanied by a boom in sales of health foods. In the background were such factors as a concern over the excessively rich diet of many present-day Japanese and an increasing proportion of older people in the population. There was still no legal definition of what constitutes health food; however, the National Institute of Nutrition classified health foods under the following three categories. 1. Nutritional supplements such as vitamins, protein, calcium, and wheat-, rice-, or corn-germ oil. 2. Health-maintenance supplements such as ginseng and dietary fibers. 3. Foods for adjusting nutritional balance such as low-sodium and diet foods. In addition to these categories, foods free of additives or raised without chemical fertilizers as well as unrefined foods such as whole wheat were also generally being referred to as health foods. The Japanese health-food industry was growing rapidly, and from the latter half of the 1970s large firms began to enter the business. However, there were no legal regulations applying specifically to health foods, and unscrupulous sales practices involving exaggerated claims of medicinal properties were becoming a problem. In 1984 the Ministry of Health and Welfare established a Health Food Policy Office to take responsibility for ensuring the safety of health foods and regulating trade practices.

MATSUMOTO Katsumi

Health Insurance Law, revision of

A revision of Japan's Health Insurance Law went into effect in October 1984. This revision was intended to provide a foundation for a stable health-insurance system for an age in which more and more Japanese people were living into their eighties and at the same time to enforce the government's basic principle of fiscal responsibility. (The government's outlays for the provision of health care had been growing steadily as the proportion of older people in the population increased.) The focal point of the revision was the introduction of a requirement that the primary insured under the system of health insurance for employed persons pay 10 percent of health-care costs. (Previously the employed person had only been required to pay an initial treatment fee of ¥800.) Other important changes included (1) revisions in the system of payment for major medical expenses, (2) approval of the use of health insurance to pay for treatment by advanced techniques previously not covered (this was limited to treatment in university hospitals and other such facilities), and (3) introduction of a health-care system for retired persons under 70 and their families (people aged 70 or over were covered by the Law concerning Health and Medical Services for the Aged). Another measure, intended to assure the appropriateness of health-care expenditures, revised the system for recognition of health-care providers so that hospitals or doctors who submitted excessive or improper claims could be denied recognition under the insurance system.

NOSE Takayuki

high-definition television

(HDTV). A new color television system being developed in Japan in the 1980s that creates sharper, more realistic images than the conventional television already in use. HDTV has 1,125 scanning lines and provides a remarkably improved picture quality with much higher resolution than the conventional 525-line system. HDTV also permits viewing on larger screens and at closer distances without loss of quality. With HDTV, analog video and audio signals are converted into digital signals for broadcast by satellite, as conventional broadcast is impossible at the frequencies required. The digital signals provide a more reliable broadcast. In January 1984, NHK (the Japan Broadcasting Corporation) demonstrated the suitability of the HDTV system for satellite broadcasting in a joint project with the Sony Corporation, Mitsubishi Electric Corporation, and other Japanese companies.

NISHIMATA Souhei

high-technology industry

The Japanese high-technology industry (including electronics, information, aerospace, biotechnology, new materials, mechatronics, and other fields) had a bright future in 1986, and its effect on the technological innovations of other industries was expected to be enormous. In the 1980s Japan was rapidly sharpening its competitive edge in such fields as electronics and mechatronics. At the same time, the United States made the Japanese system of standards and certification one of the issues of the so-called trade friction between the two nations, asserting that American high-technology products could not penetrate the Japanese market sufficiently due to restrictions that were being imposed.

IKEDA Minoru

home automation

During the 1980s there was a growing interest in Japan in home automation (the introduction of electronics and microcomputers to the household routine). Home automation is intended not only to save energy and labor, but also to provide residential alarms, entertainment, and home management conveniences. For example, an information network that makes it possible for users to do banking and other activities through home computer terminals was introduced in the Tōkyō area in 1984, and several manufacturers introduced computerized ranges that combined microwave, steam, and conventional cooking. However, full-scale home automation would have to await major changes in lifestyle and domestic architecture, and as of the mid-1980s home automation was not yet widespread in Japan.

NISHIMATA Souhei

Honshū-Shikoku bridges

In 1986 three separate chains of island-hopping bridges across the Inland Sea designed to connect Honshū and Shikoku were under construction. The easternmost route, the Kōbe-Naruto route, would link Akashi in Hyōgo Prefecture with Naruto in Tokushima Prefecture via the island of Awajishima, using two bridges. The middle route, the Kojima-Sakaide route, would link Kojima in Okayama Prefecture with Sakaide in Kagawa Prefecture, using five islands and six bridges. The westernmost route, the Onomichi-Imabari route, would link Onomichi in Hiroshima Prefecture with Imabari in Ehime Prefecture, using eight islands and nine bridges. A study of the feasibility of connecting Honshū and Shikoku by such chains of bridges was initiated in 1959, and in 1970 the Honshū-Shikoku Bridge Authority was established. In 1973, the Minister of Transport and the Minister of Construction approved the construction of the bridges, and by 1985 three of the total of seventeen individual bridges had been completed. The route scheduled to be completed first (by 1988) was the Kojima-Sakaide route.

KURAHASHI Tōru

hospice care

In Japan the English expression "hospice care" is used to refer to special care for the terminally ill, usually in a regular hospital rather than in a special facility as in other countries, and usually for only the final two to six months of life. The phrase thus refers to the concept of a special kind of care rather than a place. The brevity of the period allocated to hospice care is based on a number of emotional, social, and medical factors. It would be difficult to develop special hospice

Ichikawa Danjūrō XII

Ichikawa Danjūrō XII, performing under his new name for the first time, in the role of the Buddhist monk in *Narukami*. The court lady is played by Bandō Tamasaburō.

care facilities in Japan. One reason is the deep-rooted aversion, on the part of physician, patient, and family, to pronouncing "the sentence of death" by admitting that death is inevitable. Another is the medical fact that it is now overwhelmingly customary in Japan to face death in a hospital attended by a physician. It would be very difficult for people to accept being transferred to a special facility to die. For such reasons, hospice care in Japan is carried out by special hospice-care teams in such institutions as university hospitals and hospitals specializing in cancer. It is also carried out as a regional joint activity by some cooperating regional hospitals and clinics.
Nose Takayuki

household savings ratio

The household savings ratio is the ratio of household savings to total household disposable income after taxes, savings being defined as that part of disposable income not accounted for by consumer expenditures. (Savings includes bank deposits, stocks and bonds, life insurance, and home loan payments.) The household savings ratio in Japan from 1973 to 1978 was high—over 20 percent. After 1978 it gradually declined to 16.3 percent in 1983 and 16.1 percent in 1984. This was still higher than the savings ratios of Western nations. (The 1983 figures were 11.5 percent for France, 11.3 percent for West Germany, 7 percent for the United Kingdom, and 5.2 percent for the United States.) During the 1980s, Japan's high household savings ratio was cited by some people in the United States and other Western nations as one of the causes of the large Japanese trade surplus that had been a source of friction between Japan and its international trading partners. It was felt that the Japanese should stop saving their money and buy more imported goods. According to a survey by the Japanese government's Management and Coordination Agency, the average household savings of Japanese wage earners at the end of 1984 was ¥6.49 million (US $27,314), which was more than the average yearly income of wage-earner households (¥5.45 million or US $22,937). One reason for Japan's high savings ratio had been the youthful makeup of the Japanese population. In the 1980s, the population was aging at a rapid rate, and this trend could be expected to result in a drop in Japan's household savings ratio.
Yasuhara Norikazu

household violence

(kateinai bōryoku). In Japan this term is used almost exclusively to refer to violent acts directed by children against parents, grandparents, or other members of their own families. It usually refers to such acts as striking or kicking family members, instances of which take place repeatedly over a fairly long span of time. Cases of this kind of behavior first began to be reported in Japan around 1960, and since then it has grown to the dimensions of a serious social problem. (There have even been instances of parents killing violent children or of children killing their parents.) According to 1984 figures, children of middle-school age were the most numerous perpetrators of violence against family members. The next most numerous were unemployed youths and high-school students. Regardless of age, the overwhelming majority of violent children were male. The object of the violence in 62 percent of the cases was the mother. In 53.3 percent of the cases the immediate cause was reaction against the parent's attitude over such matters as discipline. The causes for the increasing incidence of violence against family members are harder to determine. However, the most commonly cited theory is that in the material abundance of present-day Japanese society many children are overprotected and are the objects of too much parental interference and that as a result they are lacking in the resilience needed to overcome obstacles or adapt themselves to situations in which things do not go as they had wished. According to this theory, the outbreaks of violence begin to occur when these children meet head-on with such difficulties as Japan's harsh entrance-examination competition and become frustrated or lose self-confidence. In other words, the causes of the phenomenon are deeply rooted in conditions in the home, the schools, and the society at large.
Yamagishi Shunsuke

hydroponic vegetables

The first large-scale production of vegetables in Japan by hydroponics (the use of solutions containing the necessary minerals rather than soil) was carried on by the US military forces shortly after the end of World War II. The hydroponic vegetables that are now being grown commercially in Japan include tomatoes, cucumbers, melons, *mitsuba* (honewort or wild chervil), and *kaiware daikon* (radish sprouts). The latter two are especially important, as 90 percent of the total *mitsuba* crop and 100 percent of the *kaiware daikon* is produced hydroponically. Beginning in the 1980s, computer-controlled "vegetable factories," combining hydroponics with the use of artificial light, were introduced on a trial basis. The chief crop now being grown in such vegetable factories in Japan is lettuce.

Ichikawa Danjūrō XII (1946–   )

In April 1985, Ichikawa Ebizō X (real name Horikoshi Natsuo) assumed the illustrious KABUKI acting name of ICHIKAWA DANJŪRŌ, becoming the twelfth in the line. He was born in Tōkyō as the eldest son of Ichikawa Danjūrō XI (1909–65), and his assumption of the name came on the 20th anniversary of his father's death. Performances commemorating the announcement were held at the Kabukiza during the three months of April, May, and June. The naming of a new Danjūrō also marked the 90th year since the founding of the SHŌCHIKU CO, LTD, which produces kabuki performances, and it was hoped that the event would symbolize a revival of kabuki from the slump that it had been suffering. Following the three months of performances at the Kabukiza, commemorative announcement performances were also held in the United States in Washington, New York, and Los Angeles during July and August.

imitation foods

(kopī shokuhin). A term used in Japan to refer specifically to imitation crab, scallops, squid, and other fish products. These imitations are made chiefly from a fish paste *(surimi)* derived from Alaska pollack or walleye pollack. Starch, flavorings, preservatives, dyes, and other additives are used to produce products that are almost identical in shape, color, taste, and smell to actual crabmeat, scallops, or squid fillets. The price of these imitations ranges from one-tenth to one-third of the prices of their real counterparts. Imitation crabmeat, which is used in SUSHI, soups, TEMPURA, and other dishes, is the most widely sold imitation fish product in Japan. The amount produced has been increasing steadily, and it is exported to Europe,

the United States, and Australia. From around 1984, Japanese businesses began building and operating imitation-crabmeat factories in the United States. Kibun, a fish paste manufacturer, opened one such plant in Seattle, Washington, and another in Raleigh, North Carolina. A similar plant was scheduled to open in Scotland in 1986. In addition to crab, scallops, and squid, imitation herring roe and salmon roe are also produced; the latter, however, are not made from fish paste but consist of salad oil enclosed in a gelatinous membrane derived from seaweed.

industrial policy in the 1980s

Since the 1970s the Japanese government's INDUSTRIAL POLICY had been based on utilization of the market mechanism. The functions of industrial policy had been limited to a few areas such as providing industrial vision for the future, encouraging planned reduction in production or conversion to other types of products for those industries faced with long-term difficulties as a result of the oil crises of 1973 and 1979, and encouraging the development of basic technologies in small and medium enterprises. A specific example is the law that was passed in May 1978 to aid 10 types of industries, such as aluminum refining, shipbuilding, and spinning, that were then facing difficulties. This law made possible the drawing up of plans for cooperative disposal of surplus equipment and the establishment of a cooperative fund to assure the availability of needed capital. In May 1983 this law was replaced by a new law which affected 21 other types of industries, such as paper, ethylene, and sugar, in addition to the original 10. The new law not only encouraged the cooperative disposal of surplus equipment but also cooperative production, amalgamation, and product specialization. Another law, passed in February 1986, introduced tax measures to encourage investment for technological innovation in small and medium enterprises as well as financial measures to encourage conversion of industries in the face of the rising value of the yen.

Ōmori Takashi

INS

(Information Network System). The name of the integrated services digital network (ISDN) developed by the Nippon Telegraph and Telephone Corporation (NTT). The system combines previously separate phone, facsimile, and data communication lines into a single telecommunications network, thereby providing information and visual communication simultaneously. Through a home terminal unit, users can shop by television, bank, utilize data service, and enjoy home study and other activities. An experimental model of the system was introduced to Japan in September 1984 as a 30-month experiment in the Mitaka-Musashino district of Tōkyō. Commercial service was to commence in ten locations in 1986 and in the prefectural capital cities in 1987. Digitization of lines throughout Japan was targeted for 1995 so that the INS would serve the entire country by integrating telephone and nontelephone lines. Technical characteristics of the system are digitization of electrical signals and the use of large-capacity optical-fiber cables.

Nishimata Souhei

"intelligent" buildings

The concept of the "intelligent" or "smart" building—an ultramodern office building equipped with the new technology of computer-based office operations and telecommunications systems—was developed in the United States and imported to Japan in the early 1980s. The key element in an intelligent building is provision for advanced electronic communications technology and for the systems of interconnected computers and other devices known as local area networks (LAN). As of early 1986, no intelligent buildings had actually been built in Japan; however, the Tōshiba Building, completed in 1984 in Tōkyō as the main office building for the Tōshiba Corporation, and the Honda Aoyama Building, which was completed in Tōkyō in 1985 and serves as the main office building for the Honda Motor Co, Ltd, were equipped with very advanced office automation systems that clearly anticipated those of the intelligent building. In 1986 blueprints for intelligent buildings were being drawn up by several Japanese high-technology corporations, including the Mitsubishi Electric Corporation and the Nippon Telegraph and Telephone Corporation. According to Mitsubishi's projections, 20 to 30 percent of all new Japanese office buildings would be the intelligent type by 1990. *Nishimata Souhei*

internationalization of the yen

A phrase referring to the increased use and holding of the yen in international transactions. As of the mid-1980s the level of the yen's internationalization was lower than that of the Deutsche mark. In 1985, 30 to 40 percent of Japan's export transactions were conducted on a yen basis, but import transactions were conducted almost entirely on a foreign currency basis. In capital transactions, nonresident holdings of yen-denominated assets, such as long-term bonds in yen, increased remarkably in the 1980s, while resident holdings of external yen-denominated assets, such as syndicate loans in yen, also increased rapidly. In official reserves such as foreign currency, foreign exchange, and special drawing rights (SDR) held by governments or central banks, the component ratio of yen held by foreign authorities was less than 5 percent in 1983. Benefits of an internationalized yen include facilitation of the flow of domestic and foreign capital, improved efficiency in the raising and use of funds by enterprises, and greater transactions opportunities for domestic and foreign financial institutions. In March 1985 the Council on Foreign Exchange and Other Transactions, an advisory council to the Japanese government, submitted a report on the desirability of further internationalizing the yen. The report stressed the necessity of bringing about conditions that would further the financial liberalization of Japan, making the yen an easily usable transaction currency, and stabilizing its value for an extended period. *Nishikawa Masao*

international relations in the 1980s

The most outstanding fact about Japanese foreign policy during the first half of the 1980s was that Japan cleared itself of charges that it was "a big nation economically but a small nation politically" by demonstrating that it was ready to play a positive role in international politics.

A Political Role in Troubled Areas of the World——Japan attempted to mediate in the war that had broken out between Iran and Iraq in September 1980 by sending Minister of Foreign Affairs Abe Shintarō (b 1924) on a visit to the area in the summer of 1983. The following year, the foreign ministers of Iran and Iraq and other important officials from the two countries paid successive visits to Japan. Although these exchanges did not achieve the desired result of an end to the war, they nevertheless attracted attention as a new development in Japanese foreign policy—an attempt to play a positive political role in world affairs. The Japanese government also made clear its desire to help in settling the strife that had continued in Cambodia since the end of the Vietnam War by indicating its readiness to provide monetary assistance to peace-keeping activities in the area. It also offered to send personnel to help in the event of free elections under international supervision.

Japan As a Member of the Western Alliance——In the early 1980s Japan also demonstrated in a number of ways its intention of fulfilling its responsibilities as a member of the Western alliance. For example, there were changes of emphasis in Japan's economic aid to other nations. There was an increase in aid to nations such as Pakistan, Thailand, and Turkey in the so-called troubled areas of the globe. Aid was also provided to nations like Egypt and the Sudan in response to the demands of collective security. Another clear expression of Japan's wish to cooperate with other Western nations as a member of the alliance can be seen in the "political statement" issued at the ninth summit meeting of the seven industrialized nations of Canada, France, Great Britain, Italy, Japan, the United States, and West Germany, which was held in Williamsburg, Virginia in May 1983. The fact that Japan participated in this declaration, which was a display of solidarity against the Soviet Union on the part of the seven Western nations and the fact that Japan agreed to the deployment of intermediate-range nuclear missiles in Western Europe represented a revision of the course that the nation's foreign policy had followed up to that point. This intention of playing a political role as a member of the Western alliance can also be observed in the way Japan conducted its foreign relations in Asia.

Relations with South Korea——During talks held between the Japanese and South Korean foreign ministers in August 1981, South Korea asked Japan for a large amount of financial aid, citing the burden borne by South Korea in maintaining security in the region. Negotiations reached a stalemate, and, as a result, relations between Japan and South Korea became strained. A settlement of the economic aid issue was reached during Prime Minister NAKASONE YASUHIRO's (b 1918) visit to Korea in January 1983, shortly after the inauguration of the Nakasone cabinet. This visit and South Korean President Chun Doo Hwan's visit to Japan in September 1984 marked the recovery of friendly relations between the two countries.

Relations with China——Japanese economic and technical aid to China was stepped up during this period in connection with China's program of modernization for social reconstruction, and Sino-Japanese trade was also greatly enlarged. In addition, there were great increases in programs for human and cultural exchange. The number of Chinese students and researchers working at Japanese universities grew rapidly, doubling in the period between 1980 and 1985. The friendly relations between the two countries were strained by a number of incidents such as a controversy over Japanese government approval of history textbooks (publishers were required to weaken descriptions of Japan's invasion of China in the 1930s) and a controversy over official visits by the prime minister to YASUKUNI SHRINE (seen by some as a symbol of Japan's militarism in the 1930s and 1940s). There was also the problem of Japan's large trade surplus. However, the basic movement of Sino-Japanese relations in the first half of the 1980s was in the direction of greater harmony.

Cooperation with the United States in Defense——The early 1980s was also a period of increased Japanese cooperation with the United States in the field of defense. First there was an explicit reference to an "alliance" between Japan and the United States in the joint statement issued by Prime Minister SUZUKI ZENKŌ (b 1911) and President Reagan on the occasion of the former's visit to the United States in May 1981. On this occasion, Prime Minister Suzuki also stated that defense of the 1,000-nautical-mile sea lane of communications (SLOC) between the two nations was a matter of course. This was taken a step further by Prime Minister Nakasone during his visit to the United States in January 1983, when he spoke of the "common destiny" shared by Japan and the United States. Nakasone also made a number of martial-sounding statements that created a stir in Japanese public opinion. For example, he described Japan as "an unsinkable aircraft carrier" and spoke of the possibility of blockading "four strategic straits" in a defense emergency (the latter statement was later amended to "three strategic straits," a reference to the straits of Sōya, Tsugaru, and Tsushima).

Increased cooperation between Japan and the United States in matters of defense went beyond such declarations by heads of state to include new concrete developments as well. Examples include Japan's participation, from 1980, in the RIMPAC (Rim of the Pacific) exercises and an agreement, reached in November 1983, for Japan to provide defense technology to the United States. This agreement was counter to the "three principles" prohibiting arms export that had been adhered to by previous Japanese administrations (see ARMS EXPORT, THREE PRINCIPLES OF); however, the provision of aid to the United States was made a special exception. As of 1985, the question of Japanese participation in the research for the Reagan administration's Strategic Defense Initiatives (SDI) had become the subject of a lively debate in Japan.

Despite these developments in defense cooperation, a strong feeling of dissatisfaction prevailed within the United States, and particularly within the Congress, over insufficient Japanese effort toward strengthening of Japan's own defenses, especially over the Japanese rule limiting defense expenditures to one percent of the nation's gross national product (GNP). There were people in the United States who accused Japan of "taking a free ride" when it came to defense. In 1981–82 there was even talk in Japan of "defense friction" between the two nations, and doubt was thrown on the Reagan-Suzuki statement about an "alliance" when Suzuki told reporters that the word did not have a military meaning.

Economic Friction——The single most important theme in Japanese foreign relations in the first half of the 1980s was the phenomenon referred to as "economic friction" between Japan and the United States. Trade friction between the two nations had already been intensifying since the middle of the 1970s with reference to such products as steel, color television sets, beef, oranges, automobiles, and semiconductors. In the first years of the 1980s, intensified competition from Japanese products in fields of manufacturing that had always been a source of American strength and prestige became a particularly important problem. These developments were accompanied by the emergence in the United States of a tendency to view Japan as an unyielding "rival," and there was much talk of "the Japanese threat." At the same time, the image held of the Japanese market was that of a "closed market" (an image that did not necessarily correspond with the reality), and there was increased criticism, especially in the Congress, of Japanese trade practices as "unfair."

Such sentiments were strengthened by America's extremely unfavorable trade balance with regard to Japan. This unfavorable balance of trade increased annually during the 1980s, reaching $36.8 billion in 1984 and $49.7 billion in 1985 (according to US customs statistics). The situation was to a large degree caused by foreign exchange factors such as an improving American economy and a strong dollar. Nevertheless, in March 1985, a hard-line attitude toward Japan became dominant in the US Congress, and a resolution demanding retaliatory measures was passed by a unanimous vote of the Senate. The demands for an opening up of the Japanese market were particularly strong, and the Japanese government responded to these in July 1985 with an "Action Program for Improving Market Access." However, this was not viewed as likely to have a great effect on the balance of payments. An event that did have an important impact on this situation was a decision for cooperative intervention in the exchange rate that was reached at a meeting of the finance ministers of the Five Advanced Nations (the so-called G-5 Meeting of France, Great Britain, Japan, the United States, and West Germany) on 22 September 1985. After this decision, the exchange rate began a sharp movement in the direction of a weaker dollar, a development that had a calming effect on trade friction between Japan and the United States.

Japan and the World Economy——Japan also continued to have a favorable balance of trade with the EC (European Community) nations. There was some trade friction with these nations, but one reason that it did not become as pronounced as the friction with the United States was that for a number of years Japan's trade surplus had increased on an extremely gentle curve, remaining around the $10 billion level. Nevertheless, there were strong protective currents within the EC nations which, together with the increasingly protectionist leanings within the United States, cast dark shadows on the future of the system of free world trade. The world economy now stood at an extremely important crossroad, and it was impossible to predict the future prospects of the Japanese economy. A cheaper dollar and the drop in oil prices that occurred in 1985 were combined factors that were certain to produce great fluctuations in the world economy. International expectations of Japan as an economic power were reaching a new height.

Assistance to Developing Nations——Official Development Assistance (ODA) to developing nations continued to increase as it had in the 1970s. The nations that were the objects of this assistance continued to be chiefly Asian nations, particularly the ASEAN countries (see ASEAN AND JAPAN). One noteworthy development was the rapid increase in the relative importance of China as a recipient of such aid. The amount of aid to South Korea also increased sharply beginning in 1983. Japan's economic cooperation in the effort to aid famine victims in Africa and Japanese humanitarian relief activities aimed at refugees from Cambodia and Afghanistan should also be mentioned. In relations with third-world countries, the problem of the accumulated debt of developing nations was one source of extremely high expectations of Japan as an economic power. Along with the rise of protectionist tendencies, it was this accumulated-debt problem that most threatened the future of the world economy, and it added greatly to the weight of Japan's responsibilities as an international power.

HOSOYA Chihiro

Ishibashi Masashi (1924–   )

Politician. Born in the city of Taibei (Taipei; J: Taihoku) in Taiwan, then a Japanese colony. Ishibashi graduated from the Taibei Economics Professional School in 1944, then served in the Japanese army during World War II. After being demobilized in Japan at the end of the war, he worked as a laborer at a base of the American Occupation forces at Sasebo. In 1947 he became chief secretary of the Sasebo branch of a labor union for Japanese employees of the Occupation. In 1955 he was elected to the House of Representatives from Nagasaki Prefecture as a candidate of the left faction of the JAPAN SOCIALIST PARTY. Within the party he became active as a specialist in foreign relations and defense issues. He served as the party's secretary general under the chairmanship of NARITA TOMOMI (b 1912) for seven years from 1970. In 1983 he became the ninth chairman of the party. Placing more emphasis on practicality than ideology, he worked, under the slogan "The New Socialist Party," to change the party into one that could hope to win a majority and form a government. After the July 1986 election Ishibashi resigned from his position as chairman.

Ishihara Takashi (1912–   )

Businessman. Born in Tōkyō. Ishihara graduated from the Faculty of Law and Literature of Tōhoku University in 1937 and worked for the Nissan Motor Company. In 1977 he became representative director and president of the company. A strong promoter of the automobile export trade, he succeeded in opening up markets in Britain and Mexico and in initiating local manufacturing. In April 1985 he became the representative manager of the JAPAN COMMITTEE FOR ECONOMIC DEVELOPMENT. He also served as president of the Japan Automobile Manufacturers Association and of the Japan Motor Industrial Federation.

Itakura Keiichi (1942–   )

Molecular biologist. Born in Tōkyō. Graduated from the Tōkyō College of Pharmacy. After working as a researcher in Canada, Itakura served from 1976 as a senior researcher at the City of Hope Medical Center near Los Angeles in the United States. He succeeded in synthesizing the DNA of the pancreatic hormone somatostatin and in expressing it in the colon bacillus E. coli, an epoch-making achievement in the field of artificially synthesized gene expression. He afterwards succeeded in the synthesis and expression of genes of insulin and human growth hormones, becoming recognized as one of the leading scientists of his field.

Japanese diet

The traditional Japanese diet emphasizes grains (particularly rice), fish and shellfish, seaweed, and vegetables. The intake of meat, milk and other dairy products, and fats is extremely small compared to the diet of most Western nations; however, it is nutritionally well-balanced. The fact that in Japan the death rates from heart disease and diabetes are low is said to be a result of this traditional diet. However, in the mid-1980s, forty years after the food shortages that immediately followed World War II, the Japanese diet had reached a stage that some called "an age of gluttony," and the problem had become one of an overabundant diet. According to the Ministry of Health and Welfare, the required daily calorie intake for adult males was 2,500 calories and that for females 2,000 calories. However, in 1983 it was estimated that approximately 60 percent of the Japanese people were exceeding this calorie intake. Moreover, the proportion of calorie intake attributable to fats was increasing, and the people were consuming less fish than they had traditionally. For these reasons, the Ministry of Agriculture, Forestry, and Fisheries, and the Ministry of Health and Welfare were carrying on campaigns to promote a return to the healthier traditional Japanese diet.

MATSUMOTO Katsumi

Japanese-language training for foreigners

As Japan rejoined the international community following World War II, interest in the Japanese language in other nations began to grow at a rapid pace. According to a survey conducted in 1967 by the Japanese Ministry of Foreign Affairs, Japanese was being taught at 428 institutions in 37 foreign countries. The number of teachers was 1,027 and the number of students 36,694. The corresponding figures in a survey conducted in 1984 by the Ministry of Foreign Affairs and the JAPAN FOUNDATION was 2,651 institutions, 75 countries, 7,351 teachers, and 580,943 students. Growing interest in Japan and closer international relationships would obviously cause these numbers to continue to increase in the future. The largest numbers of the foreign students of Japanese lived in nations situated around the rim of the Pacific Ocean, such as the nations of East Asia, Southeast Asia, Oceania (including Australia and New Zealand), North America, and Central and South America (see table). Until the 1970s, Japanese had been treated as what might be called a special foreign language. Now it was being recognized as an ordinary foreign language, and in some of the nations of East Asia, Southeast Asia, and Oceania it was being taught as such at the secondary-school level (chiefly in high schools). In some countries, such as South Korea, China, and Australia, Japanese had become one of the foreign languages included in college entrance examinations. Japanese was also being taught by radio and television in these countries, and there were plans to begin similar broadcasts in Canada and the United States. Some foreigners were even beginning to learn Japanese as a medium for the study of advanced technology.

Tendencies similar to those could be seen in Japanese-language

Japanese-language training for foreigners

Study of Japanese abroad by region (1984)				
Region	Number of countries	Number of organizations	Number of teachers	Number of students
Asia	19	1,159	3,920	460,689
Oceania	4	274	487	27,739
North America	2	469	1,402	40,375
Central and South America (including Mexico)	13	514	942	40,375
Europe	25	215	563	10,478
Middle East, Near East, and Africa	12	20	37	825
Total	75	2,651	7,351	580,943

Source: Japan Foundation, Kaigai nihongo kyōiku kikan chōsa (1984)

study by foreigners in Japan itself. According to a 1985 survey by the Ministry of Education, Japanese was being taught to 35,335 foreign residents of Japan by 3,258 teachers in 370 institutions, including universities and Japanese-language schools.

The administration of a Japanese-language proficiency test to foreigners residing in Japan and in various other countries began in 1984. (The test, which is supported by the Ministry of Foreign Affairs and the Ministry of Education, is administered abroad by the Japan Foundation and in Japan by the Association of International Education, Japan.) The 1985 test was taken by 15,000 people in 34 cities in 18 countries, including Japan. This was twice the number of people who had taken the test in 1984.

The Japan Foundation provides various forms of support and assistance to Japanese-language programs in foreign countries. (For example, it arranges to send native Japanese specialists in Japanese as a foreign language to teach in other countries.) Assistance to Japanese-language programs for foreigners in Japan is the responsibility of the Ministry of Education and the Agency for Cultural Affairs. The Society for Teaching Japanese as a Foreign Language, which was founded in 1962 and has headquarters in Tōkyō had 1,800 members in 1986, of whom 210 were overseas members. The society publishes Nihongo kyōiku (Journal of Japanese Language Teaching) and sponsors conferences for specialists in the field.

SHIINA Kazuo

Japanese nationality, changes in requirements for

On 25 May 1984, the Japanese Diet unanimously approved an amendment to the Nationality Law of 1950 (see JAPANESE NATIONALITY), which took effect on 1 January 1985.

During the thirty-four years after the enactment of the 1950 law, there had been substantial changes in both international and Japanese domestic circumstances. An increasing number of Japanese nationals went abroad, and a considerable number of foreigners came to establish residence in Japan because of Japan's growing economy and improvements in overseas transportation, among other reasons. As a consequence of the increased exchange of people, international marriages had also become more common, bringing about serious problems concerning the acquisition of Japanese nationality by the children of Japanese women married to foreigners, since according to the Nationality Law of 1950, nationality could be acquired only by patrilineal relationships, i.e., by jus sanguinis through the father. Also, there were criticisms of the law's provisions concerning naturalization because foreign wives of Japanese nationals could establish Japanese nationality more easily than foreign husbands of Japanese nationals.

Proposals for revision of the law became more and more frequent on the grounds that the Japanese constitution provides for the equality of the sexes and that the provisions of the Nationality Law were thus unconstitutional. Furthermore, Japan had assumed an obligation to revise its internal laws concerning the matter in order to ratify the United Nations Convention on the Elimination of All Forms of Discrimination against Women, signed in July 1980, which stipulated that women had the same rights as men with respect to the nationality of their children.

In December 1981, the Japanese government began preparing for revision of the Nationality Law by appointing a Nationality Law

Committee, responsible to the Legislative Council and composed of government officials, university professors, former diplomats, jurists, and representatives from different sectors of the community. The Committee submitted a draft for the amendment to the minister of justice in February 1983, and public hearings were held to collect opinions from civic groups, academic circles, and other interested parties. Written suggestions were also accepted. The amendment approved as a result of this process made very important changes in the Nationality Law of 1950. Major changes are enumerated below.

Acquisition of Nationality——Nationality can be acquired by birth, legitimization, and naturalization. In the first instance, a child is a Japanese national when at the time of its birth the father *or* mother is a Japanese national (article 2, paragraph 1).

A child under twenty years of age who is recognized as a legitimate child by parents of Japanese nationality is entitled to obtain Japanese nationality by submitting notification to the minister of justice (article 3).

As for naturalization, the minister of justice is authorized to grant naturalization to a foreign spouse of a Japanese national, irrespective of sex, on condition that he or she has been married to the Japanese national for three years or more and has had a domicile in Japan for one full year or more (article 7). The minister may also permit the naturalization if the alien is, despite his or her intention, unable to deprive himself or herself of his or her current nationality and the minister finds exceptional circumstances—for example in his or her familial relationship with a Japanese national, or other circumstances (article 5, paragraph 2).

There are also special rules for the acquisition of nationality, which provide that a person who was born during the period of 1 January 1965 to 31 December 1984, and whose mother was a Japanese national at the time of the person's birth may acquire Japanese nationality by notifying the minister of justice within three years after the enforcement of this law.

Choice of Nationality——A Japanese national having a foreign nationality must choose either of the nationalities (a) before he or she reaches twenty-two years of age if he or she has acquired both nationalities on or before the day when he or she reached twenty years of age or (b) within two years after the day when he or she acquired the second nationality if he or she acquired such nationality after the day when he or she reached twenty years of age. Choice of Japanese nationality is to be made either by the individual's depriving himself or herself of the foreign nationality or by a declaration in which he or she swears that he or she chooses to be a Japanese national and that he or she renounces the foreign nationality (article 14).

Loss of Nationality——A Japanese national who voluntarily acquires a foreign nationality, or who acquires a foreign nationality by reason of birth in a foreign country, loses his or her nationality retroactively as from the time of birth unless within three months after birth or the acquisition of the foreign nationality the individual (or the parents) manifests his or her volition to preserve the Japanese nationality (article 12).

Family Registration Law——In order to effect the changes called for by the amendment of the Nationality Law, a revision of the Family Registration Law of 1947 also became necessary. The major improvement was that a Japanese woman married to a non-Japanese will be allowed to establish a new *koseki* (family register), and such a Japanese woman will be allowed to take her husband's name if notification is made within six months after marriage.

NINOMIYA *Masato*

Japanese word processor

A computerized electronic typewriter designed to write and edit the Japanese language. Unlike most Western languages, which are written in a single alphabet, Japanese is written in a combination of Chinese characters (*kanji*) with two separate sets of phonetic characters (*kana*). This complex writing system made the use of Japanese typewriters a laborious process before the development of microelectronics brought about the invention of a practical Japanese word processor. With a Japanese word processor, words and whole phrases are input from the keyboard phonetically, using either the roman alphabet or one of the *kana* scripts. The processor then converts the words into normal Japanese writing composed of the three types of characters. The built-in computer dictionary of a large word processor contains more than 50,000 words permanently stored in its memory. Special words, such as proper names and technical terms, can be added to the dictionary.

The first Japanese word processor was launched in 1978 by the TŌSHIBA CORPORATION at a price of ¥6.3 million (US $29,937). As integrated circuit computers became steadily less expensive, the prices of Japanese word processors fell sharply. By the mid-1980s some portable machines were selling for less than ¥50,000 (US $210). The Japanese word processor is one of Japan's most popular electronic products. In 1985 over 1.2 million of them were sold, four times the previous year's sales, and nearly a dozen firms had developed a wide variety of machines for both home and business use.

NISHIMATA *Souhei*

Japan's growing middle class

During Japan's period of high economic growth in the 1960s and 1970s, an increasing percentage of the population come to identify themselves as part of the middle class. Several changes in the general lifestyle in Japan brought about this attitude.

First, the employment rate rose rapidly as the country's rate of industrialization progressed from 39% in 1950 to 74% in 1984. Urbanization kept pace with improvements in working conditions and helped create an increasingly homogeneous society. The typical image of Japanese workers is of families living in housing complexes in the suburbs of large cities. Secondly, the average monthly wage in 1950 was ¥63,000 (US $265.14); by 1984 it had increased to ¥305,000 (US $1,284). At the same time, wage differentials based on the size of the enterprise, an employee's age, and similar considerations had decreased.

Reflecting the higher income, consumption per household increased 3.5 times between 1950 and 1984. The levels of income and consumption for farming families increased at the same rate as those of workers in the cities.

The key index of the improved living standard was the rapid spread of consumer durables in the 1960s, particularly household electrical appliances. By 1970 major household electrical appliances were owned by 90 percent of the households in Japan, and 1984 data showed that 99 percent of all Japanese households used electric refrigerators and color television sets, 98 percent had electric washing machines, and 97 percent used vacuum cleaners. Leisure-time amusements were also being enjoyed by more people, reflecting the more prosperous situation of most Japanese. Higher education, which was available only to a select group before World War II, was offered to a greater part of the population. In 1955, the percentage of young people attending high schools and universities was 52 percent and 10 percent, respectively, but by 1985 the percentage had reached 94 percent and 38 percent, respectively. If specialized courses in special schools and technical colleges are included, 52 percent of Japanese students went on to institutions of higher learning in 1985, so that one out of every two individuals of eligible age was receiving a higher education.

YASUHARA *Norikazu*

Japan Tobacco, Inc

(Nihon Tabako Sangyō). The company that has a monopoly on the manufacture of tobacco products in Japan. Created in 1985 through the privatization of the JAPAN TOBACCO AND SALT PUBLIC CORPORATION with a capital of ¥100 billion (US $420 million). All stock is held by the government. The background to the privatization of this government industry includes a 1983 report of the Second Provisional Commission for Administrative Reform, which had mentioned privatization as one of the principles for simplification of government administration, as well as the fact that there had been increasingly strong demands for the lifting of restrictions against foreign tobacco products in the Japanese market as one step in lessening economic friction between Japan and the United States. By means of privatization, restrictions on the import and marketing of foreign tobacco products were relaxed. The sale of salt remained a monopoly that Japan Tobacco, Inc, took over from the Japan Tobacco and Salt Public Corporation. (The NIPPON TELEGRAPH AND TELEPHONE PUBLIC CORPORATION was privatized at the same time.)

Japan–United States agricultural talks

As the trade imbalance between Japan and the United States continued to become more pronounced during the early 1980s, the issue of opening up the Japanese market to foreign agricultural products remained one of the most frequently raised points of contention. In the Japan–United States Agricultural Consultations held in October 1981, the United States demanded the liberalization of imports of beef and citrus fruits beginning in April 1984. After two and a half years of protracted negotiations over this demand, an agreement was finally reached in April 1984. The agreement called for (1) a 27,600-ton increase in imports of high-quality beef over the following four years, (2) an 11,000-ton increase in imports of oranges in each of the following four years, (3) a 500-ton increase in imports of orange juice in each of the following four years, and (4) grapefruit juice import quotas based on Japanese market demand for two years, followed by freeing of imports beginning in April 1986. Beef and citrus imports for the 1987 Japanese fiscal year (ending March 1988) and beyond were to be discussed in future talks.

The US government also demanded liberalization of imports for 12 of 22 other categories of agricultural and fish products on which Japan had imposed import restrictions and submitted a complaint on the matter under the General Agreement on Tariffs and Trade (GATT). Only partial progress was made by the liberalization in April 1984 of some individual products within the 12 categories. In March 1986, negotiations on the issue were reopened; however, they did not go smoothly, for the United States demanded complete liberalization of imports on all 12 categories of products or, barring that, a gradual phase-out of restrictions, whereas Japan showed reluctance on the grounds that further reliance on imports of agricultural products would be a serious blow to domestic agriculture and would cause problems in maintaining a stable domestic food supply.

Japan and the United States also continued to negotiate about the lowering of tariffs on plywood as part of the MOSS (Market Oriented Sector Selective) talks. These negotiations were intertwined with the issue of the lowering of tariffs on plywood from Indonesia and other Southeast Asian nations, and the necessary internal adjustments within Japan proved difficult. Nevertheless, in January 1986, reductions in the tariffs were agreed upon, effective April 1987. FURUNO Masami

Japan–United States Group on Yen-Dollar Issues

In November 1983 the Japanese Minister of Finance and the American Secretary of the Treasury announced the establishment of a Joint Japan–United States Ad Hoc Group on the Yen-Dollar Exchange Rate, Financial, and Capital Market Issues to deliberate these and other issues connected with the further opening of Japan's financial market. The stated aims of the group were to achieve a greater mutual understanding of conditions in the two countries and to evaluate the factors involved in the yen-dollar exchange rate. In practice, however, such concrete measures were discussed as the deregulation and the opening up of the financial and capital markets of Japan, and the internationalization of the yen. The group submitted a report to the prime minister of Japan and the president of the United States in May 1984. NISHIKAWA Masao

Joint First-Stage Achievement Test

A standardized, multiple-choice examination given jointly by Japanese national and other public universities in January of each year since 1979 as the first stage in screening potential applicants for admission. The test covers seven subject areas in the five fields of Japanese language, social studies, mathematics, science, and foreign languages (the student chooses two subject areas each in social studies and science). The test is intended to measure the level of competence attained by the student in basic, general subjects. The student chooses the university to which he or she wishes to apply on the basis of the score achieved on this test. The individual universities then conduct their own independent entrance examinations in March as the second stage in the examination process, and admission is based on the combined results of the first- and second-stage examinations.

This two-stage process was devised in an attempt to normalize the increasingly harsh Japanese entrance-examination race. However, it was criticized for the added burden that taking two examinations places on the student, and there were strong public expressions of doubt that a multiple-choice test could measure true academic ability. As of 1985 a number of proposed reforms were being studied that would affect the way the first-stage test was administered or even its continued existence. In June 1985, the Association of National Universities decided, effective 1987, to reduce the number of subject areas covered in the five fields from seven to five

and to allow further reductions in subject matter at the discretion of the individual universities and departments concerned. At the same time, the Provisional Council on Educational Reform recommended that the joint first-stage test be replaced by another type of joint test. This new test would be open to use by private as well as public universities, and the autonomy of the individual universities would be respected by allowing them considerable freedom in the way the test was used. Implementation of this new test would be in 1989. YAMAGISHI Shunsuke

JT-60

A piece of critical plasma testing equipment constructed by the Japan Atomic Energy Research Institute (JAERI) in Ibaraki Prefecture to study nuclear fusion. (J and T stand for JAERI and tokamak, a device for confining plasma, and the figure 60 indicates the 60 cubic meters, or 2,118.6 cubic feet, of plasma held in the vacuum container.) Nuclear fusion is caused by heating deuterium and tritium at an ultrahigh temperature to a plasma state in which the atomic nuclei and electrons separate, and then confining the plasma for a given period of time at a constant density. The JT-60 is a piece of experimental equipment for the actual production of the critical state of plasma. The structure features a doughnut-shaped vacuum container that is surrounded by magnets. The whole unit, eight years in the making and completed in 1985, has a height of 13 meters (42.64 feet) and a diameter of 15 meters (49.2 feet). It weighs 5,000 metric tons (5,500 short tons). NISHIMATA Souhei

kaiware daikon

Radish sprouts, specifically sprouts of the large white radish known as daikon (see RADISHES). In Japan radish sprouts are usually served raw, either as a garnish for sashimi (raw fish) or in salads, soups, and other dishes as in the West. The name kaiware daikon (literally, split-shell radish) derives from the fact that the first two leaves of the sprout resemble a clamshell that has been split open. Consumption of radish sprouts has increased dramatically in Japan since the beginning of the 1980s, when the use of hydroponics made large-scale year-round production possible. The sprouts can be harvested one week after the seeds are planted. The large quantities of seeds needed are imported from the west coast of the United States, where they are grown on consignment.

Kaizuka Shigeki (1904–)

Scholar of Chinese history. Professor emeritus at Kyōto University. Born in Tōkyō. Kaizuka studied Chinese history under NAITŌ KONAN (1866–1934) and others at Kyōto University, where he became a professor in 1949. He is highly regarded for his studies emphasizing the importance, as historical materials, of the "oracle bones," bronze and stone inscriptions, and other Chinese archaeological finds. He organized the approximately 3,000 oracle bone fragments housed at the Research Institute for Humanistic Studies, Kyōto University, publishing the results of his research in Kyōto Daigaku Jimbun Kagaku Kenkyūjo shozō kōkotsu monji (1960, Studies on the Oracle Bones in the Institute for Humanistic Research, Kyōto University) and Kōkotsumon jidai kubun no kisoteki kenkyū (1961, Basic Studies on the Periodization of the Oracle Bones). His collected works is Kaizuka Shigeki chosaku shū, 10 vols (Chūō Kōron Sha, 1976–79). He was awarded the Order of Culture in 1984.

kamban system

Also known as the Toyota production system or the "just-in-time" (JIT) system, the kamban system is a manufacturing system created by the TOYOTA MOTOR CORPORATION to achieve a policy of rationalized production through the removal of all waste, the assurance of quality, and the reduction of costs, goals which encourage increased productivity. The kamban system includes all the accompanying technology necessary to pursue those aims, which are realized practically through the implementation of two basic principles. The first principle is that of "just-in-time" production, which means manufacturing only the necessary items at the necessary times and in necessary amounts. The second principle is "jidōka," a word used by Toyota to mean building into automation the ability to detect and stop malfunctions before the defects are passed on. Ideally, jidōka results in 100 percent quality that is built into a manufacturing system.

The *kamban* is an information-carrying device (usually a small card or other object) that serves as a tool for implementing the "subsequent-process parts pick-up" or "pull" system of production, which is the vital process of picking up from the preceding processes the proper parts at the required times and in the necessary quantities, and then producing more parts to replace those that have been taken away. The *kamban* travels with the actual parts, circulating between preceding and subsequent processes and delivering such information as the part-name, the delivery point and time, and the quantity to be made. The *kamban's* circulation times are adjusted to the number of parts being used. In this way, raw materials and supply inventories can be kept to a minimum.

The *kamban* system is used in all production processes at Toyota and by the corporation's outside suppliers as well. Items used by Toyota, the company furthest downstream in the production process, are replaced by outside suppliers. Toyota workers are able to see at a glance the inventory levels and are able to work on their own to keep inventories at a minimum. In this way the workers become active participants in the company's efforts to achieve rationalized production.

Kani

City in southeastern Gifu Prefecture on the southern bank of the river Kisogawa. Formerly a town, Kani assumed city status in 1982. The city has convenient road and rail transportation to Nagoya, and it has become a residential suburb of that city. Industries include automobile parts, electric equipment, and ceramics. Vegetables and flowers are grown here, and there is also poultry and pig farming. The Kani Municipal Museum of Local History is located in the Kukuri district. Pop: 69,630.

Kansai Bunka Gakujutsu Kenkyū Toshi

(Kansai Academic New Town). A planned new community intended as an equivalent in the Kansai (Kyōto-Ōsaka) area of the existing TSUKUBA ACADEMIC NEW TOWN near Tōkyō. The plan, being promoted jointly by the national and local governments, calls for development of a 2,500-hectare (6,175-acre) tract of land that includes parts of Kyōto, Nara, and Ōsaka prefectures. Ground-breaking ceremonies were held in October 1985. Classroom buildings for use by first- and second-year students of Dōshisha University were opened in April 1986, and the Kyōto Flower Center opened there the same month.

Kansai International Airport

A planned new international airport for the Kansai (Kyōto-Ōsaka) region. Construction of the new airport on a manmade island in Ōsaka Bay, which was to be financed jointly by private enterprise and the national and local governments, was scheduled to begin in the fall of 1986. When opened in the spring of 1993, the airport would be the first in Japan to be operated on a 24 hour basis. The Kansai International Airport Co, Ltd, the primary agency involved in its construction, was established in October 1984, when it became evident that the existing Ōsaka International Airport was unable to meet demands for increased capacity. The first stage of the plan (to be completed by 1993) called for an airport of 511 hectares (1,262 acres) with one 3,500 meter (2.2 mi) runway.

KURAHASHI *Tōru*

karaoke

(an abbreviation of words meaning literally, "empty orchestra"). Records or cassette tapes containing only the orchestral accompaniment to songs, the words being omitted. All types of music are available, including classical and folk; however, cassettes of Japanese-style popular songs, particularly the genre known as *enka*, are overwhelmingly numerous. Such orchestra-only recordings were being used by recording studios and broadcasting stations from the mid-1960s. In the 1970s, bars and other drinking places began to equip themselves with special *karaoke* cassette systems with microphones through which customers took turns singing the words to the songs. Eventually use of this equipment spread to private homes. *Karaoke* systems have powerful amplifiers, and there have been complaints of noise pollution caused by drinking establishments in residential neighborhoods.

Kōbe Universiade

The summer games of the 1985 Universiade (biyearly international sports competitions for college students) were held in the city of Kōbe, Hyōgo Prefecture, during the 12 days from 24 August to 4 September. It was the second time that the games had been held in Japan, the first having been the Tōkyō Universiade in 1967. The Kōbe Universiade was participated in by 3,949 contestants and officials from 106 countries. There were 10 competitions: track and field, swimming and diving, gymnastics, basketball, tennis, volleyball, fencing, soccer, water polo, and *jūdō*. Two new world's records were established: 49.14 seconds in men's 100 meter freestyle swimming by Matthew Biondi of the United States and 2 meters, 41 centimeters in the running high jump by Igor Paklin of the Soviet Union.

Koiso Ryōhei (1903–)

Western-style painter known for his paintings of women and groups done in a style that combines precise realism with Western classicism. Born in Hyōgo Prefecture, Koiso graduated from the Tōkyō Bijutsu Gakkō (now Tōkyō University of Fine Arts and Music). His painting *Kyōdai* (Brother and Sister) was selected for exhibition at the Teiten (Exhibition of the Imperial Fine Arts Academy) in 1925. He studied in France from 1928 to 1930, and one of his paintings was shown at the Salon d'Automne. He participated in the forming of the Shin Seisakuha Kyōkai (New Creative Association) in 1936. He taught at the Tōkyō University of Fine Arts and Music from 1950, becoming professor emeritus there in 1971. He became a member of the Japan Art Academy in 1982 and received the Order of Culture in 1983. His best-known works include *Rafu* (1937, Nude), *Sannin ritsuzō* (1954, Three Standing Figures), and *Hataraku onna* (1968, Working Women). Koiso is also known as a prolific illustrator for fiction published in both newspapers and magazines.

Kōjindani site

Archaeological site of the YAYOI PERIOD (ca 300 BC–ca AD 300) located in the town of Hikawa, Shimane Prefecture. In August 1984, 358 bronze swords dating from the 1st to 2nd centuries were discovered to have been buried there as a group. The bronze swords are medium-narrow ones, about 50 centimeters (19.7 in) in length. They were lined up in four rows in an area 4.6 by 2.3 meters (15 by 7.54 ft). This is the first discovery of such a large number of buried swords. In August 1985 a group of six DŌTAKU (bronze bells), all approximately 20 centimeters (7.88 in) high, and 16 medium-breadth bronze spearheads, ranging from 64 to 84 centimeters (25.22 to 33.10 in) in length, were discovered buried together at the same site. This is the first time that objects representing both of the two great cultural spheres of Japan's bronze age—bronze spearheads representing the Northern Kyūshū cultural sphere and *dōtaku* representing the cultural sphere of the capital provinces (the present-day Kyōto-Ōsaka-Nara area)—have been discovered in the same place. As a result, the theory that these two great cultural spheres stood in opposition to each other is being reexamined. The existence here in the Izumo area of a bronze culture is also proof of the existence at Izumo of a great political power which rivaled the YAMATO COURT.

Kuroyanagi Tetsuko (1933–)

Television personality. Born in Tōkyō. Graduated from Tōyō College of Music (now Tōkyō College of Music). Kuroyanagi joined the NHK Radio Theater in 1954, making her broadcasting debut in IIZAWA TADASU's (b 1909) radio drama series for children, *Yambō, Nimbō, Tombō* (1954–57). In television she is known chiefly as a master of ceremonies in musical shows and as a talk-show host. In 1981 Kuroyanagi published a book of reminiscences about her elementary-school years entitled *Madogiwa no Totto chan* (tr *Little Girl at the Window*, 1982), which sold 6 million copies. She used the royalties from this book to establish the Totto Fund to support a drama group for the hearing-impaired. She was appointed a UNICEF goodwill ambassador in 1984.

labor problems associated with robotization

The introduction of industrial robots and other types of microelectronic systems into industry affects employment trends, working conditions, and industrial relations, and was therefore becoming an increasingly important issue in Japan in the 1980s. The reduced employment brought about by microelectronics in Japan by the mid-1980s was being dealt with by reshuffling personnel, and thus had not yet caused any serious unemployment problems. However, it was possible that in the future older and female unskilled workers and even some skilled workers would lose their jobs because of the introduction of microelectronics. For this reason, there was an increasing number of Japanese companies in which labor and management were concluding "robot agreements," which usually consisted of clauses guaranteeing "prior consultation, personnel reassignment and occupation reshuffling, and educational training." The Japanese government was also considering the problem of robotization. In April 1984 the Employment Policy Council (a private advisory group to the minister of labor) announced five principles to be considered in conjunction with the introduction of microelectronics: (1) the stabilization and expansion of employment, (2) the improvement of the capabilities of workers to prevent maladjustment, (3) the prevention of industrial accidents and the lowering of working conditions along with the improvement of workers' welfare, (4) the establishment of a consultation system to promote better understanding between labor and management, and (5) the consideration of public opinion from an international point of view.

YOSHIKAWA Kaoru

Large-scale Retail Stores Law

Full name: Law concerning the Adjustment of Retail Business Operations in Large-scale Retail Stores. A law requiring large new stores to hold a conference for interested parties before the store actually opens. The purpose of such conferences is to reach a satisfactory agreement on the new store's size, opening date, the number of employee holidays to be scheduled, and the store's closing time. Decisions resulting from the conferences also guarantee that large retail firms will not infringe on the business of small or medium-sized stores in the surrounding area. If the provisions of this law are not observed, the Ministry of International Trade and Industry can impose the penal clauses contained therein. The law, which was enacted in March 1974, originally applied to stores of 3,000 square meters (32,100 sq ft) in certain cities designated by government ordinances and to stores of 1,500 square meters (16,050 sq ft) in other cities. In May 1979 it was decided that stores of 500 square meters (5,350 sq ft) or more should also be required to obey this law. It has been argued that the Large-scale Retail Stores Law interferes with the efficient distribution of goods and that it can be used to hinder the penetration of foreign products into the Japanese market.

IKEDA Minoru

lasers

One of the most significant developments in Japanese laser technology in the 1980s was the use of lasers in optoelectronics. More important to Japan commercially was the semiconductor laser, which is used as the light-emitting source for optical-fiber transmissions and compact disc players. A semiconductor laser consists of a flat junction of two pieces of semiconductor material. When a large electrical current is passed through such a device, laser light emerges from the junction region. With the sales explosion of compact discs, the production of semiconductor lasers was also increasing sharply in Japan.

NISHIMATA Souhei

Law concerning Health and Medical Services for the Aged

(Rōjin Hoken Hō). Since January 1973, the Japanese government's policies on health care for the aged had been based on the nation's health-insurance system and on the system for government health-care payments for the aged provided for in the Law for the Welfare of the Aged. However, as the proportion of older people in the Japanese population continued to grow, and as expenditures for health care for the aged continued to increase, the emphasis of government policies shifted toward finding a way of guaranteeing that health-care payments could be provided in the future. The Law concerning Health and Medical Services for the Aged, which went into effect in February 1983, was an attempt to deal with these problems. In addition to medical care, this law provided for such health-care services as health education, health advice, physical examinations, and rehabilitation. Medical care was to be provided to people aged 70 or above, and the other health-care services to people who were

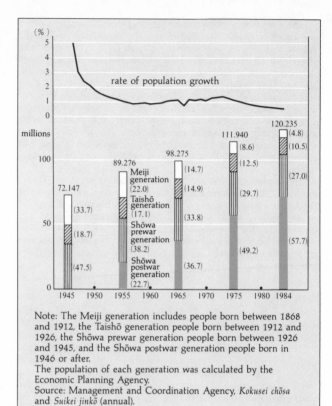

Note: The Meiji generation includes people born between 1868 and 1912, the Taishō generation people born between 1912 and 1926, the Shōwa prewar generation people born between 1926 and 1945, and the Shōwa postwar generation people born in 1946 or after.
The population of each generation was calculated by the Economic Planning Agency.
Source: Management and Coordination Agency, *Kokusei chōsa* and *Suikei jinkō* (annual).

Lifestyle in the 1980s —— Figure 1: Increased population and changing generational composition

40 or older. One notable feature of the new health-care system for the aged was the requirement that certain fees for health care be paid by the individual. (The system of free government health care for the aged that had been in effect since 1973 was abolished.) On the fiscal side, the health-care insurance system had been such that the health-insurance societies for employed persons, which had few older members, were always operating in the black, whereas government financing of health care for older persons after retirement had always been in the red. The new law introduced a system under which other health-care insurers would bear part of the burden of care for the elderly.

NOSE Takayuki

lifestyle in the 1980s

The subtitle of the 1985 *White Paper on Life in Japan*, issued by the Economic Planning Agency, reads "Forty Years after the War: Toward an Age of Maturity." What the agency is saying is that during the forty years since the end of World War II, a lifestyle of abundance had become firmly established among the Japanese and that they had now reached a period of maturity. A few quotations from this white paper will illustrate the changes that took place among the Japanese during the period.

The Aging of the Population —— With regard to population and economic circumstances, the white paper had the following to say: "The total population of Japan, which was 72.15 million in 1945, had increased continually, reaching 120.24 million by 1 October 1984—approximately 1.7 times the 1945 figure ... As for changes in the birth rate, the first baby boom had occurred in the years 1947–49. When the people born in these years reached the age of marriage and child bearing in the period 1971–74, there was a second baby boom ... As of 1985, people of the first baby boom generation had reached the ages of 36 to 38 and those of the second the ages of 11 to 14 (the sixth year of elementary school through the third year of middle school). The existence of generations with these kinds of specific population numbers affected the society in various ways ... The population of our country can be expected to continue to increase in the future. However, the population increase has moderated, the rate of increase having declined yearly since 1972." (See Figure 1.)

This decline in the rate of population increase went hand in hand

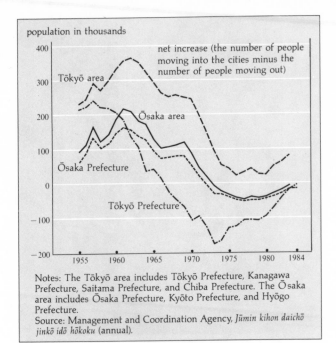

population in thousands

net increase (the number of people moving into the cities minus the number of people moving out)

Notes: The Tōkyō area includes Tōkyō Prefecture, Kanagawa Prefecture, Saitama Prefecture, and Chiba Prefecture. The Ōsaka area includes Ōsaka Prefecture, Kyōto Prefecture, and Hyōgo Prefecture.
Source: Management and Coordination Agency, *Jūmin kihon daichō jinkō idō hōkoku* (annual).

Lifestyle in the 1980s——Figure 2: Changes in urban population reflecting the U-turn or J-turn phenomenon

with a decline in the death rate, and the combination was producing marked changes in the structure of the Japanese population toward one with higher ages. According to the same white paper, "the youth population (birth to age 14) has decreased. The youth-population index, which expresses the ratio of the youth population to the population of those in their productive years (ages 15 through 64), had declined from 59.4 in 1950 to 34.9 by 1970, and although it rose briefly as a result of the second baby boom, it has declined again since 1975."

The aging of the population had been rapid. The rate of increase for the older population (65 and above) during the period 1950–59 was 1.30 times. For the period 1960–69 it was 1.37 times, and for 1970–79 it was 1.44 times. The aging rate had thus been accelerating.

And the older population had itself been aging. The population of those aged 65 or older increased 2.56 times between 1959 and 1970, and the higher the age, the higher was the rate of increase. This characteristic was remarkable—2.22 times for ages 65–69, 2.33 times for ages 70–74, 2.94 times for ages 75–79, 3.92 for ages 80–84, and 5.49 for the age of 85 or older.

Another type of change in population circumstances was changes in the direction of population movements. The concentration of population in the large cities that took place during the period of high economic growth began to subside in 1975, and by 1984 it had diminished to the levels of around 1961. In other words, high economic growth was accompanied by increased demands on the labor population from the factories and other enterprises in urban areas, and there was a great influx of the labor population into the cities. However, after Japan entered a period of stabilized economic growth, the pattern of population movement changed to one of outward flow from the three large metropolitan areas of Tōkyō, Ōsaka, and Nagoya toward regional urban areas. This is the so-called U-turn or J-turn phenomenon. (See Figure 2.)

The "Softening" of Industry——The white paper had this to say about economic circumstances. "Forty years after the end of World War II, there had been a great upward leap in living standards as a result of remarkable economic growth. The people had come to enjoy abundance in such areas as health care, education, and the conveniences of daily life. However, this process had brought with it a worsening of living conditions (the strains of a high growth rate), and they had also experienced the effects of an oil crisis on two occasions. Certainly it had not been a smooth road for the whole distance."

The Japanese economy had undergone a number of changes during these 40 years: the period of recovery from 1945 to 1954, the period of high growth rate from 1955 to 1973, and the period of

stable growth beginning in 1974 (these are the divisions used in the white paper). By the mid-1980s, the nation was in a period of stable growth in which the economic growth rate was less than 5 percent.

In the meantime, the white paper went on to say, income levels had risen considerably during the period of high growth rate, and conditions were now such that the aspirations of the Japanese could turn from an emphasis on material abundance toward an emphasis on mental and spiritual abundance. The opinions and needs of the individual had become more diverse, and cooperation among people and guarantees of fairness were becoming more important.

The industrial structure of the nation also had changed, passing from an emphasis on agriculture, forestry, and fishing immediately after World War II to an emphasis on manufacturing during the period of high growth rate, and finally to a growing importance of such tertiary industries as the service industries, including the financial, insurance, and real estate industries. This trend was referred to as the "softening" of industry.

Developments in the dissemination of information were also causing changes in the nation's industrial structure. The volume of information that poured down on people continued to increase at a great rate, whereas the volume of information digested, which had been 9 percent in 1973, was only 6.5 percent in 1983 (1984 *White Paper on Communications*). This situation was owing to a number of different factors, such as the proliferation of information from television and other mass-communication media and the development of on-line and other electronic communication tools; nevertheless, the fact remained that, while necessary information was available in abundance, there were also people who were afflicted with unnecessary information.

Changes in Middle-Class Consciousness: From "Masses" to "Partitioned Masses"——On the basis of its analysis of the circumstances, the 1985 *White Paper on Life in Japan* came to the conclusion that the majority of the Japanese had begun to develop a more diversified middle-class consciousness. In other words, they had undergone a process of maturation and individualization, moving away from "an averaging middle class" (a middle class that wants to be like everyone else) toward "a differentiating middle class" (a middle class that is aware of differences).

"It can be said," the white paper concluded, "that one of the directions that the spread of a middle-class consciousness has taken is an increasing emphasis on the needs and preferences of the individual ... The middle-class consciousness is thus moving in the direction of a greater maturity. It is undergoing a process of diversification and individualization whereby people are no longer middle class because I can do the same things as other people' ('an averaging middle class') but are rather middle class 'because I can do different things than other people' ('a differentiating middle class'). What has remained unchanged is that all this is taking place within the flow of the middle-class consciousness." These changes in values were naturally linked with changes in lifestyle. In the days of the "averaging middle class" people had been content as long as they could maintain the same levels of clothing and housing as other people in their general class, be as well informed as others, buy the same kind of household goods, and enjoy the same kind of amusements. Now, however, in the age of the "differentiating middle class," there were more and more people who wanted to be different from others in many areas of daily life in order to express their own individuality, and they were acting accordingly. What was taking place was a transition from a culture of "the masses" to a culture of "the partitioned masses."

Now there were many young people who regularly bought fashion magazines precisely because they wanted to avoid wearing the kind of clothes that were being featured in them. When it came to eating habits, it was now much easier than before for several Japanese to sit down together in a restaurant and all order different dishes according to their own tastes. As for housing, many purchasers of ready-made, mass-produced dwellings were now remodeling them in order both to adapt them to the likes and dislikes of family members and to make them better expressions of the individuality of the family as a group. When it came to education, a growing number of young people were turning their backs on the idea of going on to higher education for the mere sake of achieving an academic record and were instead enrolling in technical schools as a means of getting a job. And many housewives, in the belief that one's individuality is expressed by the kind of subjects one studies, were seeking self-improvement by enrolling in the so-called culture centers, reading educational magazines, watching educational television, and attending public lecture series.

The places where people went to amuse themselves were also becoming more diversified. For example, an increasing number of young people were now taking the tours of the hot-spring resorts that were formerly thought of as something for the elderly. And many of them were able to say that they were going to places that they themselves had discovered in a search for places where other people did not go.

People were now engaged in a search for differences that they could incorporate into a lifestyle different from that of others and express it as something of their own. Many now used the words "Have you heard of anything different?" as a standard greeting. The masses were truly becoming partitioned, and the people of "the partitioned masses" were coming into being.

However, the Japanese were still not yet ready to go beyond the kind of partitioning we are describing here—that of a "partitioned mass"—to the kind of individualism that can be seen among the peoples of the West. They continued to seek their friends in their own immediate surroundings and to gather together in groups composed of people who were the same in terms of various elements such as values, lifestyle, and standard of living. And the situation was the same within the family. There were many people who identified their own good fortune—in terms of the word *kizuna* or ties—with that of the family, maintaining a delicate internal balance of the part of themselves that was individual and the part that was family. According to a "Happiness Index Survey" that was conducted by the Hakuhōdō Institute of Life and Living, the number of Japanese who thought of themselves as "happy" amounted to 79.8 percent. Among women the figure was 83 percent. Thus, with a nation at peace, a stable economy, a high standard of living, and peace within the family, an extremely large number of Japanese considered themselves happy and were concentrating on strengthening their *kizuna* or ties with family and friends. And the likelihood was very strong that the Japanese would continue to seek not the kind of individualism that imposes conflicting demands from the standpoint of rights and duties but rather a lifestyle that would allow them to express their individuality within the shelter of the partitioned masses.

HAYASHI Hikaru

linear-motor train

The JAPANESE NATIONAL RAILWAYS began studying the feasibility of developing a linear-motor train (a superconductive, magnetically levitated system propelled by a linear electric motor) in 1962. In 1977 the Ministry of Transport agreed to the development of such a system, and by 1986 manned and unmanned trains were regularly making experimental runs at speeds of around 300 kilometers (186 mi) per hour. Facilities were being developed to supply electricity for even higher speeds. (A top speed of 517 kilometers, or 321 miles per hour, had been achieved in 1979.) The development of another type of linear-motor train was undertaken by JAPAN AIRLINES CO, LTD. This train was exhibited in 1985 at Tsukuba Expo '85, where it took paying passengers for short rides at 30 kilometers (18.6 mi) per hour.

KURAHASHI Tōru

liquid-crystal television

In 1985, 1 million liquid-crystal (LC) televisions were manufactured in Japan. A liquid-crystal television system replaces the conventional cathode-ray screen with a liquid-crystal display (LCD). Liquid crystal is a chemically synthesized organic material that changes its clarity or color in response to changes in temperature or voltage. When LC chemicals sandwiched between thin film transistors are electrically activated, they glow in the desired pattern to produce images. Liquid crystal, which was developed in the United States in the late 1960s, was first used for displays in watches and pocket calculators. In 1982 the Seikō Epson Corporation of Japan produced the first successful LC television display system. By 1984 technology in the field had developed so that Seikō could produce a pocket-sized LCD color television for the marketplace, and LCDs were leading candidates for use in superthin portable televisions and the long-awaited home television screen that can be hung on the wall.

NISHIMATA Souhei

literature in the 1980s

The first half of the 1980s saw a slump in the sales of literary works, and there were a number of other events that pointed to a state of sluggishness in literary publication in general: the literary magazine

Linear-motor train

A linear-motor train at the Japanese National Railway's Magnetic Levitation Vehicle Center in Hyūga, Miyazaki Prefecture.

Umi suspended publication in 1984, and *Bungei* changed from a monthly to a quarterly in 1986. These events also hinted at the beginning of a period of transition for the printed media as a whole. During this period of uncertainty for the publishing industry, a number of new works attracted attention, including YASUOKA SHŌTARŌ's (b 1920) *Ryūritan* (1981, A Tale of Wandering), which dealt with the history of a single family, ENDŌ SHŪSAKU's (b 1923) *Samurai* (1980), which depicted the struggle between politics and religious belief in the person of HASEKURA TSUNENAGA (1571–1622), the 17th century Japanese envoy to the West, and ŌE KENZABURŌ's (b 1935) *Reintsurī o kiku onnatachi* (1982, Women Listening to the Rain Tree) and *Atarashii hito yo mezame yo* (1983, Wake Up, New People!), the latter of which deals with how the feelings of the father of a handicapped child become dreams of a rebirth of humanity. All the above works show a deepening maturity on the part of their authors. A number of works by those authors who might be called the elders of Japanese fiction also attracted attention, including NOGAMI YAEKO's (1885–1985) autobiographical novel *Mori* (1985, The Forest), IBUSE MASUJI's (b 1898) *Ogikubo fudoki* (1982, Life in Ogikubo), ISHIKAWA JUN's (b 1899) *Kyōfūki* (1980, Mad Wind Story), NIWA FUMIO's (b 1904) eight-volume *Rennyo* (1982–83), and INOUE YASUSHI's (b 1907) *Honkakubō ibun* (1981, Posthumous Writings of Honkakubō), which traces the riddles surrounding the life and death of the 16th-century tea master SEN NO RIKYŪ (1522–91). Ibuse in particular created a stir by rewriting his early work "Sanshōuo" (1929; tr "Salamander," 1971) on the occasion of the publication of a new collected works, *Ibuse Masuji jisenshū*, 12 vols (1985–). There were a number of excellent new works that depicted the life of the individual against the backdrop of history. These included TSUJI KUNIO's (b 1925) *Ki no koe, umi no koe* (1982, The Voice of the Trees, the Voice of the Sea), SHIBA RYŌTARŌ's (b 1923) *Hitobito no ashioto* (1982, People's Footsteps), which depicts the MEIJI PERIOD (1868–1912) of the poet MASAOKA SHIKI (1867–1902) and his circle, and Kim Sokpom's (J: Kin Sekihan; b 1925) *Kazantō* (1983, Volcanic Island). There were a number of works that examined human loneliness and sensitivity by delving into the traditions of local custom and communal society that lie at the deepest layers of modern Japanese life. These included FURUI YOSHIKICHI's (b 1937) *Sansōfu* (1982, A Murmur in the Mountains) and *Asagao* (1983, Rose of Sharon), Nakagami Kenji's (b 1946) *Sennen no yuraku* (1982, A Thousand Years of Pleasure), MIURA TETSUO's (b 1931) *Oro oro zōshi* (1982, A Half-baked Story), and FUKAZAWA SHICHIRŌ's (b 1914) collection of short stories, *Michinoku no ningyōtachi* (1980, Dolls of the Deep North). All of the works just mentioned suggest the fragility of the foundation upon which the modern Japanese age of consumer culture and high technology is built. Two other such works are Hino Keizō's (b 1929) *Yume no shima* (1985, Island of Dreams), which describes the physiology of a city, and Murakami Haruki's (b 1949) *Sekai no owari to hādoboirudo wandārando* (1985, The End of the World and Hard-boiled Wonderland), which deals with the emptiness of the modern age. Tatematsu Wahei (b 1947) is another author who is noteworthy for his relentless portrayal of the collapse of the communal society, the family, and the individual, as in *Enrai* (1980, Distant Thunder).

It was among women writers that the most vigorous activity occurred during this period of a sagging market for literary fiction. New female writers appeared on the scene one after another, and a succession of women received the Akutagawa Prize (see LITERARY PRIZES): Katō Yukiko (b 1936) in 1982, Takagi Nobuko (b 1946) in 1983, Kizaki Satoko (b 1939) in 1984, and Kometani Fumiko (b 1930) in 1985. If one were looking for signs of a possible new life for Japanese literary fiction, one place to look would be among these women, with their fresh sensibilities and their international outlook. In addition to these new writers, a large number of established women writers of several generations also continued to be active during this period. The late Nogami Yaeko has already been mentioned. Notable new works by other established female writers included *Kikujidō* (1984, Chrysanthemum Page) by ENCHI FUMIKO (b 1905; Enchi was awarded the Order of Culture in 1985), *Sumidagawa boshoku* (1984, Evening on the River Sumida) by Shibaki Yoshiko (b 1914), *Heitai yado* (1982, Soldier's Inn) by Takenishi Hiroko (b 1929), *Shanhai* (1983, Shanghai) by Hayashi Kyōko (b 1930), *Katachi mo naku* (1982, Loneliness) by Ōba Minako (b 1930), and *Ikari no ko* (1985, Child of Anger) by Takahashi Takako (b 1932). A much-discussed work that combines dark wartime memories with descriptions of local customs in a village is Saegusa Kazuko's (b 1929) *Onidomo no yoru wa fukai* (1983, Dark is the Night of Demons). Three other established women writers who continued to be active were SONO AYAKO (b 1931), KURAHASHI YUMIKO (b 1935), and Kōno Taeko (b 1926). Important writers of a slightly later generation included Tomioka Taeko (b 1935), Kanai Mieko (b 1947), Tsushima Yūko (b 1947)—the daughter of DAZAI OSAMU (1909–48)—Hikari Agata (b 1943), and Masuda Mizuko (b 1948). The vitality of these women was a symbol not only of the rise of feminism and the collapse of male dominance but also of important qualitative changes that were quietly beginning to take place within the realm of the printed media.　　　　　　　　　　　　　　　　　　*ASAI Kiyoshi*

lively politics

An English expression used in Japan to refer to the lively, down-to-earth style and everyday concerns of the citizens' political movements such as the ecology movement and the local autonomy movement that arose during the 1970s. Other new citizens' movements that appeared in Japan during the latter half of the 1970s include the organic farming movement and the recycling movement. Such movements continued to be active in the 1980s. In the 1983 election for governor of Hokkaidō, a loose coalition of groups representing young people, housewives, shopkeepers, and other segments of the Hokkaidō citizenry, each group maintaining its own point of view, cooperated in selecting and supporting their own candidate and succeeded in getting him elected. In 1984 a nature-protection group composed chiefly of housewives in the city of Zushi, Kanagawa Prefecture, launched a campaign against construction of housing for American military personnel in the area. The group succeeded in recalling the mayor, who was in favor of the construction, and electing their own candidate in his place. All of these political movements conducted their campaigns in an easygoing, idiosyncratic political style marked by spontaneous creativity, bringing a new flavor to Japanese local politics.
　　　　　　　　　　　　　　　　　　NAKAMURA Kiichi

local area networks

(LAN). As of the mid-1980s, the introduction of LANs in Japan was still in the experimental stages. (A LAN is an information or office-automation network within a single business or other institution, in which computers, terminal devices, printers, telephones, facsimile machines, and other types of office equipment are joined together by means of optical-fiber or coaxial cables.) The well-known LAN called "Ethernet," which was developed jointly by three American firms (Xerox, Digital Equipment, and Intel), had been introduced to

several Japanese firms, and domestic electronics manufacturers were also developing their own LAN systems.　　　*NISHIMATA Souhei*

machine translation

In Japan, machine translation (automatic translation from one language into another by computer) was first developed primarily for English-to-Japanese translation. Systems designed in Japan follow one of two basic approaches. The "direct" method uses analysis of rules of syntax and grammar to translate one language into another, while the "transfer" approach employs an internal intermediate language as a bridge between the source language and target language.

In 1984 Bravice International, a small firm in Tōkyō, began marketing the country's first commercial Japanese-to-English translation system, which the company claims can translate simple Japanese texts into passable English at a rate of up to 3,000 words an hour. This system is based on the transfer method pioneered by an American computer software company. Other Japanese high-technology firms, including FUJITSŪ, LTD, and HITACHI, LTD, launched English-to-Japanese translation systems based on the direct method in 1984. Fujitsū's program is called ATLAS/I and Hitachi's is named ATHENE/E. By early 1986 more than ten electronics companies were developing automatic translation systems, all of which relied on the highly sophisticated syntax-analysis programs and large-scale computer dictionaries that are indispensable for any practical system of translation. The automatic language translation systems developed by 1986 still required continuous assistance from human translators, but Japanese companies were optimistic about the future of machine translation, and they were confident that by 1995 more than 80 percent of all translation work would be done by computer.　　　　　　　　　　　*NISHIMATA Souhei*

Maekawa Report

A report submitted in April 1986 by the Advisory Group on Economic Structural Adjustment for International Harmony, a private advisory group to Prime Minister NAKASONE YASUHIRO (b 1918). The report is named after the advisory group's chairman, Maekawa Haruo (b 1911), former senior deputy governor of the Bank of Japan.

Since the beginning of the 1980s, Japan's current-balance account surplus in international trade had risen to unprecedented levels. It was obvious that changes would have to be made in the nation's existing economic policies and in the economic life of the Japanese people, and the advisory group had been formed in October 1985 to study specific proposals for those changes.

The Maekawa report stated that Japan's huge trade surplus had its roots in the nation's existing economic structure, which heavily depended on exports, and recommended that Japan should aim at changing to an economic structure more in keeping with harmonious development of the world economy. It recommended that the following policies be pursued: (1) stimulation of demand in the domestic market, (2) change to an industrial structure that would contribute to international harmony, (3) further improvement of access to the Japanese market for foreign nations, coupled with stimulation of imports, (4) stabilization of international exchange rates and liberalization and internationalization of financial markets, and (5) promotion of international cooperation and contributions to the world economy commensurate with Japan's international status. A sixth set of recommendations had to do with management of fiscal and monetary policy. The government accepted these proposals, and in August 1986 it was decided to form a Task Force on Economic Structural Adjustment, headed by Prime Minister Nakasone.

Management and Coordination Agency

(Sōmuchō). An agency of the national government formed in July 1984 on the basis of a 1983 report of the Second Provisional Commission for Administrative Reform. The new agency combines the organization and functions of the ADMINISTRATIVE MANAGEMENT AGENCY with those of a part of the PRIME MINISTER'S OFFICE (the former ceases to exist). The chief purpose of this reorganization is to provide more effective overall administrative coordination of government departments. The Management and Coordination Agency is made up of five bureaus, two of which it takes over from the former Administrative Management Agency (the Administrative Management Bureau and the Administrative Inspection

Bureau) and the other three from the Prime Minister's Office (the Personnel Bureau, the Government Pensions Bureau, and the Statistics Bureau).

Maruya Saiichi (1925–)

Novelist and critic. Real name Nemura Saiichi. Born in Yamagata Prefecture. Maruya graduated from Tōkyō University, where he majored in English. In 1952, he and the critic Shinoda Hajime (b 1927) founded the coterie magazine *Chitsujo* (1952–63). It was in this magazine that Maruya serialized his first novel *Ehoba no kao o sakete* (1952–60). He won the Akutagawa Prize for his short story "Toshi no nokori" in 1968. In his fiction Maruya uses the depiction of the outward surface of daily life as a vehicle for exploring the deeper levels of human psychology. His most important works of fiction include *Tatta hitori no hanran* (1972) and *Uragoe de utae Kimigayo* (1982). His critical works include *Go-Toba In* (1973; winner of the Yomiuri Literary Prize in the same year), *Bunshō tokuhon* (1977), and *Chūshingura to wa nani ka* (1984). Maruya has also been an outspoken commentator on issues relating to the Japanese language.

Asai Kiyoshi

Matsumoto Kōshirō VIII (1910–1982)

KABUKI actor. Real name Fujima Junjirō. Son of Matsumoto Kōshirō VII (1870–1949). Born in Tōkyō. Kōshirō, who made his debut in 1926, studied under Nakamura Kichiemon I (1886–1954), afterwards becoming the latter's son-in-law. He took the stage name of Ichikawa Somegorō in 1930 and succeeded to the name of Matsumoto Kōshirō in 1949. Inheriting the acting styles of his father and father-in-law, he was noted for his combination of boldness and precision. He specialized in the roles of military commanders in historical dramas and in the *jitsugoto* (realistic) style of kabuki. Like his father, he involved himself actively in other types of drama, both Japanese and Western. He was designated as a Living National Treasure in 1975 and became a member of the Japan Art Academy in 1976. In 1981 he yielded the name Matsumoto Kōshirō to his eldest son and took the name Matsumoto Hakuō in retirement. The same year he was awarded the Order of Culture.

measures for increased domestic demand

Increased foreign demand for Japanese goods contributed much to Japan's economic growth in the first half of the 1980s, but another result was a massive surplus of the current balance account and friction with Japan's foreign trade partners. Increased domestic demand was necessary for harmonious international economic growth, and the Japanese government took measures to stimulate such demand. In a cabinet meeting on economic policy on 15 October 1985, the government approved a package of measures designed to increase domestic demand. Four measures were designated for immediate implementation: encouragement of urban development and private investment in housing, encouragement of equipment investment by private electric power and gas companies, stimulation of personal spending, and increase of public investments. Four additional goals were designated for future implementation: increased involvement of the private sector in public enterprises, wider adoption of the five-day workweek, more effective use of publicly owned land and other property, and relaxation of government regulations affecting private economic activity.

Ōmori Takashi

medical electronics equipment

With the remarkable advances being made in electronics in the 1980s, more and more medical electronics equipment was being introduced into clinics and hospitals throughout Japan. Generally speaking, this medical electronics equipment can be divided into three categories: electronically controlled imaging devices, automatic clinical analyzers, and clinical patient-monitoring systems. The first category includes the X-ray computerized-tomography (CT) scanner, the positron CT scanner, and the nuclear magnetic resonance CT scanner. The X-ray CT scanner, widely used throughout Japan, detects density changes in X-rays that have penetrated the human body and then displays images of the examined organ by computer processing. By the end of 1985, approximately 3,500 X-ray CTs had been introduced into Japanese hospitals, and the Japanese had the highest percentage in the world of patients

using the machine. The positron CT scanner monitors positrons emitted from radioisotopes injected into the human body, and the nuclear magnetic resonance CT scanner uses specific electromagnetic waves emitted from the human body under strong magnetic fields to provide images. In 1983, the Ministry of Health and Welfare granted permission to the Tōshiba Corporation to begin production of nuclear magnetic resonance CT scanners, and by 1985 40 machines were in use in Japan. In addition to these imaging devices, there were more than 10,000 pieces of ultrasonic diagnostic equipment in use in Japan by the mid-1980s.

The second category of medical electronics equipment, that of automatic clinical analyzers for blood and urine, is very instrumental in saving lives in situations demanding emergency treatment, and automatic clinical monitoring systems are indispensable for the intensive care of patients suffering from strokes, heart ailments, or cancer.

Nishimata Souhei

middle-class consciousness

The results of a 1958 "Public Opinion Poll on the National Life" taken by the Prime Minister's Public Information Office showed that of those individuals responding to the question, "Given the current living standards in Japan, which group do you feel your family is in?" 72 percent chose either upper-middle, middle-middle or lower-middle class. In 1973 this figure exceeded 90 percent. Further examination of the 90 percent of the Japanese who called themselves "middle class" revealed a pattern of upward mobility: those who thought of themselves as lower middle-class decreased from 32 percent of the population to 22 percent, while the middle-middle class rose from 37 percent to 61 percent and the upper-middle class grew from 3 percent to 7 percent of the Japanese population. No marked changes occurred in this ratio between the 1973 oil crisis and 1985, and the figures for 1985 showed that a total of 89 percent of the population still considered themselves as part of this general category. The upper-middle class continued to compose 7 percent of the population, although the middle-middle decreased to 54 percent and the lower-middle rose to 28 percent.

Yasuhara Norikazu

mokkan discovered at Asuka palace site

In 1985 a number of ancient wooden tablets (*mokkan*) were unearthed in the village of Asuka, Nara Prefecture, at the eastern side of a site traditionally said to be that of the palace Asuka Itabuki no Miya. When archaeologists from the Kashihara Archaeological Institute made an excavation measuring three by five meters (9.8 by 16.4 ft) alongside a ditch that marked the eastern boundary of the palace, a total of 1,082 fragments of wood were unearthed, among which were approximately 100 *mokkan* with characters written on them in black. These *mokkan* were cleaned and then deciphered with the aid of infrared photography and other such techniques. Identified among the writings were a number of personal and place names, including those of Prince Ōtsu (663–686) and Prince Ōtomo (648–672; see KŌBUN, EMPEROR) and of the provinces of Ise and Owari. Three of the *mokkan* contain a date corresponding to 681, the 10th year of the reign of Emperor TEMMU (d 686). Some scholars think that the *mokkan* were materials used in the compilation of the chronicle NIHON SHOKI. The discovery of such a large number of *mokkan* has made it almost a certainty that the upper layer at the traditional Itabuki no Miya site consists of the remains of another palace, Asuka Kiyomihara no Miya.

Monju

An experimental fast breeder reactor that was being constructed in the 1980s by the Power Reactor and Nuclear Fuel Development Corporation in the city of Tsuruga, Fukui Prefecture. Monju was expected to reach critical mass in the spring of 1991, with a thermal output of 714,000 kilowatts. This reactor was to follow the reactor named Jōyō, which reached critical mass in April 1977 and has a thermal output of 100,000 kilowatts. According to the government's long-range plans for the development and use of atomic energy, Monju was slated for practical utilization by about 2010. However, the high cost of power generation and the lack of a reprocessing technique, in addition to a slowdown in the scale of nuclear development, threatened to delay the plans for this fast breeder reactor.

Morishita Yōko

Morishita Yōko performing with Rudolf Nureyev in a 1984 production of *Swan Lake* in Macerata, Italy.

Moonlight Project

A national project launched by Japan's Ministry of Trade and Industry (MITI) in 1978 to encourage research and development in the field of energy-efficient technology. MITI's Agency of Industrial Science and Technology was responsible for the project. Japan was increasingly concerned over the possibility of energy shortages after the oil crisis of 1973, and the Energy Conservation Law of 1979 required Japanese industries to reduce their energy consumption by 7 percent. The law also encouraged the development of energy-saving technology and aided existing endeavors such as the Moonlight Project. The project was dubbed "Moonlight" to suggest that even energy as slight as that in a beam of moonlight should not be overlooked as a possible source of power. Under the Moonlight Project, efforts were taken to develop more efficient energy-producing and energy-using technologies that would enable the currently available resources to yield more energy. The Moonlight Project had five major areas of interest: magnetohydrodynamic power generation, advanced gas turbines, advanced load-leveling storage battery systems, fuel-cell power generation, and commercial Stirling engines. Other areas were also being considered.

NISHIMATA Souhei

Morishita Yōko (1948–)

Ballerina. Born in Hiroshima Prefecture. Morishita, who began learning ballet at the age of 3, studied under Tachibana Akiho (b 1934), Matsuyama Mikiko (b 1923), and Marika Besobrasova. She was the first Japanese to win a gold medal in the International Ballet Concours at Varna in Bulgaria (1974). Morishita is active as a leader of the Matsuyama Ballet Company, which she joined in 1971, as is her husband, the ballet dancer Shimizu Tetsutarō (b 1948), who is the son of Matsuyama Mikiko. She has made many appearances abroad, and her performances with Rudolf Nureyev won enthusiastic reviews. Her specialties include *Giselle*, *Swan Lake*, and *Don Quixote*. She received a Laurence Olivier Award in 1985.

MOSS approach

(market oriented sector selective approach). An approach adopted in discussions between the United States and Japan concerning the issue of the opening of the Japanese market. This approach includes investigation of the actual status of the Japanese market in individual fields, the location of possible barriers to market entry, and the discussion of possible remedial measures. Modeled after the Japan–United States Group on Yen-Dollar Issues, which was established in November 1983, the MOSS approach has been in use since January 1985 in the fields of telecommunications, electronics, medical equipment and pharmaceuticals, and forest products. Substantive and continuous negotiations have been conducted on a monthly basis according to this scheme. In 1986 it appeared highly possible that this system would henceforth be applied to other fields of interest to the United States.

NISHIKAWA Masao

Munakata

City in northern Fukuoka Prefecture, northern Kyūshū. A town since 1954, it became a city in 1981. Situated in an agricultural area with cultivation of rice and MIKAN (a tangerine-like citrus fruit) as well as chicken farming. Electrification of the Kagoshima line of the Japanese National Railways led to the construction of a succession of large-scale housing projects in the area, and the city is now essentially a suburb of the cities of Fukuoka and Kita Kyūshū. In 1966 the national Fukuoka University of Education was moved here. There is also a campus of the private Tōkai University. Pop: 60,972.

museums

In recent years Japan has seen the construction of a large number of prefectural and municipal museums that emphasize exhibits of the works of local artists and regional folk arts. As of March 1985 there were 2,417 museums in Japan, 370 of which were built between 1980 and 1984. The rest of this article will be devoted to a brief description of the most important of these recently opened institutions.

Ainu Museum (Ainu Minzoku Hakubutsukan). Private museum in the town of Shiraoi in southwestern Hokkaidō. Opened in 1984. Contains clothing, dishes, and other objects used by the Ainu people in daily life. Also features live performances of Ainu songs and dances.

Fukui Prefectural Museum (Fukui Kenritsu Hakubutsukan). Prefectural Museum in the city of Fukui, Fukui Prefecture. Opened in 1984. The museum contains exhibits showing the history of Fukui Prefecture from the age of fossils to modern times as well as collections of folk crafts, agricultural tools, and other artifacts associated with daily life. It is equipped with video disc display facilities.

Fukuoka Prefectural Museum of Art (Fukuoka Kenritsu Bijutsukan). Prefectural museum in the city of Fukuoka, Fukuoka Prefecture. Opened in 1985. The museum has collections of paintings by SAKAMOTO HANJIRŌ (1882–1969) and Nakamura Ken'ichi (1895–1967), both of whom were born in Fukuoka Prefecture. There is also a collection of over 5,000 sketches by members of the Ogata family, who were employed as painters by lords of the Fukuoka domain during the EDO PERIOD (1600–1868). The museum's library of books concerning art is one of the largest in Japan.

Fukushima Prefectural Museum of Modern Art (Fukushima Kenritsu Bijutsukan). Prefectural museum in the city of Fukushima, Fukushima Prefecture. Opened in 1984. The museum features a collection of works by 20th century American artists and a collection of works by the artist Sekine Shōji (1899–1919), who was born in the prefecture. There are 300 woodblock prints by Saitō Kiyoshi (b 1907), who was also born in the prefecture.

Historical Village of Hokkaidō (Hokkaidō Kaitaku no Mura). Prefectural museum in Sapporo, Hokkaidō. Opened in 1983. Consists of buildings from the period of settlement in Hokkaidō during the late nineteenth and early twentieth centuries. The buildings have been restored and moved to the site.

Hyōgo Prefectural Museum of History (Hyōgo Kenritsu Rekishi Hakubutsukan). Prefectural museum in the city of Himeji, Hyōgo Prefecture. Opened in 1983. Exhibits concerning the history and culture of Hyōgo Prefecture. A permanent exhibit on HIMEJI CASTLE uses videotapes and models to give a detailed explanation of the castle's construction and history. There is a "firsthand experience" section, where the visitor may try on armor or court ladies' ceremonial dress, as well as a videocassette library on the history of the prefecture.

Ishikawa Prefectural Museum of Art (Ishikawa Kenritsu Bijutsukan). Prefectural museum in the city of Kanazawa, Ishikawa Prefecture. Opened in 1983. The museum contains a collection of articles handed down by the MAEDA FAMILY, rulers of the Kaga domain during the EDO PERIOD (1600–1868), including a colored, pheasant-shaped incense burner by the 17th century ceramic artist NONOMURA NINSEI (fl mid- 17th century). There are also important examples of KUTANI WARE and a collection of works by Matsuda Gonroku (1896–1986) and other artists whose names are associated with Ishikawa Prefecture.

Iwate Prefectural Museum   (Iwate Kenritsu Hakubutsukan). Prefectural museum in the city of Morioka, Iwate Prefecture. Opened in 1980. The museum is composed of a general exhibition hall containing materials on the archaeology, history, folk customs, and natural history of Iwate Prefecture and a modern art exhibition hall featuring works by Yorozu Tetsugorō (1885–1927) and other artists from Iwate Prefecture.

Japan Ukiyo-e Museum   (Nihon Ukiyo-e Hakubutsukan). Private museum in the city of Matsumoto, Nagano Prefecture. Opened in 1982. The museum holds a collection of approximately 100,000 woodblock prints ranging from early UKIYO-E works to modern prints collected over five generations by the Sakai family (rich merchants based in the city of Matsumoto).

Kagoshima City Museum of Art   (Kagoshima Shiritsu Bijutsukan). Municipal museum in the city of Kagoshima, Kagoshima Prefecture. Reopened in 1985. (The original museum, which had been built in the grounds of Tsurumaru Castle in 1954 was torn down and replaced by the present one, completed in 1985.) The museum contains a collection of paintings by KURODA SEIKI (1866–1924), FUJISHIMA TAKEJI (1867–1943), WADA EISAKU (1874–1959), and others. There are also collections of ceramics, sculpture, and the calligraphic exercises known as *bokuseki*.

Kagoshima Prefectural Museum of Culture: Reimeikan   (Kagoshima Ken Rekishi Shiryō Sentā Reimeikan). Prefectural museum in the city of Kagoshima, Kagoshima Prefecture. Opened in 1983. The museum contains exhibits on the Kagoshima area from its beginnings to modern times under such headings as archaeology, folklore, history, literature, and arts and crafts. Approximately 3,000 of the 40,000 articles held by the museum are exhibited at one time. Reimeikan (literally, "Dawn Hall") is a name chosen for the museum in a popular contest, the word *reimei*, or dawn, having long been used in poetic names referring to the area.

Kōbe City Museum   (Kōbe Shiritsu Hakubutsukan). Municipal museum in the city of Kōbe, Hyōgo Prefecture. Opened in 1982. The museum contains exhibits concerning Japanese cultural exchanges with foreign nations from ancient times to the present, with an emphasis on the role of the port city of Kōbe. There are also exhibits of NAMBAN ART centering on the collection of Ikenaga Hajime (1891–1955), a wealthy landowner.

Kōbe Science Museum   (Kōbe Shiritsu Seishōnen Kagakukan). Municipal museum in the city of Kōbe, Hyōgo Prefecture. Opened in 1984. The museum features exhibits concerning the most recent achievements of science and technology arranged under four themes: the science of forces and mechanisms, the science of energy, the science of the environment, and the science of information. There is an interactive exhibit of both industrial and "intelligent" robots. There is also a planetarium, which has a dome 20 meters (65.6 ft) in diameter.

Kubosō Memorial Museum of Arts   (Izumi Shi Kubosō Kinen Bijutsukan). Municipal museum in the city of Izumi, Ōsaka Prefecture. Opened in 1982. A collection of premodern Japanese and Chinese works of art, including paintings, decorative arts, ceramics, lacquerware, and bronze mirrors, donated to the city of Izumi by Kubo Sōtarō III (1926–84), head of the textile firm Kubosō. The collection includes 2 pieces classified as National Treasures and 28 classified as Important Cultural Properties.

Kushiro City Museum   (Kushiro Shiritsu Hakubutsukan). Municipal museum in the city of Kushiro, Hokkaidō. Opened in 1983. The museum contains materials from all periods of Kushiro's history, as well as ecological exhibits concerning the Kushiro marshes and the Japanese crane (*tanchō*).

Kyūshū Ceramic Museum   (Saga Kenritsu Kyūshū Tōji Bunkakan). Prefectural museum in the town of Arita, Saga Prefecture. Opened in 1980. A collection of ceramics of historical, artistic, or industrial importance produced in various parts of Kyūshū, including Old Karatsu, early Imari, and Nabeshima wares. Works by contemporary Kyūshū artists are also exhibited.

Little World Museum of Man   (Ningen Hakubutsukan Ritoru Wārudo). Private museum in the city of Inuyama, Aichi Prefecture. Opened in 1983. A new type of museum, featuring outdoor exhibits, and designed to show the traditional cultures of peoples from all over the world and reveal the things that unite them as human beings. The exhibits in the main building are organized under five themes: evolution, technology, language, society, and values. The building is equipped with animated video displays. The outdoor exhibits consist of over 20 dwellings of various peoples of the earth, which were moved to the museum and restored to their original state.

Mie Prefectural Art Museum   (Mie Kenritsu Bijutsukan). Prefectural Museum in the city of Tsu, Mie Prefecture. Opened in 1982. The museum's collection centers on Japanese modern paintings of the MEIJI PERIOD (1868–1912) and after. There are also works by earlier artists such as SOGA SHŌHAKU (1730–81) and Iwahashi Kyōshō (1832–83), whose names are associated with Mie Prefecture. Sculptures by Giacomo Manzú and others are displayed in an outdoor setting.

Miyagi Museum of Art   (Miyagi Kenritsu Bijutsukan). Prefectural museum in the city of Sendai, Miyagi Prefecture. Opened in 1981. A collection of modern and contemporary art, including works by Takahashi Yuichi (1828–94), Matsumoto Shunsuke (1912–48), Wassily Kandinsky, and Paul Klee, along with works by other artists whose names are associated with Miyagi Prefecture.

Munakata Taisha Treasure House   (Munakata Taisha Shimpōkan). An addition to the treasure house or museum at the Munakata Hetsumiya Shrine in the town of Genkai, Fukuoka Prefecture, one of the MUNAKATA SHRINES. Opened in 1980, the new treasure house is connected to the original treasure house, which was opened in 1964 and is now used for storage. The collection consists mainly of over 100,000 articles from the 4th to 10th centuries that were excavated at the OKINOSHIMA SITE. All the items have been classified as either National Treasures or Important Cultural Properties. There is also a collection of some 3,000 old documents known as the Munakata Monjo.

Museum of Fine Arts, Gifu   (Gifu Ken Bijutsukan). A prefectural museum in the city of Gifu, Gifu Prefecture. Opened in 1982. A collection chiefly of modern art, including important works of both Japanese and Western artists. A special feature is the collection of 177 works by Odilon Redon. Other artists represented include Maeda Seison who was born in Gifu Prefecture, Pierre Renoir, and Juan Miro.

Museum of Modern Art, Toyama   (Toyama Kenritsu Kindai Bijutsukan). Prefectural museum in the city of Toyama, Toyama Prefecture. Opened in 1981. A varied collection of 20th century art, containing works by Henri Toulouse-Lautrec, Pablo Picasso, Henri Matisse, and Marc Chagall, as well as a collection of posters by Kamekura Yūsaku (b 1915) and other artists. The museum is also dedicated to the preservation of local traditional arts.

Museum of Oriental Ceramics, Ōsaka   (Ōsaka Shiritsu Tōyō Tōji Bijutsukan). Municipal museum in the city of Ōsaka. Opened in 1982. The museum was established to accommodate the Ataka Collection, which was donated to the city by the 21 companies of the Sumitomo Group. The collection contains approximately 1,000 ceramic works from China and Korea, including 2 pieces classified as National Treasures and 12 as Important Cultural Properties.

Nagano City Museum (Nagano Shiritsu Hakubutsukan). Municipal museum in the city of Nagano, Nagano Prefecture. Opened in 1981. A general museum containing exhibits on the geology, archaeology, history, and folklore of the NAGANO BASIN arranged to emphasize the relationship between human beings and nature.

Nara Prefectural Museum, Kashihara Archaeological Institute (Nara Kenritsu Kashihara Kōkogaku Kenkyūjo Fuzoku Hakubutsukan). Prefectural museum in the city of Kashihara, Nara Prefecture. Opened in 1980. The museum is attached to the Kashihara Archaeological Institute, which was established in 1938. It houses a collection of artifacts unearthed in Nara Prefecture, including stone implements, earthenware, HANIWA, bronze mirrors, and armor dating from the PALEOLITHIC through the MUROMACHI PERIOD (1333–1568).

Niigata Science Museum (Niigata Ken Shizen Kagaku Kan). Prefectural museum in the city of Niigata, Niigata Prefecture. Opened in 1981. The museum features exhibits of the interactive type, which create a personal experience for the viewer. Themes include the world of nature, science and technology, the human senses, and changes in Niigata Prefecture as seen from the standpoint of industrial history.

Sendai City Museum (Sendai Shi Hakubutsukan). Municipal museum in the city of Sendai, Miyagi Prefecture. Opened in 1985. Contains exhibits of artifacts associated with the history of the DATE FAMILY, rulers of the Sendai domain during the EDO PERIOD (1600–1868) as well as exhibits concerning HASEKURA TSUNENAGA (1571–1622) and other early Japanese Christians.

Shimonoseki City Art Museum (Shimonoseki Shiritsu Bijutsukan). Municipal museum in the city of Shimonoseki, Yamaguchi Prefecture. Opened in 1983. A collection of works by local painters, most notably works by KANŌ HŌGAI (1828–88), one of the forerunners of modern Japanese-style painting, who was born in Shimonoseki. There is also a collection of French art nouveau glassware and a collection of Near Eastern (chiefly ancient Egyptian) funerary figurines, glass, and jewelry.

Tochigi Prefectural Museum (Tochigi Kenritsu Hakubutsukan). Prefectural museum in the city of Utsunomiya, Tochigi Prefecture. Opened in 1982. The chief themes of the museum are the natural history and culture of Tochigi Prefecture, including archaeology, history, folklore, arts and crafts, physical geography, and plants and animals. A special feature is a spiral ramp leading from the first to the second floor, which is used for exhibits showing the vertical distribution of plants and animals in the NIKKŌ region.

Usa Site Museum (Ōita Kenritsu Usa Fudoki no Oka Rekishi Minzoku Shiryōkan). Prefectural museum in the city of Usa, Ōita Prefecture. Opened in 1981. The museum, which is located in a historic site containing six keyhole-shaped tomb mounds (KOFUN) of the "front-square and rear-round" type, has exhibits relating to the history of the Usa and Kunisaki regions from the YAYOI PERIOD (ca 300 BC–ca AD 300) to the HEIAN PERIOD (794–1185), the history of the HACHIMAN cult, special forms of BUDDHIST ART associated with the region, and local folk practices.

Mutō Kiyoshi (1903–)

Structural engineer. Born in Ibaraki Prefecture. Graduated from Tōkyō University. Mutō taught at Tōkyō University from 1927, becoming professor emeritus in 1963. He was also director of the Mutō Institute of Structural Mechanics. Mutō perfected a method of aseismic calculation by which the effect of earthquake forces on the structure of buildings could be determined. He thus made it possible to erect extremely tall buildings in Japan, a country whose frequent earthquakes had formerly made this impossible. He was involved in the construction of many of Japan's high-rise buildings, including the 36-story Kasumigaseki Building, the first such building in Japan (Tōkyō, 1968, 147 meters or 482 feet), and the 60-story Sunshine Building (Tōkyō, 1978, 240 meters or 787 feet). He was the head of the Architectural Institute of Japan from 1955 to 1957 and the head of the International Association for Earthquake Engineering from 1963 to 1965. He received the Architectural Institute of Japan Award in 1970 and was awarded the Order of Culture in 1983. His books include the *Taishin sekkei shirīzu* (Aseismic Design Series), 5 vols (Maruzen, 1963–77).

Nakamura Kanzaburō XVII (1909–)

KABUKI actor. Real name Namino Seiji. Born in Tōkyō. Kanzaburō made his debut in 1916 with the stage name Nakamura Yonekichi, changed his name to Nakamura Moshio in 1929, and became Nakamura Kanzaburō XVII in 1950. Inheriting the acting styles of his older brother, Nakamura Kichiemon I (1886–1954), and his father-in-law, Onoe Kikugorō VI (1885–1949), he became known for his wide range of roles and rich power of expression. In 1970 he became a member of the Japan Art Academy, and in 1975 he was designated as a Living National Treasure. In 1980 he was awarded the Order of Culture. He is best known for his acting in such classic kabuki roles as the title roles in *Hōkaibō* and *Kamiyui Shinza* and as Matsuō in *Terakoya*. He also specialized in such modern kabuki pieces as *Ippon-gatana dohyōiri* and *Kurayami no Ushimatsu*.

Nakano Kōichi (1955–)

Bicycle racer. In Colorado in 1986 Nakano won the pro sprint in the World Cycling Championship for the tenth time in succession, a record for successive victories. He was born in Fukuoka Prefecture (his father was also a bicycle racer) and graduated from Yame Industrial High School. He made his debut as a racer in 1975 and in 1976 was named rookie of the year. Afterwards he won a succession of important Japanese races, including the Cycling Crown (Keirin'ō) and the Japan Championship. His first victory in the World Cycling Championship came in 1977, the first year he entered the race.

Nakazato Tsuneko (1909–)

Novelist. Real name Nakazato Tsune. Born in Kanagawa Prefecture. Nakazato graduated from Kanagawa Girls' Higher School. She established herself as a writer with the encouragement of the novelist YOKOMITSU RIICHI (1898–1947). In 1938, with her short story "Noriai basha," she became the first woman to win the Akutagawa Prize. After World War II, she wrote a number of novels describing international marriages, including *Mariannu monogatari* (1946; title later changed to *Bochi no haru*) and *Kusari* (1959), which deals with her own daughter's marriage to an American. In her works of the 1970s and 1980s she moved from a refined description of the inner workings of human life to a more symbolic style of writing, as in *Utamakura* (1973; winner of the Yomiuri Literary Prize in the same year). In 1974 Nakazato received the Japan Art Academy Prize, and she became a member of the academy in 1983.

ASAI Kiyoshi

National Bunraku Theater

(Kokuritsu Bunraku Gekijō). A theater established by the government for the performance of Japan's traditional puppet theater (BUNRAKU). Opened in March 1984. Located in the Nihombashi district of Minami Ward, Ōsaka, the theater has five stories above ground, two below ground, and seats 753 people. The theater was established in Ōsaka because of the city's history as the birthplace of bunraku. It is dedicated to the preservation, promotion, and spread of bunraku as well as to the training of new performers. Regular performances are scheduled six times a year. In addition to the main theater, there is a smaller hall (159 seats), which doubles as a place for rehearsals and training. There is also a room for exhibits. The main theater, which is also used for KABUKI and other traditional performing arts, has a revolving stage and *hanamichi* (ramp through the audience) and is fully equipped with all the special features used in bunraku performances.

National Nō Theater

(Kokuritsu Nōgakudō; formal name Kokuritsu Gekijō Nōgakudō). A theater dedicated to the performance of the traditional Japanese dramatic forms of NŌ and KYŌGEN. Located in the Sendagaya district of Tōkyō. The decision to establish such a theater was made at a cabinet meeting in 1956, but construction did not begin until 1980, and the theater opened in September 1983. The theater, which has two floors above ground and one below ground, was built at a total cost of over ¥4.59 billion (US $19.33 million). The theater on the first floor seats 591 people. A separate theater on the second floor, intended for training, will accommodate 200 people. The total number of scheduled performances per year is 54, including regular Nō performances twice a month, educational and special performances once a month each, and bimonthly *kyōgen* performances. However, with the addition of other special performances, the theater was open 262 days in 1985. The primary goals of the National Nō Theater are the performance and preservation of the art of Nō, the training of actors and musicians, and Nō study and research.

National Personnel Authority recommendations in the 1980s

The National Personnel Authority makes annual recommendations to the Japanese government concerning salary levels and working conditions for public service employees, who have neither collective bargaining rights nor the right to strike (see NATIONAL PERSONNEL AUTHORITY RECOMMENDATIONS). Government financial difficulties caused the authority's 1982 salary recommendations to be shelved, and the 1983 and 1984 recommendations were also frozen. The recommendations for 1985 were put into effect in July of that year (three months after the April date recommended), and the full 5.74 percent recommended increase was implemented for the first time in four years. The government promised to do its utmost to implement the previously frozen recommendations by 1986. The first complete revision of the public employees' wage scale in 28 years was undertaken as recommended by the authority. This revision was intended to respond to diversification of types of occupations and other changes in personnel organization. A new special administrative personnel wage scale covering air traffic controllers and other new occupations was prepared, and the administrative personnel wage scale was altered from an 8-grade system to an 11-grade system.
                                                          YOSHIKAWA Kaoru

national secrets bill

(kokka himitsu hōan). Also known as the antispy bill *(supai bōshi hōan).* A bill introduced in the Diet in June 1985 by the LIBERAL DEMOCRATIC PARTY but withdrawn in December of the same year. The full name of the proposed legislation was Law concerning Prevention of Spy Activities affecting National Secrets. The Liberal Democratic Party insisted that the law was necessary since Japan had no laws aimed at the control of spying and that in the absence of such a law spying activities were left to proceed unchecked. However, the proposed law's definition of "national secrets" was vague, and there were fears that it would infringe on the people's right to be informed as well as some danger that it would interfere with the legitimate information-gathering activities of the news media. For these reasons, there was strong opposition from the press, the opposition parties, legal and scholarly circles, and the general public.

The stated purpose of the law was the protection of "those matters pertaining to defense or foreign relations which it is necessary to keep secret for the sake of the defense of Japan." More specifically these included (1) defense policies, plans, and activities, (2) the organization, equipment, duties, and deployment of units of the Self Defense Forces, and (3) policies relating to foreign relations. In all such categories, any information that had not been officially made public by the government was declared to be a national secret. The maximum penalty provided for violation of the law was capital punishment. Lesser penalties included imprisonment with labor and imprisonment without labor for fixed terms.

In February 1986, the Liberal Democratic Party began preparing a revised version of the bill in order to reintroduce it in the Diet. The revision was completed in May as the "defense secrets bill." The party made early passage of the revised bill part of its platform in the July 1986 election, claiming that in the revision "national secrets" had been limited to "defense secrets." The opposition parties remained opposed to the bill, charging that the framework of the revision did not differ from that of the original version.
                                                          NOMURA Jirō

National Trust Movement

General term for a number of separate Japanese movements based on the idea of the National Trust that was introduced in Great Britain in 1895. Citizens of an area, or the local government, make a broad appeal for funds to buy land in order to preserve some part of their natural or historical environment. The first such movement in Japan began in December 1964, when a citizens' group in the city of Kamakura in Kanagawa Prefecture purchased a tract of land in the hills behind the Tsurugaoka Hachiman Shrine in order to stop a planned housing development. The best-known examples are the movements to preserve the Shiretoko Peninsula in Hokkaidō and the Tenjinzaki area of Wakayama Prefecture. In the Hokkaidō example, a movement began in March 1977 in the town of Shari to buy up a tract of land on the Shiretoko Peninsula, where part of a virgin forest had been cut down, and restore it to its natural state. This movement centered in the town government. By March 1986, nine years later, funds totaling over ¥270 million (US $1.495 million) had been collected from 25,069 people, and 355.5 hectares (approximately 878 acres) of land had been purchased. (The movement was scheduled to continue until its goal of 472 hectares, or some 1,166 acres, had been purchased.) In the case of Tenjinzaki, citizens of the city of Tanabe began raising funds in February 1974 in order to buy up land and protect the area's natural setting from housing developments. As of 1985, the group had already purchased 8,500 square meters (about 2 acres) in the heart of the Tenjinzaki area with the cooperation of the city and prefectural governments, and the drive was still being continued with the goal of buying up the remaining land. During the 1980s movements of this kind spread throughout Japan, assuming various forms, such as the preservation of historic urban districts, the establishment of bird sanctuaries, and the preservation of natural seacoasts. In February 1983 a loosely knit nationwide organization called the Japanese Union of National Trust Movements was formed. Beginning in 1985, revisions in the tax system made it possible for national trusts recognized as nonprofit organizations by the national and local governments to receive special income-tax treatment.

negative ceiling

In the 1980s, all Japanese government ministries and agencies were required to adhere to strict ceilings when submitting budget claims to the Ministry of Finance so that the government's announced goal of "fiscal responsibility without increased taxation" could be realized. In fiscal year 1982 the government established a ceiling of a zero-percent increase from 1981's figures. Beginning in 1983, "negative ceilings" were established. Budget claims for 1983 were required to be 5 percent lower than they had been in 1982 (certain expenditures, such as those for economic cooperation and national defense, were not subject to the negative ceiling). Severe restrictions in fiscal year 1986 called for a 10 percent reduction in ordinary expenses from the previous year, and a 5 percent decrease in investment expenditure. While this system was effective in reducing annual expenditures, it deprived the Japanese government of some of the financial flexibility necessary for making policy changes required by new problems.
                                                          ŌMORI Takashi

new international round

Preparations for the eighth multilateral round of negotiations for the General Agreement on Tariffs and Trade (GATT) were begun in the spring of 1986. This new round of negotiations was launched at a meeting of finance ministers of the 92 participating nations held at Punta del Este in Uruguay in September 1986. The Uruguay Round, named after the host country, had been proposed at the economic summit conference of developed nations held in Williamsburg, Virginia, in May 1983 because the tariff concessions established during the previous Tōkyō Round were scheduled to expire in 1987 and because continuing countermeasures against protectionism were required. In November 1983, Japan became the first nation to agree to a new international round; the EC (European Community) agreed a year later, in November 1984. The date for beginning the round was not set until October 1985, however, because of the insistence of developing nations that their concerns be given priority and that service trade be excluded from the topics for negotiation. The main topics scheduled for discussion were follow-up matters agreed upon at the previous Tōkyō Round such as tariff concessions and nontariff barriers, matters not addressed during that round such as safeguards (emergency import restrictions), matters of particular concern to developing countries, and such subjects as service trades, high technology, merchandise trade, and intellectual proprietary rights, areas which were not included in the earlier framework of GATT and about which the United States was eager to negotiate with other countries, since it was highly competitive in these fields.

NISHIKAWA Masao

new materials

In the 1980s both government and industry in Japan were giving high priority to the development of new materials and associated processing technologies because of their potential technical and competitive advantages. In the broadest sense, the term "new materials"—or the alternate term "exotic materials"—refers simply to alternatives to existing materials. One example is gallium arsenide, an alternative to silicon as a material for manufacturing electronic chips. However, the specific definitions of these terms can vary greatly depending on what is meant by "new" or "exotic." In Japan "new materials" usually means metal alloys, organic and inorganic compounds, or their composites, whose physical and chemical functions are enhanced by revolutionary changes in manufacturing processes and production technology.

Developing new materials is one of the major goals of the Research and Development Project of Basic Technologies for Future Industries that is being promoted by Japan's Ministry of International Trade and Industry. In this project, new materials are divided into four areas: function polymers, microcrystalline metals, composite materials, and advanced ceramics (referred to in Japan as "fine ceramics").

Function polymers include high-performance engineering plastics such as polyamide resin, polyacetal resin, polycarbonate resin, polyphenylene oxide, polybutyrene terephthalate resin, fluoroplastic, and other similar materials. These plastics, which are valued for their mechanical strength and resistance to heat and chemical corrosion, have wide applications for machinery, electronics, aerospace, and automobiles, to name a few fields.

The most important of the microcrystalline metals, which are based on rapid solidification technology, are the amorphous metals. Shape-memory alloys are another example of microcrystalline metals. This type of alloy transforms its shape when heated but regains the original form when cooled off.·

Composite materials include hybrid materials with plastic and metal matrices, and those based on other materials, such as carbon, boron, and aluminum. Examples include a carbon fiber reinforced metal and an aluminum-lithium alloy, both of which are used for aircraft frames.

Examples of advanced ceramics, which result from a reaction-bonding calcination of chemically synthesized inorganic compounds, include almina-ceramic, used in the production of integrated circuit boards, silicon carbide, and partially stabilized zirconia. Advanced ceramics are used for electronics, medical equipment, and automobile parts.

There were discrepancies between laboratory practices and the actual manufacturing processes needed to create new materials from the existing basic materials; however, Japanese government analysts predicted that by the year 2000 the gross sales of new materials would exceed ¥5 trillion (US $21 billion, based on 1985 exchange rates).

NISHIMATA Souhei

new social indicators

(NSI). A set of social indicators compiled by the Japanese government beginning in 1986. Just as the gross national product (GNP) and other economic indicators are used to measure a nation's level of economic activity, many nations compile social indicators to determine the level of their people's welfare. These social indicators provide a comprehensive system of statistical measurements of conditions in various aspects of society or the national life, using nonmonetary as well as economic factors. Social indicators for Japan have been compiled annually by the Japanese government since 1974. The new social indicators introduced in 1986 were selected in light of changes in the national life and changes in the people's awareness. Japan's new social indicators were designed, according to a government statement, as "a system which will enable us to know precisely the present state and points-at-issue of national life." The new indicators include measurements of personal awareness and structural changes in society as well as

international comparisons, in addition to the normative indicators already in use.

Broadly speaking, the new social indicators fall into three categories: "spheres of life," personal awareness, and concerns and interests. The "spheres of life" (which were called "social goals" in the old set of indicators) are divided into eight areas: health, environment and safety, economic stability, home life, working life, school life, regional and social activities, and learning and cultural activities. The category of personal awareness includes measurements of such indicators as satisfaction with present life and attitudes toward material as opposed to spiritual well-being. The category of concerns and interests includes such areas of concern as the "internationalization" of Japanese society, the flood of information provided by new electronic media, increased life span, urbanization, and life differentials in terms of such factors as place of residence, employment, age, and sex.

YASUHARA Norikazu

Nippon Telegraph and Telephone Corporation

(Nippon Denshin Denwa; NTT). A corporation established on 1 April 1985, when the NIPPON TELEGRAPH AND TELEPHONE PUBLIC CORPORATION came under private management. According to the recommendations of the 1983 report of the Second Provisional Commission for Administrative Reform, the corporation's existing managerial structure was altered to improve efficiency. Initially, all stock in the corporation was held by the government, but up to two-thirds of the stock was eventually to be transferred to private ownership. As of April 1985, NTT was the largest enterprise in Japan, with a capital of ¥780 billion (US $3.277 billion) and 320,000 employees. As a result of private management, NTT would be able to offer new services to users, and competition would be introduced into the previously monopolistic field of telecommunications.

IKEDA Minoru

Nishikawa Yasushi (1902–)

Calligrapher. Professional name Nishikawa Seian. Born in Tōkyō. Graduated from Keiō University, majoring in Chinese literature. Nishikawa was the son of the calligrapher Nishikawa Shundō, and he studied calligraphy under his father from childhood. As a student in Beijing (Peking) in 1940, he studied Chinese literature and ancient Chinese bronze and stone inscriptions. Nishikawa became a leading figure in contemporary Japanese calligraphy, both as a scholar of Chinese calligraphy and for his own calligraphy in styles based on the Chinese angular, standard style (J: kaisho) of the Six Dynasties period (222–589) and the style of the ancient bronze and stone inscriptions. He received the Japan Art Academy Prize in 1955 and became a member of the academy in 1969. In 1985 he was awarded the Order of Culture. His books include Shina no shodō (1940; The Calligraphy of China) and Sho no hensō (1960; The Changing Face of Calligraphy).

nonsmokers' rights

(ken'enken). In Japan, as elsewhere, the issue of nonsmokers' rights (the right of nonsmokers not to be forced to inhale the tobacco smoke of people smoking around them) became one of the important social issues of the 1970s and 1980s. In 1978 a citizens' action group called the Japan Action for Nonsmokers' Rights was formed. The activities of this group were mainly aimed at securing nonsmokers' rights by demanding regulation of smoking in public places. One of its chief targets was the Japanese National Railways (JNR). Among other things, the group demanded that at least half the passenger cars on the JNR's trains be designated as no-smoking cars, and in 1980 it initiated a "nonsmokers' rights lawsuit" to force the railroad to comply. The trial resulting from this lawsuit was concluded in March 1986, and a decision was expected in October of that year. The influence of the lawsuit could already be seen in the JNR's decision, effective October 1980, to designate one non-reserved-seat car on each of its high-speed Shinkansen trains as a no-smoking car. The JNR afterwards gradually began to set aside no-smoking cars on its other trains. The nonsmokers' rights movement spread throughout the nation, and, among other achievements, it succeeded in having smoking banned in the waiting rooms of all national and other public hospitals. The All-Japan Antismoking Liaison Council was formed in 1978 as a loose nationwide federation of nonsmokers' rights groups. The number of participating groups had grown to 43 by the end of 1985. The Liaison Council was instrumental in having one week in April declared No-smoking Week beginning in 1984. It was also active in carrying on international exchanges with similar groups in other countries, and the sixth World Conference on Smoking and Health was scheduled to be held in Tōkyō in November 1987.

nuclear fuel cycle facility

A planned combined nuclear facility that would be composed of a nuclear fuel reprocessing plant (to be operational by 1995), a facility for onshore disposal of low-level radioactive waste (to be opened in 1991), and a uranium enrichment plant (to be operational by 1991). The village of Rokkasho on the Shimokita Peninsula, Aomori Prefecture, was chosen as the chief candidate for the location of the facility, and the governor of Aomori Prefecture approved a proposal to that effect from the Federation of Electric Power Companies in April 1985. However, opponents of the plan pointed out that since there were problems of economy with respect to fast-breeder reactors using reprocessed plutonium as a fuel, and since there was a worldwide surplus of uranium for use in fueling power plants, there was not such an urgent need for the reprocessing plant and the uranium enrichment plant. Accordingly, they said, there was some danger that the proposed facility would turn out to be not a nuclear fuel cycle facility but a radioactive-waste storage facility, for which there was a more obvious need. There were also opponents of the proposal who charged that, under the pretext of revitalizing the depopulated area around Rokkasho, a facility whose safety was still a matter for dispute was being forced on the area.

nuclear power plants

As of the end of 1985, 31 commercial nuclear power plants were operating in Japan, 16 with boiling-water reactors and 15 with pressurized-water reactors; their total capacity was 23.63 million kilowatts. Japan had thus become the world's fourth-largest generator of nuclear power, following the United States, France, and the Soviet Union. Atomic energy was Japan's single largest source of power in 1985, generating 156.9 billion kilowatt-hours of electricity, or 26 percent of the nation's total power. Seventeen additional nuclear power plants were under construction or being planned as of the end of 1985, and their generating capacity would total 17.06 million kilowatts. It was estimated that by 1995 the added power-generating capacity of all nuclear power plants planned by the Japanese government would see nuclear power plants producing 48 million kilowatts and providing 35 percent of Japan's total generated power. The average rate of operation for the country's nuclear power plants in 1984 was 74 percent, the highest in the world. Until the end of the 1970s, Japan had depended on the light-water-reactor technology of the United States, but beginning in the early 1980s the construction of these plants and attendant safety measures were undertaken domestically. Japan still depended on the United States and Europe for most of the enriched uranium used for fuel; however, a uranium enriching plant, scheduled for completion in 1987, was being constructed by the Power Reactor and Nuclear Fuel Development Corporation, and in the future the nation would be able to be more self-sufficient in this regard. *Nishimata Souhei*

nuclear waste

Of all the forms of radioactive waste produced by nuclear power plants, certain types of industry, and medical and research facilities, the waste produced by nuclear power plants has become the most serious social and political problem. This is true in Japan as it is in other advanced nations. The amount of radioactive waste produced by nuclear power plants and the degree of danger involved set them apart from other such facilities. Radioactive waste is classified by the amount of radiation, usually into the two categories of high- and low-level radiation but sometimes into three categories by the addition of medium-level radiation. Regardless of the amount of radiation, the problem of how to dispose of the waste has become an important issue. In 1980 the Japanese government announced plans to dispose of low-level nuclear waste in the Pacific Ocean. However, there was strong opposition from the governments of South Pacific nations as well as from fishermen, and the plan was eventually dropped in 1985. At the same time, when the Power Reactor and Nuclear Fuel Development Corporation announced plans in 1984 to construct a storage facility in the town of Horonobe, Hokkaidō, for vitrified high-level nuclear waste, the people of the

locality were caught up in a storm of arguments for and against, and in 1986 the issue still remained unsettled. *Iwadare Hiroshi*

Nukatabe no Omi sword inscriptions

Inscriptions on the blade of an iron long-sword found in Okadayama Tomb Number One in the city of Matsue, Shimane Prefecture, in 1915. The sword was badly rusted, and rust-removal operations were carried out at the Gangōji Cultural Properties Research Center. In 1983, X-ray studies revealed an inscription of ten or more characters in silver inlay on the blade of the sword. The first four characters turned out to be a personal name, Nukatabe no Omi, thus proving the existence of the district official *(gunji)* of that name who is mentioned in the *Izumo fudoki*. This discovery is expected to provide valuable material for future studies of the relationship between the YAMATO COURT and the Izumo region in the latter half of the 6th century. The rounded pommel of this sword resembles a pattern that has been unearthed in tombs in the southwestern part of South Korea.

office automation

Office automation (the use of computers and other electronic communication and information-storage equipment to improve productivity and efficiency within a business office) requires special equipment in Japan. Word processors, telexes, and optical character readers, for example, have to be specially designed in order to handle the Japanese language. As of the mid-1980s, office automation was making remarkable progress yearly, and the production of office automation equipment yielded a profit of ¥3 trillion (US $12.6 billion) in 1983. This figure was expected to double by 1988; it was estimated that approximately ¥2 trillion would be spent for ordinary office machinery, including Japanese word processors, and ¥4 trillion on such equipment as computers and facsimile machines. *Nishimata Souhei*

Office of Trade and Investment Ombudsman

(OTO). The name of an ombudsman system established by the Japanese government in January 1982 to handle complaints concerning procedures related to import inspections, direct investment in Japan, and other issues connected with the further opening of the Japanese market to foreign trade. The system is operated jointly by 14 government ministries and agencies, with the Economic Planning Agency taking a leading role. Complaints can be filed in person or by proxy with one of the involved offices or with a Japanese embassy or consulate overseas. Two hundred and twenty-one complaints had been received by November 1985. *Nishikawa Masao*

official development assistance

In the first half of the 1980s, the most notable change in Japan's official development assistance (ODA) to developing nations (see FOREIGN AID POLICY) was an increase in aid to nations in the so-called troubled areas of the globe. There was a marked increase in aid to Pakistan, Turkey, Egypt, the Sudan, and Somali as well as to members of the Association of Southeast Asian Nations (ASEAN). China also became one of the major recipients of Japanese aid in connection with its program of liberalization and modernization. Aid to China in 1983 amounted to US $290 million. A total of US $4 billion in aid over a seven-year period was also promised to South Korea on the occasion of Prime Minister NAKASONE YASUHIRO's (b 1918) visit to that nation in January 1983.

In 1977 Japan had launched a plan to double its ODA by 1980, and this goal had been met: ODA had increased from US $1.42 billion in 1977 to US $3.3 billion in 1980. In January 1981 Japan announced a new medium-range plan for doubling its ODA again, this time over a five-year period. However in 1981 and 1982 the amount of Japan's ODA fell below that of the previous year for two years in a row. ODA for 1983 was US $37.61 billion, an increase of 24.4 percent over the previous year. This 1983 figure placed Japan third among the 17 member nations of the Development Assistance Committee (DAC) of the Organization for Economic Cooperation and Development (OECD). (The first and second nations were the United States and France.) Japan's ODA for 1984 was US $4.32 billion, second to that of the United States. However, Japan's ODA as a percentage of its gross national product (GNP) was low: in 1984 the figure was 0.35 percent, placing Japan eleventh among the members of the DAC. Japan also ranked low in the so-called grant element, an index of the generosity of conditions for assistance—sixteenth among the DAC nations. NISHIKAWA Masao

official discount rate

In March 1980, Japan's official discount rate was raised to 9 percent after having been raised to 7.25 percent only the month before. However, the rate was lowered to 8.25 percent in August of the same year, as it was clear that the Japanese economy had entered a period of recession. By October 1983 the official discount rate was 5 percent, having been lowered three more times in the intervening period. After October 1983 the rate remained unchanged for two years and three months owing to such factors as a continued upturn in business conditions and the need to prevent lowered domestic interest rates from acting as a spur to the falling value of the yen. In January 1986, the official discount rate was lowered to 4.5 percent. This was a response to a rapid rise in value of the yen accompanied by stagnation in domestic business conditions following the meeting of the finance ministers of the five advanced nations (the United States, Japan, West Germany, France, and the United Kingdom) in September 1985. In March and April of 1986 Japan and the United States both lowered their discount rates. As of the summer of 1986, the rate had remained at 3.5 percent since April.

ŌMORI Takashi

Ogura Yuki (1895–)

Japanese-style (NIHONGA) painter specializing in graceful family scenes and pictures of women. Born in Shiga Prefecture (her maiden name was Mizogami Yuki). Ogura graduated from Nara Women's Higher Normal School in 1917, majoring in Japanese and Chinese literature. In 1920, while working as a teacher, she began studying painting under YASUDA YUKIHIKO (1884–1978). Her painting Kyūri (Cucumbers) was selected for an Inten exhibition (see JAPAN FINE ARTS ACADEMY) in 1926, and she afterwards showed paintings at Inten exhibitions regularly. In 1976 she became a member of the JAPAN ART ACADEMY. She received the Order of Culture in 1980. Her best-known works include Yuami onna (1938, Bathing Women), Oyako (1961, Mother and Child; winner of the Japan Art Academy Prize in 1962), and Maiko (1969, Apprentice Geisha).

Okuda Genso (1912–)

Japanese-style (NIHONGA) painter. Real name Okuda Genzō. A specialist in landscapes in an original style blending the ink painting tradition of China and Japan with the color expression of Western painting. Okuda was born in Hiroshima Prefecture. After graduating from middle school, he began studying painting with Kodama Kibō (1898–1971). His painting Sannin no josei (Three Women) was selected for the BUNTEN exhibition in 1936. He became a member of the Japan Art Academy in 1974 and received the Order of Culture in 1984. His best-known paintings include Taigetsu (1949, Waiting for the Moon) and Bandai (1962, Mt. Bandai; winner of the Japan Art Academy Prize in 1963).

"100 Best Waters of Japan"

The name of a nationwide campaign conducted by the Environment Agency in 1985 for the purpose of arousing public interest in preserving the purity and quality of Japan's water supply. On the basis of this survey, the "100 Best Waters of Japan" (Meisui Hyakusen) were selected. The survey emphasized the measures that the residents of the districts concerned were taking to preserve the quality of their water resources. Among the waters selected were those of the Eight Springs of Oshino in Yamanashi Prefecture, which are fed by water from Mt. Fuji that has filtered through the soil, the Miyamizu of Hyōgo Prefecture, another soil-filtered water, which is famous as the water used in making the sakes of the Nada district, and the mountain-stream water of Mitake, which is one of the sources for the drinking water in Tōkyō.

The Environment Agency's campaign was aimed at preserving the purity of Japan's water resources as a whole and was not concerned with water for any specific purpose such as drinking. Earlier, in 1984, the Ministry of Health and Welfare had carried out a project aimed at improving the quality of the piped water supplied in Japanese cities. The ministry made a list of the requirements of good

drinking water and rated the cities of the nation on the quality of their water supply. Thirty-two cities among those with populations of 100,000 or above were designated as having good water. Public drinking water in the northern Kantō and Chūbu regions was found to be good, whereas the water in the cities of Tōkyō, Ōsaka, and Kita Kyūshū was found to have a disagreeable taste.

one-percent defense ceiling

A government policy limiting Japan's defense spending during any one year to one percent of the nation's gross national product (GNP) for that year. The policy was established in a cabinet meeting in 1976.

When the Defense Agency adopted the Outline of the National Defense Program (which established defensive strength levels to be attained) in October 1976, the cabinet of Prime Minister MIKI TAKEO (b 1907) decided at a cabinet meeting to "aim" at keeping defense spending within one percent of the GNP "for the present." In 1985 it began to look as if this ceiling might be exceeded, and the question of whether this was to be allowed became an important political issue. Some segments of the LIBERAL DEMOCRATIC PARTY, as well as certain intellectual groups, began to advocate abolishing the limit entirely. Increasingly strong demands from the United States for more cooperation from Japan in matters of defense had coincided with a slowing of Japan's economic growth. Also, the international situation was becoming critical, with increasing tension between the United States and the Soviet Union. There were those who criticized the ceiling itself as irrational, pointing out that the original decision had contained the qualifications "for the present" and "aim."

A proposal was advanced within the government to compensate for a possible abolition of the ceiling by raising the Defense Agency's Mid-term Defense Program Estimate to the status of a government plan and approving the total amount of the five-year expense of the plan. This would mean approving defense spending over five-year periods, a system which could be substituted for the yearly one-percent ceiling as a brake on defense spending. The status of the Mid-term Estimate was indeed raised in September 1985; however, public opposition to abolition of the one-percent ceiling remained deep-rooted, and, at the insistence of a part of the leadership of the Liberal Democratic Party, the abolition of the ceiling was shelved. FUKUSHIMA Yasuto

One Village, One Product Movement

(Isson Ippin Undō). A plan for the vitalization of local industry that was promoted by Hiramatsu Morihiko (b 1924), the governor of Ōita Prefecture. The slogan One Village, One Product was first used in November 1979. The idea of the plan was that each town or village in the prefecture would choose a local product, typically an agricultural product, and that sales of this product would be promoted on the national market, resulting in the vitalization of local industry and further development of the towns and villages themselves. Similar plans were adopted in other parts of Japan, including Okinawa and Fukushima prefectures and Hokkaidō. In 1984 the Small and Medium Enterprise Agency of the central government's Ministry of International Trade and Industry began an attempt to spread this type of revitalization of local industry even further under the general slogan Village Vitalization Enterprise (Mura Okoshi Jigyō). This effort of the central government focuses on the development of unused resources and the reevaluation of traditional Japanese industries for the purpose of stimulating employment in depopulated areas. NAKAMURA Kiichi

opening of Japan to foreign attorneys

In order to practice law in Japan, an attorney must be a member of the JAPAN FEDERATION OF BAR ASSOCIATIONS as well as a local prefectural bar association. An attorney must also qualify by passing the national LAW EXAMINATION. Attorneys from other nations have complained that Japan's is a closed system and have demanded that foreigners also be allowed to practice law in Japan. Debate over this issue had become entwined with the larger issue of economic friction between Japan and Western nations, and there had been strong criticism of Japan, particularly from the United States. The Japan Federation of Bar Associations had formerly maintained the position that foreign attorneys could not be indiscriminately allowed to practice because of differences between the Japanese legal system and those of other countries. However, on 9 December 1985 it announced a policy of admitting foreign attorneys into legal practice under certain conditions. The most important conditions were (1) reciprocity (practice would be limited to attorneys from nations that also admitted Japanese attorneys), (2) the foreign attorneys would be registered with the Japan Federation of Bar Associations and placed under its guidance and supervision, (3) their practice of law would be limited to the law of their own country and the law of third nations to be designated by the minister of justice, and (4) foreign attorneys were prohibited from forming partnerships with Japanese attorneys.

The Japanese government followed up the federation's announcement by introducing in the Diet a special bill concerning the practice of law by foreign attorneys. This bill was approved by a unanimous vote in May 1986. The government aimed at putting the new law into effect by April 1987; however, as of the end of May 1986 a definite date for the opening of Japan to foreign attorneys had still not been set.   NOMURA Jirō

optical-fiber transmission

A number of important optical-fiber transmission projects were undertaken in Japan in the 1980s. (Optical-fiber transmission refers to a communication system that uses light signals passed through optical fibers instead of electrical signals or radio waves. Such a system consists of a light-emitting device, which converts electrical signals to optical signals, an optical-fiber cable, repeaters, which boost signals at regular intervals along the route, and a light-receiving device which converts the optical signals to electrical signals.)

The first fibers suitable for communications were made by Corning Glass Works in 1970, and the first commercial systems were installed in the United States around 1980. Fiber-optics technology was introduced to Japan shortly thereafter, and Japanese firms made rapid progress in research and development in the new field of optoelectronics. One notable achievement was the trunk line for an optical-fiber cable transmission system throughout Japan, which was constructed by the Nippon Telegraph and Telephone Corporation (NTT) in 1984. This trunk-cable system, called F-400, extends 3,400 kilometers (211 mi) and carries information at the rate of 400 million bits per second, enough for 5,760 telephone lines. It was put into commercial service as part of NTT's Information Network System (INS).

The transmission capacity of F-400 varies according to communication demands along the route. Between Tōkyō and Ōsaka the system consists of 12 main fiber cables that carry 70,000 telephone circuits, or 720 videoconference circuits, at one time. Optical signals are emitted from indium-gallium-arsenide-phosphorous semiconductors and are regenerated at every 20–25 kilometers (12–16 mi).

Another major optical transmission project underway in the mid-1980s was a submarine cable between Japan and the United States. This transpacific cable, which would carry about 7,500 telephone lines, was to be laid by the American Telephone and Telegraphy Company (AT&T) of the United States and the KOKUSAI DENSHIN DENWA CO, LTD (KDD) of Japan. It was expected to be completed by 1988. Smaller-scale optical-fiber highways, as well as local area networks, were being constructed in various parts of Japan. The demand for optical fiber was increasing to such an extent that the total length of optical-fiber cables in use in Japan was expected to reach 1.33 million kilometers (825,930 mi) by 1989.   NISHIMATA Souhei

organ transplants

Although organ transplants are now recognized as miracle cures for patients with severe diseases of the vital organs, such as the heart, liver and kidney, Japan is still a developing country as far as transplants are concerned. The number of kidney transplants performed in Japan as of 1986 was less than one-tenth of the number of operations performed in the United States. The number was still lower for heart transplants: only one case had been reported. This first and (as of 1986) last heart transplant to be performed in Japan took place in 1968, and the patient died after 83 days. Because the brain-dead donor's heart was still functioning when it was removed from the patient's body, the heart surgeon who perfomed the operation was accused by some of murder. (The concept of brain death was slow in being accepted in Japan.) Formal charges were never brought, but since that incident, heart transplants have been treated as taboo by the Japanese medical community. The resulting scarcity of suitable donors has been an additional impediment to heart

transplant operations. As new government guidelines for defining brain death gradually become accepted by Japanese society, heart transplants might have a second chance in the near future.
                                    NISHIMATA Souhei

Ōtsuki Bumpei (1903–   )

Businessman. Born in Miyagi Prefecture. Ōtsuki graduated from the Faculty of Law of Tōkyō University in 1928 and worked for the Mitsubishi Mining Company. Ōtsuki played a leading role in the economic rebuilding of Japan after World War II and subsequently in helping the nation cope with international economic conditions. He became president of the MITSUBISHI MINING & CEMENT CO, LTD, in 1973 and representative director and chairman of the board in 1979. In May 1979 he became president of the Japan Federation of Employers' Associations (NIKKEIREN).

overseas direct investment

Overseas direct investment can take the form of the establishment of a local corporation overseas, capital participation in an existing foreign corporation, the acquisition of real property, or the establishment of branch offices. Until the early 1970s, Japanese enterprises expanded primarily into countries in Southeast Asia, where labor costs were low. From the latter half of the 1970s, however, Japanese companies have chiefly gone into developed countries in order to alleviate trade friction and secure an overseas market.

During the 1980s, Japan decreased its share of resource-developing and labor-intensive investments in developing countries while it expanded its share of technology-intensive manufacturing investments in electrical machinery and appliances, transportation, and other machineries.

The amount of overseas investment in 1981 reached US $8.9 billion, greatly exceeding the previous levels of US $4–5 billion. This figure remained at about $8 billion in 1982 and 1983. In 1984 Japanese overseas investments were valued at $10.155 billion. The figure for 1985 was $12.217 billion. In view of the tendency toward a higher yen value, the increase was expected to continue, or even accelerate. A regional breakdown of Japanese overseas investment in 1985 reveals that US $5.495 billion (45 percent of the total) was invested in North America, $2.616 billion was invested in Central and South America, $1.930 billion was invested in Europe, and $1.435 billion was invested in Asia. The remainder was allotted to various other regions.   IKEDA Minoru

Ōya Sōichi Library

Library consisting chiefly of a collection of weekly and monthly magazines assembled by the social commentator ŌYA SŌICHI (1900–1970). Located in Setagaya Ward, Tōkyō. Founded as the Ōya Library in 1971, the name being changed to the present one in 1978. There are approximately 6,500 titles and 240,000 individual issues in the collection, which includes magazines of the 100 years from the Meiji period (1868–1912) to the present. A subject index to articles in approximately 2,000 of the titles has been published as Ōya Sōichi Bunko zasshi kiji sakuin sōmokuroku, 13 vols (1985).

parcel delivery service

(takuhaibin). Parcel delivery services, which provide door-to-door transportation of small packages by truck—primarily for individuals—have achieved a tremendous increase in popularity in Japan. In fiscal year 1984, 385,000 packages were handled by such truck parcel delivery services.

Packages are picked up at the individual's home upon a request by telephone, or they can be left at a designated pickup point, typically a rice shop or a "convenience store" in the customer's neighborhood. This kind of parcel service was introduced to Japan in 1974. After the Yamato Transport Company entered the field in 1976, using the trade name Takkyūbin, it grew rapidly, and various trucking companies have agreed to cooperate in establishing a broad network. Large terminals, in which automatic machines facilitate sorting, have been constructed in major Japanese cities for this rapid transport system. There is radio communication with the trucks, and the number of days required for delivery (usually one or two) can be clearly stated. The fee schedule is simple, being determined by the number of packages, the distance involved, and the weight of the packages.

The availability of this high-quality service has not only caused people to shift their patronage from parcel post and the parcel service of the Japanese National Railways to parcel delivery by trucks, but it has also helped to create an increased demand for the transport of small packages. Consumers' rights in this field are administered by the Ministry of Transport.   KURAHASHI Tōru

part-time workers
The number of part-time workers in Japan increased during the 24 years between 1960 and 1984. While full-time employees of non-agricultural and nonforestry industries doubled during the 24 years after 1960, the number of those working less than 35 hours per week increased 3.5 times during the same period, and their ratio to all employed persons rose from 6.3 percent to 11.1 percent. Male part-time employees increased by 1.8 times in the period, and their ratio to all working males was about 5 percent, showing little fluctuation. Female part-time employees, on the other hand, showed a notable 5.8-fold increase, growing from 8.9 percent to 22.1 percent of the total female work force.   YASUHARA Norikazu

personal computers
Personal computers (known in Japanese as *pasokon*) were introduced to the Japanese market in 1979. The availability of these low-cost computers, intended for personal enjoyment as well as for business, started a sales boom, and domestic production of personal computers doubled annually through 1984. In 1985 1.2 million personal computers were produced in Japan. The figure for 1986 was expected to be 1.35 million. The leveling-off in the growth rate of personal computers after 1984 was due to the introduction of the Japanese word processor and the low-cost game computer that is referred to in Japanese as the family computer *(famikon)*. Japanese production of these family computers exceeded that of personal computers in 1985.   NISHIMATA Souhei

Pia
A biweekly entertainment guide for the Tōkyō metropolitan area. Published by Pia, Ltd. The magazine, which was first published in 1972, includes essential information (what, who, when, where, whom to contact) on movies, plays, concerts, art exhibits, lectures, and other events in Tōkyō and neighboring prefectures. Circulation in 1985 was 460,000. The president of Pia, Ltd, founded the magazine together with a group of friends while in his fourth year at college. The magazine was a monthly until August 1979, after which it began biweekly publication. As of 1985, it had an equal number of male and female readers, 35 percent of whom were employed and 17 percent each high-school and college students. The average age of the readers was 27.5. Publication of a Kansai (Kyōto-Ōsaka area) edition of *Pia* began in 1985. Its content is the same as that of the Tōkyō-area edition except that the information centers on entertainment in the Kansai area. The magazine claimed a 1986 circulation of 100,000 for this edition.

place-name preservation movement
The Law concerning Addresses for Dwellings, which went into effect in 1962, was intended to impose a degree of order on Japan's complex and often inconsistent system of addresses for dwellings and other buildings. As a result of the law, a new system of numbered designations for the districts and subdistricts where the already-numbered buildings could be found was gradually put into effect in many of Japan's larger cities and some of its towns and villages (rural areas and the city of Kyōto were not affected). In this new urban address system the existing named districts (*machi* or *chō*) within a city or ward were divided into numbered subdistricts called *chōme*. These were divided into numbered blocks called *ban*. The ultimate unit was the building number or *gō*, and thus the new system introduced a four-part pattern of district-*chōme-ban-gō*, the latter three parts commonly being written as numbers (e.g., Kotake 2-4-8). The new system officially did away with many district or subdistrict names that had deep historical, natural, or local-color associations. Movements to preserve the old place names rose up in many sections of the country. The old system had been inconvenient in terms of private life, government, and business. Large numbers of families had often been included in the same unsubdivided district, many of the division names had been confusingly similar in sound

or writing, and the numbers had not corresponded logically with the location of the buildings. The law that went into effect in 1962 thus had practical benefits. Nevertheless, there were strong feelings in many areas that poetic traditional names had been replaced with drab official designations, resulting in a loss of the sense of local community. Many residents joined associations for the preservation of place names, and some cases were taken to court. By 1983 the opposition had become so vigorous that the Ministry of Home Affairs issued a guidance memorandum stating that henceforth in implementing the new system the feelings of residents should be carefully considered and name changes that ignored historical and cultural associations should be avoided.

plant and animal breeding
Japanese plant and animal breeding technology has traditionally maintained high standards. The National Experiment Station of the Ministry of Agriculture, Forestry, and Fisheries, the agricultural experiment stations of the individual prefectures, and the agriculture departments of Japanese universities have achieved remarkable results, particularly in the breeding of paddy rice, vegetables, fruit trees, and silkworms. In the past most of this experimentation involved the improvement of varieties by means of cross-breeding; however, in recent years rapid advances in biotechnology have opened up the possibility of revolutionary ways of developing new varieties that would have been unthinkable a few years before.

One example of a technique that was developed in Japan is a technique for the cultivation of anthers. Anthers are artificially cultivated and then used for the development of full-scale plants. In the breeding of rice plants, for example, the fixation of hereditary characteristics that would take nine to ten generations by ordinary methods can be achieved using this technique in only one generation. The technique has been used in experiments aimed at developing super-multiple-crop varieties of rice and has already led to the successful development of new varieties of strawberries with almost 50 percent higher yields. Another new technique that is being widely used is one for the development of hybrids by cultivating fertilized embryos.

Research combining cell fusion and the rearrangement of genomes with traditional breeding techniques has also been making progress, and in 1986 Japanese researchers were the first in the world to succeed in using cell fusion to develop new vegetables that can actually be eaten and have economic value. These new vegetables were regenerated from calluses derived after fusion of Chinese cabbage and red cabbage cells.

The Ministry of Agriculture, Forestry, and Fisheries has announced a plan for the development of biotechnological breeding. The ministry has emphasized cooperation between the government and private sectors, stating that the gene resources developed in breeding experiments so far should be made available to private business. In April 1983 the ministry organized a breeding technology study meeting in which 15 business firms participated.

The Seeds and Seedlings Law of 1978 put into effect a system for the registration of new varieties that might well be described as a patent law for plants. In 1982 Japan ratified the International Convention for the Protection of New Varieties of Plants.

Japan has also been active in the introduction of new varieties from the United States and other countries, and imports of hybrid seeds have been increasing annually.   FURUNO Masami

plan to limit school classes to 40 pupils
A government plan to reduce the limit on the number of pupils per class in Japan's public elementary and middle schools from the 45-pupil limit that was in effect in 1980 to 40 pupils by 1991. The formal title of the plan, which went into effect in 1980, is Fifth 12-Year Plan for the Improvement of Class Grouping and Teaching Conditions. It is part of a larger plan for overall improvement of the quality of school education during the 1980s. As of 1985, the proportion of classes that still had more than 40 pupils was 22 percent in elementary schools and 59 percent in middle schools. The plan had been frozen as a result of budgetary restrictions recommended in the first report (1981) of the Second Provisional Commission for Administrative Reform; however, it was scheduled for complete implementation beginning in 1986.

plan to move the Tōkyō Metropolitan Government Office

Because the existing Tōkyō Metropolitan Government Office in the Marunouchi district near the geographical center of urban Tōkyō was becoming cramped, a proposal was made in 1983 to move the office to Shinjuku, a business and entertainment district and one of Tōkyō's so-called urban subcenters. The proposal was advanced by Tōkyō Governor Suzuki Shun'ichi (b 1910) as part of a plan to build a new metropolitan government building that would be more fitting to the nation's capital and largest urban area. In November 1983 a private advisory council to the governor recommended the move to Shinjuku. However, in December 1984, an official advisory council submitted to the governor a report discussing the relative merits of either building a new office in Marunouchi or moving to Shinjuku. The Tōkyō legislature was divided on the issue because it affected vested interests in the districts concerned; however, the move to Shinjuku was finally approved on 30 September 1985. If the plan was put into effect, it would be the first move for the Tōkyō government office in 90 years, and 13,000 metropolitan employees would be moving to the "subcenter" at Shinjuku to do their work. The governor described the move as a step toward making Tōkyō a multicentered metropolis. *Nakamura Kiichi*

politics in the 1980s

The LIBERAL DEMOCRATIC PARTY (LDP) was in power throughout the years 1980–85. Three men in turn held office as prime minister: ŌHIRA MASAYOSHI (1910–80), SUZUKI ZENKŌ (b 1911), and NAKASONE YASUHIRO (b 1918). Each of them served simultaneously as the president of the Liberal Democratic Party. This meant that there had been an unbroken succession of Liberal Democratic cabinets for the 30 years since the party's founding in 1955. However, in the general elections for the lower house (the House of Representatives) held in 1983 under the Nakasone cabinet, the Liberal Democrats failed to win a majority. The party narrowly managed to extricate itself from this crisis by forming its first coalition cabinet with the NEW LIBERAL CLUB, a conservative party that had been organized in 1976 by defectors from the LDP. With the decline of the LDP, Japan, too, had finally arrived at the age of coalition government. In addition, the influence of TANAKA KAKUEI (b 1918), the former prime minister who had resigned in 1974, remained strong within the party, controlling appointments of party and Diet officials as well as the appointment of cabinet ministers. In political circles this situation was referred to as "the Tanaka rule" (Tanaka *shihai*). However, former Prime Minister Tanaka was struck down by illness in February 1985, and his influence declined rapidly.

The Suzuki Cabinet —— In May 1980 the JAPAN SOCIALIST PARTY, the leading opposition party, brought a vote of no confidence in the lower house against the Ōhira cabinet, which was then in power. Since the LDP had a majority of seats in the house, the no-confidence vote was expected to fail. However, LDP house members who were critical of the political posture of the Ōhira cabinet absented themselves from their seats during the vote, and the motion passed. In these extraordinary circumstances, Prime Minister Ōhira immediately dissolved the House of Representatives. This meant a general election for the second year in a row. It happened that 1980 was also the year for the regular election for the upper house (the House of Councillors), which is held every three years. As a result, combined general elections for the upper and lower houses were held in June of that year. Shortly after the election campaign had begun, Prime Minister Ōhira died suddenly of a heart attack. The result of the elections was that the Liberal Democratic Party won an overwhelming majority in both the House of Councillors and the House of Representatives. The Prime Minister's dramatic death had aroused the sympathy of the voters. The LDP had recovered its "stable majority" in both houses. Suzuki Zenkō, who belonged to the same faction as Ōhira, was chosen as his successor. The LDP's party rules call for its president to be chosen by election. However, on this occasion he was chosen by negotiation among the party's factions in order "to avoid internal dissension so soon after having recovered a stable majority." The Suzuki cabinet was inaugurated in July 1980. It was Japan's 70th cabinet since the establishment of the cabinet system in 1885, and Suzuki was the 44th prime minister. Suzuki was close to former Prime Minister Tanaka, and as a result his appointments of party officials and cabinet ministers had a strong "Tanaka coloration." His political attitude was referred to as "the politics of harmony." Suzuki himself empha-

sized this idea in the following words. "My politics is the politics of negotiation, the politics of the pursuit of fairness. Japan has achieved economic development, and the living standard of the people has been raised. However, there are still people in unfortunate circumstances who must struggle to make a living. Rather than pursuing a politics of even greater abundance, we must turn ourselves toward solutions for the unhappiness and discontent of the unfortunate." The "politics of harmony" was at least partly a stance toward the situation within the LDP, for during the year and a half of the Ōhira cabinet there had been repeated internal disputes between party factions.

Plans for a Coalition Government —— In the meantime, the Japan Socialist Party, the KōMEITō, and the other opposition parties were faced with the task of rebuilding their party organizations following their defeat in the combined general elections. As they faced the election, the various parties had issued "plans for a combined or coalition government" in preparation for the LDP's failure to achieve a majority. For example, in January 1980, the Japan Socialist Party and the Kōmeitō reached an agreement on an outline of political principles and policies for a possible coalition government in the advent of the collapse of single-party rule by the LDP. However, with their defeat in the elections, they were forced to start all over again. This election also occasioned a deepening of the split between the Japan Socialist Party and the JAPAN COMMUNIST PARTY. Afterwards the Kōmeitō and the DEMOCRATIC SOCIALIST PARTY both began to show interest in a coalition with the LDP.

Prime Minister Suzuki's Resignation —— At first the Suzuki cabinet enjoyed the stability afforded by such conditions as an absolute majority in the Diet, an attitude of party unity within the LDP, and a reduced constituency for the opposition parties. Its policies emphasized administrative reform and financial rebuilding. However, Prime Minister Suzuki was lacking in leadership. This weakness was particularly conspicuous in the area of foreign affairs, where there was a succession of blunders. In May 1981 the prime minister visited the United States for talks with President Reagan. In the joint statement issued on this occasion, the first clear mention was made of an "alliance" between the two nations. In an interview with reporters after the talks, the prime minister said that "alliance" did not have a military meaning, a statement that opened up a controversy. Itō Masayoshi (b 1913), then minister of foreign affairs, made the statement that "the United States–Japan Security Treaty does exist, so it is only natural that military questions would be included," thus revealing a lack of unity within the cabinet. In the end, Itō resigned as foreign minister. This incident was the beginning of a downturn in Japanese-American relations. In October 1982, Prime Minister Suzuki suddenly announced his resignation. This was right before the November election for Liberal Democratic Party president, in which he had been expected to seek reelection. Chief among the reasons for Suzuki's resignation was that party unity had collapsed, with criticism coming from within the party that he was too much under the control of former Prime Minister Tanaka. Another was that his policies had come to a dead end. In addition, he had not been able to respond quickly to the problem of economic friction with other nations. In particular, charges came from within the party that he was responsible for relations with the United States having become worse than at any time since World War II.

The Nakasone Cabinet —— In the election of the Liberal Democratic Party president held in November 1982, Nakasone Yasuhiro was chosen as Suzuki's successor. The faction that Nakasone led ranked fourth within the party. For this reason, it was only with the assistance of the top-ranking Tanaka faction (led by former Prime Minister Tanaka) and the second-ranking Suzuki faction (led by former Prime Minister Suzuki) that he succeeded in being elected. The majority of Nakasone's cabinet appointments and the majority of party and Diet posts under his administration were filled by members of the Tanaka faction. Thus his cabinet was even more dominated by the Tanaka faction than the Suzuki cabinet had been. Nakasone's basic political attitude was expressed by the phrases "a government that is easy to understand" and "a government that speaks to the people." One of the most important features of the Nakasone cabinet as it began was a display of leadership in foreign affairs, including an emphasis on the alliance with the United States. Another was that the initiative in domestic politics was in the hands of the Tanaka faction. However, the rate of support for the Nakasone cabinet shown in public opinion polls continued to be maintained at high levels compared to cabinets in the past. Prime Minister Nakasone took the stance that Japan now stood at its most

Preservation of historic districts

The front gate to the Aoyagi family residence, one of the samurai residences dating back to the Edo period that have been preserved in Kakunodate, Akita Prefecture.

important turning point since World War II. This came from a consciousness that Japan, which had undergone various reforms during its occupation by the United States and its allies, had now reached the point that it embodied problems and contradictions in every sphere of its national life—politics, economics, culture, education, and so on. On top of this the prime minister advocated "an overall balancing of accounts for postwar politics." The year 1983 was a year of decisive political battles. In April came the 10th unified local elections, in June the 13th regular election for the House of Councillors. In the election for the House of Councillors, the Liberal Democratic Party won an overwhelming majority. On the strength of this, Nakasone dissolved the House of Representatives, and the 37th general election was held in December. The result was a decisive defeat for the LDP, in which it failed to win a majority of seats. Calls came from within the party for the prime minister's resignation, and for a while confusion reigned. However, in the end a coalition was established with the opposition party known as the New Liberal Club, and the second Nakasone cabinet was formed. This was the Liberal Democratic Party's first experience of being forced to resort to a coalition. This general election was popularly referred to as the "Tanaka verdict election" or the "Lockheed verdict election." The reason for this was that the election had occurred soon after former Prime Minister Tanaka, who had been a defendant in a trial resulting from the LOCKHEED SCANDAL, had been sentenced to four years in prison (October 1983). It followed that one of the main issues in the election was "the ethics of politicians," and this is one of the things that led to the defeat of the Liberal Democratic Party.

Toward a Full-Scale Changing of the Guard——In October 1984, Prime Minister Nakasone was reelected without opposition as president of the Liberal Democratic Party, and his second reorganized cabinet was formed. On this occasion an anti-Nakasone group within the party had attempted to put forward Nikaidō Susumu (b 1909), the vice president of the party, as an opposition candidate, but this attempt had collapsed when former Prime Minister Tanaka opposed it. Once elected, Prime Minister Nakasone gave even greater emphasis to his slogan calling for "an overall balancing of accounts for postwar politics" as he set about grappling in earnest with such problems as administrative reform, educational reform, strengthening of defenses, and finding a solution to Japan's trade friction with other nations.

In June 1986, Nakasone dissolved the House of Representatives with a view to recovering a stable majority in the Diet, and combined general elections for the upper and lower houses were held in July. The LDP won a resounding victory and took complete charge of state affairs. Because the LDP rules prohibit a third term as party president, Nakasone was expected to retire in October 1986, when his term of office was due to expire. However, all factions of the LDP concurred in granting a one-year extension until October 1987.

With an eye to the period "after Nakasone," various movements within the party became active. The so-called new leaders, all in their sixties, began jockeying for position as the next party leader (and thus the next prime minister). The leading candidates included Miyazawa Kiichi (b 1919), minister of finance, Takeshita Noboru (b 1924), secretary general of the LDP, and Abe Shintarō (b 1924), chairman of the general council of the LDP. In the Japan Socialist Party, which suffered a grave defeat in the combined elections, Chairman Ishibashi Masashi (b 1924) and all other members of the executive committee resigned, and Doi Takako (b 1928) was elected party chairperson, becoming the first female party leader in the history of modern Japanese politics.

Observers anticipated a period of transition, with the reigns of power eventually passing to the new leaders. As the politicians who entered the political scene in the period of confusion following World War II and who continued to support conservative government policies gradually retired, the changing of the guard was seen as ushering in a new era of Japanese politics.

KUNIMASA Takeshige

preservation of historic districts

Various efforts aimed at the restoration of historic urban districts, towns, and villages or their preservation from the demolition that accompanies urban renewal operations continued to grow in Japan in the 1980s. The Ancient Cities Preservation Law (Law concerning Special Measures for Preservation of Historic Natural Features in Ancient Cities) had already been enacted in 1966; however, the areas it affected were limited to the ancient capitals of Nara and Kyōto and certain other historic towns and villages. In the 1970s the preservation movement spread to historic districts in all regions of Japan, and a nationwide organization was set up. In 1975, a revision of the Law for the Protection of Cultural Properties (see CULTURAL PROPERTIES LAW) opened the way for application of that law to the preservation of urban districts and other groups of historic buildings, and throughout the 1970s and on into the 1980s the number of places where local governments joined together with citizens' groups in attempting to deal with the problem continued to grow. Beginning in 1976, the Agency for Cultural Affairs cooperated with local governments in selecting areas for designation as "Preservation Districts for Groups of Historic Buildings." As of March 1986, there were 22 districts that had been so designated throughout Japan. These included groups of *samurai* residences from the EDO PERIOD (1600–1868) such as those in the town of KAKUNODATE in Akita Prefecture, the remains of post-station towns from the same period, as in the Tsumago district of the town of Nagiso in Nagano Prefecture, groups of houses built by foreign residents in Kōbe's Ikuta Ward, and historic groups of farmhouses such as those in the village of Shirakawa in Gifu Prefecture.

product imports

A term used to refer to the importation of goods (mainly manufactured products) other than mineral fuel, raw materials, and agricultural products. Specifically, it usually refers to the importation of goods included in categories 2 through 9 of the Standard International Trade Classification. The ratio of product imports to total imports is called the product import ratio. In the case of Japan, this ratio was 29.8 percent in 1984, lower than that of other countries (the product import ratio in the United States in 1984 was 62 percent and in Great Britain it was 67 percent). This low ratio was one of the issues in the so-called trade friction between Japan and the United States, and in 1985 the Japanese government urged Japanese industries to increase the rate of product imports from the United States and other nations. The low ratio was largely due to Japan's lack of natural resources and its dependence on imported oil and coal as sources of energy. Japan's low product import ratio may also be a reflection of the country's large domestic market and the absence of neighboring industrialized countries. While the ratio remained low, Japan's product import value had increased from US $105 per capita in 1975 to US $341 by 1984. Since the income and price elasticities of product imports are high, the stronger the growth of the Japanese economy and the yen value, the greater is the expected product import value. The importation of intermediate goods, such as steel and nonferrous metals, rather than raw materials from countries rich in resources, and of machine parts from young industrialized Asian countries were both expanding greatly. Further international industrial adjustment of this sort would also become a key factor in the acceleration of product imports.

NISHIKAWA Masao

proportional representation system

(hirei daihyōsei). A new system of representation for the nationwide constituency for candidates-at-large in ordinary elections for the House of Councillors. The system was created by revisions to the Public Office Election Law, which went into effect on 18 August 1982. Its official designation is a "proportional representation system based on prioritized lists of names." What this means in practice is that each political party that qualifies to put forward candidates-at-large for the election submits in advance a list of the names of those candidates, arranged in order of preference. Under this new system, the qualified parties are those that are able to satisfy at least one of the following three conditions. 1. The party has five or more members in the Diet. 2. The party gained at least four percent of the total valid votes cast in either the most recent election for the House of Representatives or the most recent vote of the prefectural or national constituencies for the House of Councillors. 3. The party has at least 10 candidates for the nationwide constituency, the local constituency, or a combination of the two. Each party registers a list of candidates arranged in order of preference for election, and in the election the voters write in the name of the party they prefer. The seats are distributed among the parties in proportion to the number of votes received by each of them in accordance with "d'Hont formula." The first election held after the revised system went into effect was the 13th ordinary election for the House of Councillors on 26 June 1983. Eighteen parties submitted lists of candidates for the nationwide constituency in this election. With the implementation of the new system, the custom of candidacy by intellectuals and other well-known individuals that had been the ideal of the nationwide constituency for the House of Councillors ceased to exist. In late 1985, possible revisions to the new system were being discussed because it worked to the advantage of a number of smaller parties that were formed after it had been put into practice and thus conflicted with the interests of the existing parties.

NAKAMURA Kiichi

Provisional Council on Educational Reform

(Rinji Kyōiku Shingikai). An advisory council set up by the cabinet of Prime Minister NAKASONE YASUHIRO (b 1918) in September 1984 for the purpose of making recommendations on basic policies for reforming Japan's educational system. The council was to report directly to the prime minister. Ever since taking office, Prime Minister Nakasone had made educational reform one of his highest priorities, along with administrative reform. Since 1952 the Ministry of Education had referred all instances of the planning and implementation of educational reforms to the CENTRAL COUNCIL FOR EDUCATION. The establishment of an advisory council directly responsible to the prime minister was thus a departure from custom, and it was said to be a demonstration of Prime Minister Nakasone's strong resolve with regard to educational reform. However, it was unclear what sort of educational reforms the prime minister had in mind, and in fact he had explained in a statement in the Diet that he would leave the matter entirely to the deliberations of the provisional council. The council was made up of 25 members supported by a staff of 20 specialists, most of whom had academic experience. The chairman of the council was Okamoto Michio (b 1913), former president of Kyōto University. Very few of the council members were specialists in education, most of them being former bureaucrats, specialists in economics, and university professors specializing in fields other than education. The council submitted its first report in June 1985 and its second report in April 1986. The stated basic aim of the reports was to explore the ideal educational system for the 21st century and to hammer out policies for combating a series of social problems in the nation's schools that was being referred to as Japan's "blight in the schools." The scope of the reforms being contemplated was broad, touching upon such matters as higher education, especially relating to college entrance examinations, measures for improving the quality of elementary and middle-school teaching by means of teacher-training programs, and plans for making Japanese education more responsive to the newer information systems and to the nation's need to integrate itself into the world community.

YAMAGISHI Shunsuke

reapportionment issue

During the 1970s and 1980s the problem of inequalities in the apportionment of seats in the national Diet among election districts became a serious constitutional issue in Japan. If election districts with a large number of voters, such as those in large cities and surrounding areas, and election districts with a small number of voters, such as those in rural villages, both elect the same number of representatives to the legislature, then one vote from the rural district has a greater relative weight in electing one member of the legislature than one vote from the city district. Such a situation runs counter to a basic principle of the Constitution of Japan, which guarantees equality under the law. Hence the necessity to apportion the number of seats in the legislature allotted to each election district to the number of voters in that district is clear.

In order to fulfill this responsibility, the cabinet and the Diet are obligated to review the relationship between the population of each district and the number of representatives allotted to it on the basis of the national census that is conducted every five years and to carry out a prompt reapportionment. However, Japan's period of high economic growth in the 1960s led to rapid population movements, which made proportional representation more difficult to maintain, and the apportionment issue also directly affected the interests of incumbent representatives in various districts. Owing to factors like these, Japan went from the 1960s to the 1980s without a thorough reapportionment.

In the meantime, the Supreme Court ruled in April 1976, in a case involving elections for the House of Representatives, that an inequality of 1 to 4.99 in the value of individual votes was unconstitutional. In the 1980 House of Representatives election, the disparity between the value of a single vote in the underpopulated Hyōgo Fifth District and the heavily populated Chiba Fourth District was 3.94 to 1, even though a reapportionment had been carried out in 1975. In November 1983, the Supreme Court in effect ruled that this disparity was unconstitutional when it stated, "the inequality in the value of votes has reached a degree that is contrary to the requirements of the constitution." In the 1983 House of Representatives election, the disparity between the two districts was 4.40 to 1. On 17 July 1985, the Supreme Court declared that this disparity was "unconstitutional." The majority opinion did not mention a specific numerical value. However, it stated that the standard for the judgment of unconstitutionality was that the inequality had reached "a degree that would not normally be thought reasonable, even taking into account the various factors that might ordinarily be considered in the Diet." Nevertheless, according to advance figures from the census that was conducted as of 1 October 1985, the greatest disparity between election districts was already more than 5 to 1.

Having received the Supreme Court's judgment of unconstitutionality, the Diet, in May 1986, passed an amendment to the Election Law that would reduce the greatest disparity to approximately 3 to 1. However, partly because of the differing opinions and tactics of the various political parties, the Diet was unable to agree on the changes that were necessary if the principle of equality of the vote that was the basis of democracy was to be maintained.

NAKAMURA Kiichi

recycling movement

In Japan, as in other nations, there has been a popular movement aimed at the reuse of used articles in order to preserve natural resources. The Japanese economy achieved an extremely high rate of growth beginning in the 1960s. During this period the Japanese people seemed to be vying with one another in the successive purchase of new goods, throwing away articles that were still usable without regard to the waste of natural resources. However the oil crisis of 1973 brought the lesson that there was a limit to these resources. There arose a new trend toward using natural resources wisely and attempting to reduce the amounts of discarded materials, which had been continually on the increase. The recycling movement was part of this new trend. In addition to the usual recycling of paper, bottles, and other common materials, the movement in Japan was associated with flea markets, rummage sales, and other outlets for the sale of used clothing or other household items. One such outlet was the "recycling shops" that appeared in many parts of the country. These shops sold used articles at a low price, either on consignment or by buying them outright. As of the end of 1985 there were approximately 1,000 of them in Japan. Another flourishing phenomenon was associations for the exchange of unwanted articles.

IWADARE Hiroshi

refusal to be fingerprinted

All foreigners above the age of 15 who have been granted resident status in Japan for a term of one year or more are required by the Alien Registration Law of 1952 (see ALIEN REGISTRATION), as amended in 1982, to register as aliens within 90 days of the beginning of the term of residence and to renew their registration every five years. A mandatory requirement at the time of registration is that the fingerprint of the left forefinger be imprinted on three documents: (1) the original registration document, which is preserved by the local government authority concerned (city, town, village, or ward), (2) the registration certificate that the individual must carry, and (3) a fingerprint card, which is preserved by the Ministry of Justice. Failure to abide by this requirement is punishable by up to one year of imprisonment with labor or a fine of up to ¥200,000 (US $840 at 1985 exchange rates).

This mandatory fingerprinting requirement applies not only to the first registration but to each subsequent reissuance of the registration certificate every five years. Many of the Koreans who constitute a majority of the foreigners resident in Japan have opposed the fingerprinting requirement on the grounds that fingerprinting is the treatment given criminals and that it is an infringement of human rights.

The Ministry of Justice maintains that fingerprinting is the most accurate method of verifying identity and that it is absolutely necessary for accurate alien registration and the prevention of such unlawful acts as the forging of registration certificates. However, some of the foreigners who object to the practice have refused to be fingerprinted. (As of August 1984 there were 36 such cases. By November 1985 the total had climbed to 1,671 people, partly due to a large number of registration renewals in the intervening year.) In June 1984, in the first verdict among 8 cases then being prosecuted, an American college teacher was found guilty in the Yokohama District Court and fined ¥10,000 (US $42). In August of the same year a Korean resident of Japan was fined ¥10,000 in the Tōkyō District Court, and these cases were followed by others that also ended in guilty verdicts. At the same time, the Ministry of Justice was refusing to grant readmission to Japan to persons who had left the country temporarily after refusing to be fingerprinted.

As of the summer of 1986, strong opposition to fingerprinting continued; however, the Ministry of Justice had no plans for abolishing the practice.   NOMURA Jirō

Reizei Family Library

A library in Kamigyō Ward, Kyōto, built by the Reizei family for the maintenance and preservation of the Reizei family documents and other such materials. Established in April 1981. The purposes of the library were to preserve the Reizei family residence, a unique example of a Japanese noble-family mansion, along with its surroundings, to preserve books and documents handed down by the family, and to preserve and make known to the public the traditions of flower arrangement and other ceremonial observances that had been in the family for hundreds of years. The Reizei family documents had first been made public in February 1980, when Reizei Tametō (1914–86), 24th head of the family, opened a storehouse that had remained unopened for 800 years by imperial order. A survey of the contents revealed a large number of books and documents. In 1986 these had still not been completely cataloged, but there were approximately 20,000 individual items. The overwhelming majority were literary materials, including collections of WAKA poetry (a specialty of the Reizei family) and related materials such as diaries and letters. Also included were poems and letters in the handwriting of emperors. Three of the items, including a copy, in the handwriting of FUJIWARA NO SADAIE (1162–1241), of the 10th-century *waka* anthology KOKINSHŪ, were certainly destined to be classified as National Treasures.

residual quantitative import restrictions

The General Agreement on Tariffs and Trade (GATT) prohibits restriction of imports by means of quotas except under certain conditions such as serious deficits in the balance of trade or the necessities of economic growth in developing nations. Nevertheless, many nations continue to impose such restrictions in order to protect certain domestic industries. These quotas are referred to as residual quantitative import restrictions. In the 1980s there were strong demands from the United States for the abolition of Japan's residual import

restrictions, especially those on agricultural products. In 1985 Japan had residual import restrictions on 27 categories of products—22 categories of agricultural and fishery products and 5 categories of mining and manufacturing products. Of the latter, 4 categories of leather and leather products were liberalized in April 1986, leaving the 22 categories of agricultural and fishery products (4 categories of which were fishery products) and 1 category of mining and manufacturing products (coal). (The Japanese government's 1985 Action Program for Improving Market Access had postponed action on leather products, pending further negotiations under GATT; however, when the United States government pointed out that GATT had already prohibited quantitative import restrictions and threatened to take retaliatory measures, the Japanese government decided on liberalization of these types of products.)

Although residual import restrictions were illegal under GATT unless specifically exempted, Japan was not alone in continuing to impose them. The United States had such restrictions on 7 categories of products, West Germany on 14, and France on 46. In 1986 the feasibility of liberalizing Japan's residual quantitative import restrictions on agricultural and fishery products was being studied by the Ministry of Agriculture, Forestry, and Fisheries, and similar studies with regard to coal were being conducted by the Agency of Natural Resources and Energy.   NISHIKAWA Masao

restoration of fiscal balance

Japan's FINANCE LAW of 1947 prohibits the issuance of national bonds for other than such specific purposes as financing public works projects. However, since 1965 national bonds have been issued continuously. The importance of national bonds stepped up in 1975, when a special law was passed permitting national bonds to be issued as a means of offsetting revenue shortages. This law resulted in a budget that was dependent on national bonds for 34.7 percent of its revenue in 1979. An economic plan adopted in 1983 sought to eliminate this reliance on deficit-financing bonds and to reduce the degree of government dependence on public borrowing in order to restore fiscal balance by 1990. By 1985, through strict control of annual expenditures, the government's dependence on national bonds had been reduced to 22.2 percent. The ratio of interest payments on public borrowing to total annual expenditures, however, was 19.5 percent, which resulted in even tighter government finances. Restoration of a balanced budget was difficult to achieve, and there were some who questioned whether this was, in fact, appropriate, since expenditures had already been reduced to the maximum degree and since it was clear that domestic spending would have to be stimulated in order to reduce Japan's surplus in the current balance account in international trade.   ŌMORI Takashi

restructuring of the Japanese National Railways

By the middle of the 1980s, the JAPANESE NATIONAL RAILWAYS' (JNR) share of Japanese passenger and freight traffic had been decreasing annually for a number of years. Between 1965 and 1984, the JNR's share of passenger traffic dropped from 46 percent to 23 percent, and in the same period its share of freight traffic dropped from 30 percent to 5 percent. Since 1964, the first year that the JNR had finished with a financial loss, its cumulative deficit had mounted steadily: in 1984, the railway's net loss was over ¥1.65 trillion (US $6.95 billion), its cumulative deficit exceeded ¥12.28 trillion (US $51.62 billion), and its long-term debt ¥21.83 trillion (US $91.86 billion).

The Ministry of Transport and the JNR took steps to remedy the situation. The Special Accelerating Law for Restructuring of JNR Management was enacted in 1980, and the Japanese National Railways Reform Commission was organized in June 1983. Such efforts, however, proved effective only in preventing a worsening of the deficit, and it was clear that it would be extremely difficult to reduce the cumulative debt if existing policies were continued. Therefore, in July 1985 the Japanese National Railways Reform Commission proposed a drastic reform plan whereby the company's passenger division would be divided into six districts, all of which were to be placed under private management. The six districts were Hokkaidō, Higashi Nihon (Eastern Japan), Tōkai, Nishi Nippon (Western Japan), Shikoku, and Kyūshū. Measures would be taken to relocate in other firms the 93,000 employees made idle by this plan. Part of the long-term and other debts, which amounted to over ¥37.30 trillion (US $156.98 billion), would be liquidated by creating new corporations and by selling JNR land; the balance would fall on the shoulders of the taxpayers.

In October 1985, the government established a "Fundamental Policy for Restructuring of the JNR" and began drawing up the related legislation. Pending the Diet's approval of these bills, the Japanese National Railways was to be divided up and placed under private management by 1987. *KURAHASHI Tōru*

retrial

In the Japanese judicial system the court of first instance for most cases is a district court. If there is dissatisfaction with its decision, the case may be appealed to a high court as the court of second instance. If there is also dissatisfaction with its decision, an appeal can be made to the Supreme Court as the court of third instance. The system is the same for both criminal and civil procedure.

An appeal to the Supreme Court must be based on constitutional issues or conflict with precedent, and, even with the full use of the system of three hearings, there are sometimes cases in which erroneous decisions have been issued. The means for correcting such errors is retrial. The procedures and the conditions for initiating a retrial are set forth in the Code of Criminal Procedure. There must be new evidence sufficient to overturn the final judgment, and it must be clear evidence. Because of these strict conditions the number of cases in which retrials had been initiated had been extremely small.

However, in 1975 the Supreme Court relaxed these conditions slightly when it ruled that a retrial could be initiated in cases in which there was evidence to support a rational demonstration that "the final judgment was questionable." After this judgment was handed down by the Supreme Court, the number of retrials being initiated increased. The Menda case of July 1983, the Saitagawa case of March 1984, and the Matsuyama case of July 1984 are three examples of cases in which the defendants were eventually found not guilty after once having received a guilty verdict involving the death penalty. *NOMURA Jirō*

rice production in the 1980s

During this period, the consumption of RICE in Japan continued to decrease as the Japanese people kept up their gradual move away from rice as the main food staple. According to Japanese government figures, the per capita rice consumption in cities with populations of 50,000 or over was 86.5 kilograms (190.3 lb) in 1963, 45.3 kilograms (99.7 lb) in 1980, and 41.6 kilograms (91.5 lb) in 1985. In order to hold down the resulting surplus of rice, the Ministry of Agriculture, Forestry, and Fisheries began regulating rice production in 1970. The price of rice sold by producers to the government was controlled by government policy in keeping with the surplus, and in the mid-1980s it was hardly rising at all.

Regulation of Production—— In 1978, as part of a long-range plan covering approximately 10 years, the Ministry of Agriculture, Forestry, and Fisheries began implementing a policy of restructuring the use of paddy fields. Producers were asked to convert temporarily from rice to other crops such as wheat and barley, soybeans, vegetables, and fruits. Every year a certain percentage of the nation's total area of paddy fields was designated as not to be used for rice that year. This target figure was apportioned among the prefectures, and then each prefecture further apportioned its quota among its cities, towns, and villages. The total area targeted for conversion to other crops was 391,000 hectares (966,000 acres) in 1978–79, 535,000 hectares (1,321,000 acres) in 1980, 631,000 hectares (1,559,000 acres) in 1981–82, 600,000 hectares (1,482,000 acres) in 1983–84, 574,000 hectares (1,418,000 acres) in 1985, and 600,000 hectares (1,480,000 acres) in 1986. In the period 1980 to 1983 there was a poor rice harvest for four years in a row, and the areas targeted for conversion in 1983–86 were adjusted accordingly. There was a better than 100 percent annual achievement of goals from the start of the program through 1986. At the end of 1985, the Ministry of Agriculture, Forestry, and Fisheries was engaged in a study of what approach to take in regulating rice production in 1987 and after. Judging from supply and demand conditions for rice, it seemed likely that it would be necessary to convert an additional 100,000 hectares (220,000 acres) of land.

In 1984 the government also began implementing a system of encouraging the use of rice for other than staple food purposes. (At the outset the chief alternative use was as a material for processed foods such as crackers.) This system was actually part of the crop-conversion program. Instead of being asked to convert from rice to other crops, producers were asked to convert to industrial-use rice. This approach had the advantage that paddy fields could be used as they were and did not need to be converted to the dry fields necessary for crops other than rice. The government provided supports for the production of industrial rice at the rate of ¥70,000 (US $294 at 1985 exchange rates) per metric ton.

Rice Prices—— The price that producers got from the government for their rice rose very slightly (in 1983 it was up 1.75 percent from the previous year, in 1984 2.2 percent, and in 1985 there was no increase). The price per metric ton in 1985 was ¥311,133 (US $1,307). The price that consumers paid the government was increased continuously (in 1983 there was no increase over the previous year, but the increase in 1984 was 3.76 percent). The price per metric ton in 1985 was ¥305,450 (US $1,283). The difference between the government's buying and selling prices was shrinking, and there were also rapid decreases in government expenditures for foodstuff controls (see FOODSTUFF CONTROL SPECIAL ACCOUNT). *FURUNO Masami*

Sagara Morio (1895–)

Scholar of German literature. Born in Yamagata Prefecture. Graduated from Tōkyō University. Sagara taught at Tōkyō University from 1947, becoming professor emeritus there in 1956. He helped found the Japanese Society for German Literature in 1947, and served as its chairman from 1947 to 1957. His most important works include *Doitsu chūsei jojishi kenkyū* (1948) and *Doitsu bungaku shi* (3 vols, 1970). He is also known as the compiler of the *Sagara Grosses Deutsch-Japanisches Wörterbuch* (1958). His many translations of German literature into Japanese include a translation of Goethe's *Faust* (1955) and a translation of the *Nibelungenlied* (1955). He was awarded the Order of Culture in 1985. *ASAI Kiyoshi*

Saitō Eishirō (1911–)

Businessman. Born in Niigata Prefecture. Saitō graduated from the Faculty of Economics of Tōkyō University in 1935, worked for the Mitsubishi Mining Company, and then moved to Nippon Seitetsu in 1941. In 1950, when this company was divided into Yawata Seitetsu and Fuji Seitetsu, Saitō remained with the former and became senior managing director in 1968. He retained this position when the two companies were merged to form the NIPPON STEEL CORPORATION in 1970. Saitō became president of the company in 1977 and chairman of the board in 1981. Recognized as one of the leaders of the Japanese steel industry, Saitō also served as chairman of the Japan Iron and Steel Federation. In 1986 Saitō was appointed the sixth chairman of the Federation of Economic Organizations (KEIDANREN).

Sakamoto Tarō (1901–)

Historian. Professor emeritus at Tōkyō University and member of the Japan academy. Born in Shizuoka Prefecture. Graduated from Tōkyō University. Sakamoto is noted for his positivistic studies of ancient Japanese history based on the actual record, particularly his close examination of such basic materials of ancient Japanese history as the 8th and 9th century chronicles called the RIKKOKUSHI and the 7th and 8th century legal codifications called *ritsuryō*. His specialty was the study of the *ritsuryō* as a system. His contributions to his field include the training of many younger scholars of ancient Japanese history and the editing and revision of the *Shintei zōho kokushi taikei* (see KOKUSHI TAIKEI). His works include *Taika no Kaishin no kenkyū* (1938, A Study of the Taika Reform), *Nihon kodaishi no kiso kenkyū*, 2 vols (1964, Basic Studies of Ancient Japanese History), and *Shōtoku Taishi* (1979). He was awarded the Order of Culture in 1982.

sarakin

(salary loan). General term used in Japan for the type of financial establishment that lends money to white-collar and other salaried workers on the strength of their salary alone, without security but at high rates of interest. Since such establishments are much easier to borrow from than banks, the number of users has grown rapidly, with a correspondingly rapid growth in the salary-loan business. *Sarakin* first began to appear in Japan in the 1950s. In 1983 the total number of such businesses in Japan had reached 220,000. Because of the ease of borrowing, increasing numbers of people borrowed large sums of money, and, partly owing to the high rates of interest, increasing numbers of them became unable to pay the money back. There was a succession of incidents in which borrowers committed suicide and even cases in which the borrower's entire family either committed suicide together or disappeared. Growing public demand for regulation of the salary-loan business resulted in passage of the so-called Sarakin Regulation Law, effective 1983. (This law is in actuality composed of two laws, the Amended Law concerning Regulation of Financing, Deposits, and Interest and the Money-Lending-Business-Regulation Law.) The law establishes lower ceilings on the interest charged for loans, changes the regulation of loan-establishment proprietors from a reporting system to a registration system, and prohibits coercive collecting practices. In addition, partly owing to a decrease in loans by other financial establishments to salary-loan businesses, there was a succession of bankruptcies of *sarakin* establishments of all sizes starting in 1984, and as of March 1986 the number of registered establishments in Japan had been reduced to approximately 50,000.　　　　*IWADARE Hiroshi*

school allergy

A condition, increasingly prevalent among Japanese schoolchildren, in which the child is unable to attend school for emotional reasons. As the time for school approaches, the child develops headaches, fever, or vomiting and becomes unable to leave home. This problem began to surface in Japan in the early 1960s. Various changes in the home and school educational environment have been cited as causes. One of these is the competition for school entrance examinations, which has become increasingly intense in Japan from the 1960s. Another is the growing number of children who, because of overprotection, have not fully developed self-confidence even after reaching middle-school age. The problem is particularly prevalent among middle-school pupils. According to a Ministry of Education survey, the number of middle-school pupils who had missed 50 or more days of school for emotional reasons in 1974 was 7,310. In 1983 the number had increased to 24,059. The corresponding numbers for elementary-school pupils were 2,651 in 1974 and 3,840 in 1983.

school violence

Violent acts committed by students, either against other students or against teachers, were a serious problem in Japanese schools —chiefly middle schools and high schools—during the first few years of the 1980s. In 1984 the number of incidents of school violence handled by the police was 1,683. This was 442 fewer incidents than the previous year, or a decrease of 20.8 percent. Two or three years earlier, there had been many middle and high schools that had conducted their graduation ceremonies under police protection. It was probably safe to say that the problem had already peaked.

Especially disturbing among the violent acts in the schools were those committed against teachers. In 1984 there were 742 incidents. This figure, too, represented a decrease, there being 187 fewer incidents than the year before (a decrease of 20.1 percent). However, there had been only 191 such incidents in 1978, thus it could hardly be said that there were now few acts of violence being committed against teachers.

The schools, under the guidance of the Ministry of Education, were making progress in their attempts to cope with acts of violence and other forms of misbehavior. However, the measures taken by the schools often involved constraints on dress and hair styles, the enforcement of minute regulations, and other forms of strict control of the students, and there was opposition from students and some parents.　　　　*YAMAGISHI Shunsuke*

Second Provisional Commission for Administrative Reform

(Dainiji Rinji Gyōsei Chōsakai). A Japanese government advisory commission formed in March 1981 to investigate and make recommendations concerning the government's administrative structure and administrative services for the purpose of adapting to a period of lower economic growth for the nation. The chairman of the commission was DOKŌ TOSHIO (b 1896), former chairman of the Federation of Economic Organizations (KEIDANREN). The commission was composed of 9 members drawn from the financial community,

former government officials, labor, the press, and the academic community. They were supported by a staff of 21 specialists, 56 councillors, and 6 advisors. The group as a whole was divided into specialist committees for the purpose of carrying out investigations and studies of every aspect of administrative reform.

By the time it submitted its Final Report, the commission proper had held 121 meetings. Its First Report (an Emergency Report), containing interim recommendations for the reduction of yearly government expenditures, was submitted in July 1981; its Second Report, dealing with the reorganization of the government's regulatory functions, was submitted in February 1982; its Third Report (Basic Report), proposing reforms of the nation's three large PUBLIC CORPORATIONS (the *sankōsha*) and the reorganization and consolidation of government ministries and agencies, was submitted in July 1982; and its Fourth Report, in which it called for the establishment of a Special Advisory Council on Enforcement of Administrative Reform, which would function after the Provisional Commission itself had disbanded, was submitted in February 1983. The commission submitted its Final Report in March 1983, disbanding on the 15th of that month.

The basic principle of the commission's Final Report was "restoration of fiscal balance without increased taxation." It stressed such matters as "reorganization and rationalization of departments and bureaus," "the relationship between administrative reform and fiscal balance," "reorganization of the regional branch offices of the central government," "reorganization and rationalization of subsidies," and "the partition and privatization of the three public corporations." The reports contained many abstract expressions such as "constraint" and "rationalization" and had little to say about specific reforms. It was criticized by some for advocating reductions in administrative organizations and curtailment of administrative services.

Prime Minister NAKASONE YASUHIRO (b 1918) promised to give maximum regard to the commission's reports. On 1 July 1984 he combined the Administrative Management Agency with parts of the Prime Minister's Office to form the Management and Coordination Agency. As for the three public corporations, the privatization of the JAPAN TOBACCO AND SALT PUBLIC CORPORATION and the NIPPON TELEGRAPH AND TELEPHONE PUBLIC CORPORATION was put into effect in April 1985, and the breakup and privatization of the JAPANESE NATIONAL RAILWAYS was scheduled for April 1987.　　　　*NAKAMURA Kiichi*

seed bank

Japan's first seed bank (a facility for long-term storage of many different varieties of seeds) was begun in 1966 at the National Institute of Agricultural Science's Division of Genetics, and full-scale activity has been carried on since 1978 at the Germ Plasm Storage Center of the National Institute of Agrobiological Resources. The Germ Plasm Storage Center has one of the world's most advanced storage-factor control systems. Temperature is maintained at a constant minus 10 degrees Celsius (14 degrees Fahrenheit) and the relative humidity is kept at 30 percent. As of 1985 some 38,000 varieties of seeds were being stored. A particular variety of seed can be withdrawn from storage automatically by entering its number into the system. The center was designated by the International Board for Plant Genetic Resources of the United Nations as one of the central seed banks for Asia, and construction was begun to increase its storage capacity from 50,000 to 150,000 varieties. The center was originally only open to use by research facilities of the central government; however, in January 1986 it was opened to private organizations. The center is also active in carrying out exchanges with seed banks in other nations.　　　　*FURUNO Masami*

Seikan Tunnel

(Aomori-Hakodate Tunnel). A railway tunnel under the Tsugaru Straits connecting the Oshima Peninsula in Hokkaidō with the Tsugaru Peninsula in Aomori Prefecture and thus linking the islands of Hokkaidō and Honshū. Under construction since 1964 by the Japan Railway Construction Public Corporation, the tunnel was completed in March 1985. This is the longest undersea tunnel in the world, with a total length of 53.85 kilometers (33.5 mi). The actual portion under the sea is 23.3 kilometers (14.5 mi), and the deepest point is 240 meters (787 ft) below sea level. The tunnel was scheduled to be operational in 1988, and track construction and other work was still being carried out in 1986.

Originally, the JAPANESE NATIONAL RAILWAYS (JNR) was to have operated the tunnel. However, the company's financial difficulties and sharply increased deficit halted progress on the projected extension of the high-speed Shinkansen (New Trunk Line) to Hokkaidō. As a result, the JNR had no plans for the use of the tunnel, and the issue of what to do with the project remained unresolved in 1986.

The Deliberative Council on the Seikan Tunnel Issue, established by the government and composed of experts from various fields, presented four possible plans for the tunnel. One of these was for conventional train service by a private railroad; the other three involved different types of car-train transport. In 1986, a liaison committee of the Ministry of Transport was studying the potential demand for and the economic feasibility of car trains, together with problems that such a major enterprise might face.

KURAHASHI Tōru

semiconductors

As of the mid-1980s, Japan was the second-largest semiconductor-manufacturing country in the world, surpassed in sales volume only by the United States. (Integrated circuits—commonly called ICs or chips—based on semiconductors are key components of computers, and they are essential to new products that range from pocket televisions to video games.) Japan's semiconductor production in 1985 totaled ¥553 billion (US $2.3 billion) or about 39 billion units, and its production of ICs totaled ¥1.782 trillion (US $7.48 billion) or about 9 billion units. Rating the world's semiconductor manufacturers on the basis of sales, Dataquest, a US research firm, ranked the following companies as the top ten: (1) NEC, (2) Motorola, (3) Texas Instruments, (4) Hitachi, (5) Tōshiba, (6) Philips, (7) Fujitsū, (8) Intel, (9) National Semiconductor, and (10) Matsushita. Significantly, half of the top ten companies in the industry were Japanese.

More than 50 percent of Japanese-made semiconductors were exported to overseas markets, mainly on the North American continent. The large number of semiconductors exported to the United States exacerbated the trade imbalance between the two countries, and as Japanese VLSIs (very large-scale integrated circuits), particularly the 256K dynamic RAM (random access memory), were estimated to comprise over 70 percent of the American market, the semiconductor conflict grew increasingly serious after 1985. The electronics industry in the United States appealed to the Department of Commerce and the US Trade Relations Office, claiming that Japanese manufacturers were dumping chips on the market. In August 1986 a five-year semiconductor accord was signed by the United States and Japan. While the agreement, which was intended to reduce dumping and open the Japanese semiconductor market to foreigners, seemed to improve trade relations between the two countries, there was still some concern that the terms of the accord would prove difficult to enforce.

Meanwhile, research and development for future semiconductor devices was continuing in Japan. Future electronic devices would include superlattice devices, three-dimensional ICs, and hardened ICs for extreme conditions such as those that might be encountered in space.

NISHIMATA Souhei

Shibaki Yoshiko (1914–   )

Novelist. Real name Ōshima Yoshiko. Born in Tōkyō. Shibaki graduated from Tōkyō Prefectural First Girls' Higher School. She won the Akutagawa Prize for her short story "Seika no ichi" in 1941. After World War II she again received critical attention for the depiction of the manners and customs of Tōkyō's SHITAMACHI district in her short story "Susaki paradaisu" (1954). The three novels *Yuba* (1960), *Sumidagawa* (1961), and *Marunouchi Hachigōkan* (1962), form an autobiographical trilogy dealing with the lives of the author's grandmother and father as well as her own. Many of Shibaki's works describe the lives and traditional arts and crafts of the people of the *shitamachi* district. *Seiji kinuta* (1972) is a collection of her short stories. In 1981 Shibaki received the Japan Art Academy Prize, and she became a member of the academy in 1983. ASAI Kiyoshi

Shinkai 6000

A deep-sea submarine being planned by the Japan Marine Science and Technology Center (JAMS-TEC) as a high-performance research vessel with a maximum underwater depth of 6,500 meters (21,320 ft). Basic designing was scheduled to begin in 1986 and the

Shin Kokugikan

vessel was expected to be completed by 1989. Its overall length was to be about 10 meters (32.8 ft), and it was to measure 3 meters (9.8 ft) in both width and height, thus making it a little larger than the existing Shinkai 2000. The forward part of the new submarine was to have a pressure shell of titanium alloy with an internal diameter of 2 meters (6.56 ft) that would accommodate two operators and a researcher. In addition to the exploration of mineral resources on the ocean floor, the vessel was expected to contribute to earthquake prediction studies through its observation of the Japan Trench, which is the focal region of many major earthquakes.

NISHIMATA Souhei

Shin Kokugikan

(New Kokugikan or New National Sport Arena). SUMŌ wrestling stadium. Located in the Ryōgoku district of Sumida Ward, Tōkyō, and opened in January 1985. Operated by the Japan Sumō Association. The arena has three floors above ground, two below ground, and seats 10,879 people when used for *sumō*. Three of the six annual main *sumō* tournaments are held here in January, May, and September. The *sumō* ring *(dohyō)* can be lowered beneath the floor so that the stadium can be used for other purposes. The complex also contains a Sumō Museum, a Sumō Training School, and a Sumō Clinic. (The old Kokugikan in the Kuramae district of Taitō Ward, Tōkyō, has been torn down, and the site is now under the control of the Tōkyō Metropolitan Water Department.)

Shirase

A Japanese icebreaker built for observation and research conducted in the Antarctic. The ship, built in 1982 and named for SHIRASE NOBU (1861–1946), the pioneer Japanese explorer of the Antarctic, set off on its maiden voyage to Antarctica in November 1983; it docked at the Shōwa Station in the Antarctic on 6 January 1984. Equipped with the latest electronic devices, the *Shirase* is 134 meters (439.52 ft) long, 28 meters (91.84 ft) wide and 14.5 meters (47.56 ft) deep, with a displacement of 11,600 tons and a shaft horsepower of 30,000. The propulsion system runs on diesel oil and electricity. The ship's ice-breaking capacity, which classifies it as Arctic Class 4.1 (a Canadian standard based on a ship's capacity to break through a four-foot-thick piece of ice), is twice that of the retired research icebreaker, the *Fuji*, which had a displacement of 8,570 tons.

shōchū boom of the 1980s

In the early 1980s there was a sudden boom in sales of the cheap Japanese distilled liquor known as *shōchū*. In 1983 consumption of *shōchū* surpassed that of whiskey, making it the third-largest-selling alcoholic beverage in Japan after beer and *sake*. *Shōchū* is a native Japanese distilled liquor made from grain, sweet potatoes, or other starches. Its alcoholic content ranges from 20 to 35 percent. The most important factor in the *shōchū* boom was the sudden popularity among young people of a mixed drink called *chūhai* (*shōchū* mixed with sweet carbonated beverages). Another factor was *shōchū*'s cheapness. (This cheapness was partly owing to the low rate at which *shōchū* was taxed—9 to 14 percent compared to 14 to 40 percent for *sake*, 49 percent for beer, and 28 to 50 percent for whiskey.)

Sixtieth year of the emperor's reign

Emperor Hirohito receiving congratulations from children at the ceremony celebrating the anniversary of his accession to the throne. Next to the emperor is Prime Minister Nakasone Yasuhiro.

Shōchū sales declined steadily during 1985 (though total sales for the year remained higher than in previous years), and there were signs that the boom was beginning to abate.

sixtieth year of the emperor's reign

Emperor HIROHITO (b 1901; r 1926–) began the sixtieth year of his reign on 25 December 1985. Hirohito had become the 124th emperor of Japan (in the traditional count, which includes a number of nonhistorical emperors) on 25 December 1926 following the death of Emperor TAISHŌ (1879–1926; r 1912–26). His reign was given the era-name Shōwa, and thus in the Japanese calendar 1985 was the year Shōwa 60. Hirohito was Japan's longest-reigning emperor, having surpassed the record set by Emperor MEIJI (1852–1912; r 1867–1912) as of June 1972. He was also the longest-lived emperor. As of 13 July 1985 he had lived 30,757 days and thus had broken the record of the previous longest-lived emperor, GO-MIZUNOO (1596–1680; r 1611–29). The emperor became 85 on 29 April 1986. On that day a government-sponsored ceremony celebrating his 60 years of reign was held in the Shin Kokugikan sports arena in the Ryōgoku district of Tōkyō. Special gold, silver, and copper coins were also issued to commemorate the event.

software copyright

Protection of proprietary rights to computer software has been claimed under existing laws such as patent and copyright laws, but these laws have proved insufficient. In Japan there have been a number of cases in which developers of software for computer and video games have sued each other for violation of the copyright law, and in December 1982 the Tōkyō District Court handed down a decision ruling that the software that embodies the content of video games is analogous to a written work. As of late 1985, the Ministry of International Trade and Industry was studying the feasibility of a law based on the idea of rights to software use.

NOMURA Jirō

soy milk

(tōnyū). A health food. A white liquid made from soybeans, which resembles cow's milk. Soy milk is made by grinding soybeans that have been soaked in water, adding more water, and heating. The resulting milk is strained through cloth. Soy milk also represents an intermediate stage in the manufacture of TŌFU, as the latter is essentially soy milk that has been solidified by the addition of a congealing agent called *nigari*. Soy milk, which is rich in protein and iron, has long been consumed in Japan as a health drink; however, production and sales increased markedly during the 1980s (several large food companies began producing it) as a result of the growing public interest in health foods. Commercial soy milk, which is sold in paper cartons like cow's milk, is made more palatable by removing most of the soy odor. It is available plain or in such flavors as orange and coffee. Soy milk is also used in the manufacture of processed foods such as noodles, ice cream, and soups.

sports in the 1980s

International games and Japan. Both the 1980 summer Olympic Games in Moscow and the 1984 summer games in Los Angeles were anomalous in that political confrontations between East and West were carried into the sports arena. The Japanese amateur sports world was greatly divided over the issue of participation in the Moscow games. In 1980 the Japan Olympic Committee continued a search until just before the deadline for national entries for some way of allowing a small number of athletes to participate at their own expense; however, the committee finally decided against permitting participation, taking into consideration the wishes of the Japanese government, which had been requested by the US government to cooperate with its boycott of the games. Japan sent 308 athletes to the Los Angeles games. They participated in 18 competitions and won 10 gold medals.

The summer games of the 1985 Universiade were held in Japan in the city of Kōbe. The financing of these games was modeled on that of the Los Angeles Olympics, in which operating expenses were covered on a commercial basis by payments for television broadcasting rights, support from sponsors, and admissions proceeds rather than by tax money. In the Kōbe games, approximately half the operating expenses were covered by support from business firms.

In 1986 the first Winter Asian Games were held in the city of Sapporo. A total of 431 athletes and officials from seven nations participated in the seven competitions.

The issue of amateurism. Public debate continued to grow concerning the kind of sports competitions that are named after a business firm or a commercial product. The JAPAN AMATEUR SPORTS ASSOCIATION failed to regulate this practice, and the use of amateur sports for the purposes of commercial advertising continued to flourish. In May 1986, in keeping with a worldwide trend toward participation by professional athletes in amateur games, the association adopted a new sports charter to replace its existing set of standards for amateurism. The biggest change in the new charter was a clause allowing the individual associations for the various sports to establish their own standards for membership. For example, the qualifications for soccer players would now be decided by the Japan Soccer Association. (In Japan, unlike some other countries, the individual associations had previously been required to adhere to the overall standards of the Japan Amateur Sports Association.) The new charter would in effect open up Japanese amateur sports to participation by professionals, allow contestants to receive prize money, and make it possible for both athletes and coaches to be paid for participating in amateur meets.

Sports for the sake of recreation. As the proportion of older people in the Japanese population continued to grow, accompanied by an increasing public concern for better health, there was a corresponding growth of interest in sports that can easily be enjoyed by ordinary people. The number of people of middle age or above who were enjoying sports was especially on the increase. Middle-aged women made a particularly good showing in exercise-capacity tests conducted by the Ministry of Education. According to the Leisure Development Center's *White Paper on Leisure* (1985), the number of Japanese who were engaging in jogging, pool swimming, baseball, or catch was estimated to exceed 20 million. The number of tennis players was 15 million and the number of golfers 11.5 million.

MATSUMOTO Katsumi

standards and certification system

In Japan, as in many other countries, a system of standards and certification is imposed for various products through laws and regulations for the protection of consumers. Such standards are applied to foods, medical and pharmaceutical products, farm, forest, and mining products, as well as to such manufactured products as electrical appliances and telecommunications equipment.

The Japanese system of standards and certification has been criticized for creating nontariff barriers to foreign traders attempting to gain access to the Japanese market. To counter this criticism, in March 1983 the government adopted a policy of nondiscrimination which called for the normalization of certification procedures so as to put domestic and foreign producers on an equal footing. Amendments to seventeen laws were enacted on the basis of this decision. Improvements in the system of standards and certification were also included in economic policies adopted in April 1984 and April 1985.

The Action Program for Improving Market Access, which was adopted in July 1985, saw the government making additional substantial improvements, including the further relaxation of restrictions, the introduction and subsequent expansion of a self-certification system, the use of foreign inspection agencies, and consideration of the opinions of interested foreign concerns.

NISHIKAWA Masao

Suisei

A space probe launched in August 1985 by the National Laboratory for Space Science of the Ministry of Education to observe Halley's Comet. *Suisei* (the name means "comet" in Japanese) was the tenth Japanese scientific satellite to be launched by an M-3SII type solid fuel rocket from the launching site at Uchinoura, Kagoshima Prefecture. The satellite weighed 140 kilograms (308 lb) and carried an ultraviolet-ray camera. Its primary objective was to observe the vast mass of hydrogen clouds which cluster around the comet. Together with *Giotto*, launched by the European Space Agency (ESA) in July 1985, and the two *Vegas* launched by the Soviet Union in December 1984, *Suisei* played a leading role in the international observations of Halley's Comet. On 8 March 1986, *Suisei* passed within 15,000 kilometers (9,315 mi) of the comet.

NISHIMATA Souhei

Sunshine Project

A national project begun in 1974 by Japan's Ministry of International Trade and Industry (MITI) to develop energy resources that could serve as alternatives to petroleum. Japan is poor in energy resources and depends on imported fossil fuels for 80 percent of its energy. The worldwide oil crisis of 1973 and the subsequent skyrocketing of oil prices brought about a serious depression in the Japanese economy. After the oil crisis, Japan's energy policy shifted to an active search for new energy sources in order to decrease the nation's dependency on oil as much as possible.

The Sunshine Project concentrates on five technological areas: solar energy development, including solar heat power generation, photovoltaic power generation, and solar cells; geothermal power generation; coal liquefaction and gasification; hydrogen energy; and windmill power and ocean-thermal-difference power generation. Research and development is underway at many institutions belonging to MITI's Agency of Industrial Science and Technology.

NISHIMATA Souhei

Takahashi Nobuko (1916–)

Japan's first woman to hold the title of ambassador (ambassador to Denmark, 1980–83). Born in Changchun, Manchuria. Takahashi graduated from Tōkyō Women's Christian University and Waseda University. After the end of World War II she worked for a period as an interpreter for the allied Occupation forces. In 1947 she entered the Ministry of Labor, becoming head of the Women's and Young Workers' Bureau (now Women's Bureau) in 1965, a position that she held until 1974. She served for two years from 1976 as assistant director general at the International Labor Office in Geneva. She describes her experiences as a female diplomat in two autobiographical works, *Junēbu nikki* (1979, Geneva Diary) and *Demmāku nikki* (1985, Denmark Diary).

Takayama Tatsuo (1912–)

Japanese-style (NIHONGA) painter. Though he was briefly influenced by Gauguin, Takayama is known mainly for color compositions dispensing with lines, in which he depicts nature as part of an imaginary landscape. Born in Ōita Prefecture, he graduated from the Tōkyō Bijutsu Gakkō (now Tōkyō University of Fine Arts and Music). While he was still a student there, his painting *Onsen* (Hot Spring) was selected for exhibition at the Teiten (Exhibition of the Imperial Fine Arts Academy) in 1934. He studied under MATSUOKA EIKYŪ (1881–1938), and in 1937 founded a group called the Rusō Gasha together with a number of Eikyū's other students. This group dissolved after Eikyū's death the following year, and in 1941 Takayama participated in the organization of another group, the Issaisha. In 1946 his painting *Yokushitsu* (Bath) won a special Nitten (Japan Art Exhibition) prize. In 1972 he became a member of the Japan Art Academy, and in 1975–77 he was chairman of the board of directors of Nitten. He received the Order of Culture in 1982. His best-known works include *Mine* (1957, Knoll), *Hakuei* (1959, White Haze; winner of the Japan Art Academy Prize in 1960), and *Kyū* (1964, Haven).

Takehara Han (1903–)

Performer of the Japanese-style dance, and a specialist in the style known as *jiuta-mai*. Real name Takehara Yukiko. Born in Tokushima Prefecture. Takehara began studying the *jiuta-mai* in Ōsaka in 1914 under Yamamura Chiyo and made her debut in the piece called *Bōshibari* in 1918. In 1930 she moved to Tōkyō and mastered the KABUKI dance, studying under Fujima Kanjūrō VI (b 1900) and Nishikawa Koisaburō (b 1909). With a graceful figure and a remarkable talent, she is known for the refined style of her dancing. She is particularly celebrated for her dancing in such pieces as *Yuki* and *Aoi no Ue*. She became a member of the Japan Art Academy in 1985. She published *Nochi no yuki*, a book of essays, in 1978.

tariff reductions

The seventh round of multilateral trade negotiations under the General Agreement on Tariffs and Trade (GATT) was held from 1973 to 1979. Because the negotiations were launched by a declaration approved at a GATT ministerial meeting in Tōkyō in September 1973, the entire series of negotiations is referred to as the Tōkyō round. The actual negotiations were held mainly in Geneva with the participation of 99 nations. It was decided that tariffs were to be lowered evenly over an eight-year period beginning in January 1980. The average rate of reduction on tariffs for mining and manufacturing products among the participating nations was 33 percent. Japan lowered its tariffs by 50 percent on 2,600 categories of mining and manufacturing products worth US $24.7 billion in imports. The final average tariff rate resulting from this eight-year series of reductions was expected to be a little over 4 percent for the United States, a little under 5 percent for the European Community, and a little under 3 percent for Japan, the lowest of all. In addition to tariff reductions, this round of negotiations also included talks on a wide range of other subjects, including reduction or abolition of nontariff trade barriers, the liberalization of trade in agricultural products, and favorable treatment for developing nations. It was also decided to hold an eighth round of multilateral negotiations in the future.

However, in 1984 Japan's trade surplus reached an unprecedented US $37 billion. Critics in other nations asserted that Japan's closed market was the cause of this huge surplus, and there were increasing demands for the opening of the Japanese market. The Japanese government responded to this criticism by introducing an Action Program for Improving Market Access, and one of the items given highest priority in this program was the lowering or abolition of tariffs. The government decided on a basic 20 percent lowering of tariffs on 1,792 categories of products (mostly mining and manufacturing products). Some other categories of products were designated for either reduction or abolition of tariffs, bringing the total number of product categories affected to 1,853.

NISHIKAWA Masao

tax-exempt savings

In Japan interest earned through four types of small savings deposit plans is exempt from federal and local income taxes. The four plans are the "*maruyū*" and "*tokubetsu maruyū*" plans, both of which are available through banks and securities companies, the "*zaikei chochiku*," a special savings system for employed individuals, and the postal savings system. The *maruyū* plans, which include fixed-term deposits and certain other types of accounts, and the *tokubetsu maruyū* plans, which include national and local bonds, both earn tax-free interest on deposits of up to ¥3 million (US $12,600 in 1985). *Zaikei chochiku* accounts earn tax-free interest on deposits of up to ¥5 million (US $21,000). Postal savings accounts earn tax-free interest on deposits up to ¥3 million. It is possible for an individual to earn tax-free interest on the maximum allowable deposit in all four types of accounts. Thus the total possible tax-exempt savings for an individual is ¥14 million (US $58,800). In 1983 about 60 percent of all Japanese private savings fell under these plans. While they served to protect small savers, there were problems in verifying that the allowable maximums were not exceeded by individuals establishing accounts under more than one name. Controls were tightened on these accounts, and stricter requirements for personal identification and other regulations were introduced in 1986. An overall reform of the entire system of taxation was being considered in 1986, and the advisability of retaining the tax exemptions on these savings plans was being questioned. *Ōmori Takashi*

tax reform proposals

In the mid-1980s, a number of inequalities in Japan's existing system of taxation were being pointed out by critics. Direct taxes were heavier than indirect taxes. (In the 1986 general budget, the ratio of direct to indirect taxes was 73.8 to 26.2.) Direct taxes were calculated on a steeply progressive scale. (As of April 1986, the tax rate ranged from 10.5 percent to 70 percent in 15 stages.) Wage earners were unfairly burdened as compared to small and medium enterprise owners and farmers. (Some critics asserted that 100 percent of workers' wages was subject to taxation as opposed to 60 percent of the income of small and medium enterprises and 40 percent of farm income.) To correct these inequalities, Prime Minister NAKASONE YASUHIRO (b 1918) committed himself in 1985 to carrying out the most drastic reformation of Japan's tax system since the end of World War II. In September of that year, a government tax study commission was set up. Its inquiries, which were still in progress in the summer of 1986, emphasized such points as a reduction in both personal and corporate taxes, a thorough reexamination of the question of indirect taxes, and a reform of the existing system of tax exemption for interest on certain types of small deposits. The government planned to incorporate tax reforms based on the study commission's report in its proposals for the 1987 budget. *Ōmori Takashi*

technopolis

An English word coined in Japan to refer to a number of planned cities—urban concentrations of high technology—that were being proposed by the Ministry of International Trade and Industry (MITI) in the mid-1980s for realization some ten years hence. The proposal was first made in "The Vision of MITI Policies in the 1980s," a publication issued by MITI's Industrial Structure Council in March 1980. It was subsequently transformed into a long-range plan, and in April 1983 it became a definite government policy with passage of the so-called Technopolis Law (more properly, Law for Accelerating Regional Development based upon High-Technology Industrial Complexes). The proposed technopolises would be organic combinations of an industrial sector, an academic sector, and a residential sector, all featuring the most advanced technology. More specifically, they would be located near existing mother cities with populations of 150,000 or above, and the technopolises would be designed to attract high-technology industry in such fields as semiconductors and computers, as well as related universities and research institutions, eventually developing into cities of 40,000 to 50,000 people. In 1984, 14 areas, including the Hamamatsu area of Shizuoka Prefecture, were designated for the development of such technological cities, and as of March 1986 the number had been increased to 18. *Nakamura Kiichi*

teletext

Japanese television broadcasters, including NHK (the Japan Broadcasting Corporation), NTV (Nippon Television Network Corporation) and Fuji (Fuji Telecasting Co, Ltd), began providing large-scale teletext services at the end of 1985, and the service was expected to be available throughout Japan soon thereafter. Teletext is the generic name for a type of electronic home information delivery system in which textual or graphic information on a variety of subjects (e.g., news, weather, finance, shopping) is sent to home

television sets by means of multiplex television broadcast. The teletext signals are sent using the so-called vertical blanking interval between the picture frames of the regular television broadcast. The viewer uses a decoder to have the textual matter appear on the screen instead of the video image of the television that is being broadcast at the same time. Teletext can also be used to superimpose captions on regular television programs, and in 1983 NHK began offering experimental subtitled programs for the hearing-impaired in the Tōkyō and Ōsaka areas. Teletext differs from the similar type of service known as videotex in that it is a one-way system that does not allow the user to communicate directly with the information provider. *Nishimata Souhei*

Terada Jirō (1915–   )

Tenth chief justice of the Japanese Supreme Court. Born in Aichi Prefecture. Terada graduated from the Faculty of Law at Tōkyō University. He served as chief judge concurrently on the Ōtsu District Court and the Ōtsu Family Court, as secretary-general for the Supreme Court, and as chief judge on the Nagoya and Tōkyō high courts. He became an associate justice on the Supreme Court in 1980 and was chief justice from 1982 to 1985. In a strongly conservative Supreme Court, he won the support of many other justices for his sound opinions, one example being his ruling of unconstitutionality in a case involving unequal apportionment of House of Representatives election districts. *Nomura Jirō*

test-tube babies

Japan's first test-tube baby was a baby girl weighing 2,544 grams (5.6 lb), who was born on 14 October 1983 in the Tōhoku University Hospital in Sendai. A team led by Dr. Suzuki Masakuni, professor of obstetrics and gynecology at the university, extracted an ovum from the ovary of a married woman who had been trying unsuccessfully for eight years to have a baby, fertilized it in a test tube with sperm from the husband, and then implanted it in the womb. The success of this first test-tube fertilization inspired a succession of similar attempts in other Japanese hospitals. By February 1986 a total of 25 babies had been born by this method, including two sets of twins. All of these pregnancies were brought about by the existing method, in which the ovum is fertilized in a test tube and then cultured for approximately two days before being returned to the womb. However, in November 1985 a baby girl was born using a new method, in which the ovum was returned to the mother's fallopian tube immediately after being inseminated. There had been only one report of the use of this method in the United States, and this was its first use in Japan. In the case of the first test-tube baby, certain segments of the mass media reported the names of the parents, and a fierce debate was aroused over the subsequent invasion of their privacy. In later cases, both parents and child were given fictitious names. Japan's first test-tube baby died of pneumonia on 10 November 1985. *Nishimata Souhei*

Tezuka Osamu (1926–   )

One of the leading comic-strip authors of post-World War II Japan. Born in Ōsaka Prefecture. A graduate of the Ōsaka University Medical School and holder of an MD, Tezuka made his debut as a newspaper comic-strip artist in 1946 while still a university student. Influenced by Tagawa Suihō (b 1899) and Walt Disney, he broke new ground in such fields as the comic-strip novel and comic-strip science fiction. An extremely prolific artist, Tezuka has produced a wide range of comics for both adult and juvenile audiences. His best-known series include *Janguru taitei* (Jungle Emperor; known in English as *Kimba, the White Lion*), *Ribon no kishi* (Knight of the Ribbon; known in English as *Princess Knight*), and *Tetsuwan Atomu* (Mighty Atom; known in English as *Astro Boy*). In 1954 he began producing a long-continuing series entitled *Hi no tori* (Phoenix 2772). This series is an attempt to deal in comic-strip form with some of the deepest issues of human life, and Tezuka has described it as his lifework. In 1962 Tezuka began making animated versions of his own works for television and movies. His works in both comic-strip and animated form have received praise from critics, and in 1985 he was awarded the Tōkyō Citizen's Award for Cultural Distinction.

theater in the 1980s

One of the most noteworthy developments in the modern Japanese theatrical world in the first half of the 1980s was the emergence of the so-called Third Generation of the New Theater. This Third Generation followed the First Generation, which emerged in the 1960s—represented by such playwrights as KARA JŪRŌ (b 1941), Suzuki Tadashi (b 1939), and TERAYAMA SHŪJI (1936–83)—and the Second Generation, which first became active in the 1970s—represented by Tsuka Kōhei (b 1948), Yamazaki Tetsu (b 1947), and Takeuchi Jūichirō (b 1947). The most important playwrights of the Third Generation were Noda Hideki (b 1955), whose name was associated with the theatrical troupe called Yume no Yūminsha, Watanabe Eriko (b 1955) of the troupe called 30 O (Sanjū Maru), and Kisaragi Koharu (b 1956) of the troupe called NOISE. Two younger playwrights whose activities also stood out were Kawamura Takeshi (b 1959) of the troupe called Daisan Erochika and Kōkami Shōji (b 1958) of the troupe called Daisan Butai. The theater of these playwrights treats both reality and human beings as consisting of many levels and many points of view. As a result, many of their dramas have a complex, Chinese-box-like configuration, often containing a number of plays within the play. At the same time, they are rich in comic sensibility.

The performances in foreign countries by modern Japanese theatrical troupes that had attracted so much attention in the 1970s became even more diverse in the early 1980s. There were repeated performances in Europe and the United States by such troupes as Terayama Shūji's Tenjō Sajiki, Suzuki Tadashi's SCOT (formerly Waseda Shōgekijō), and Ōta Shōgo's (b 1939) Tenkei Gekijō. There were also performances abroad of Ninagawa Yukio's (b 1935) Japanese-style productions of *Medea* and *Macbeth*. In addition to these overseas performances, there was an international avant-garde drama festival in Japan called the Toga Festival, which was held annually beginning in 1982 in the village of Toga in Toyama Prefecture under the leadership of Suzuki Tadashi. Another type of international theatrical event of the 1980s was the staging in Europe of new productions of operas designed by two Japanese producers— the *kabuki* actor Ichikawa Ennosuke (b 1939) in Paris in 1984 and the theatrical producer Asari Keita (b 1933) in Milan in 1985. The day when such traditional theatrical forms as *kabuki* and *Nō* were the chief representatives of Japanese culture abroad was beginning to come to an end.

Another noteworthy tendency in the Japanese theatrical world in the 1980s was the great popularity of American and British musicals. In addition to revivals of older Broadway hits, many new American and British musicals were being performed in Japanese-language versions by Japanese performers in Tōkyō within one or two years of their original productions. In 1980 alone there were Japanese productions of *Peter Pan, Sweeney Todd, Evita, Nine, Chicago, La Cage aux Folles,* and *Baby.* Especially active in the production of musicals was the theatrical company Shiki under the leadership of Asari Keita. The Shiki production of *Cats* was performed in Tōkyō for one year beginning in 1983 and in Ōsaka for one year and four months beginning in 1985. The combined total of 960 performances was the longest run for a musical in Japanese history. There was also a gradual increase in the number of original Japanese musicals, including such outstanding works as Saitō Ren's (b 1940) *Shanhai bansukingu* and Kuramoto Sō's (b 1935) *Kinō Kanashibetsu de.*

SENDA Akihiko

third sector

A term used in Japan to refer to joint enterprises funded by both the government and the private sector in order to further regional development. When the government (the first sector) carries out long-term regional development plans, certain aspects of the projects are often limited because of severe annual budget restrictions. With private enterprise (the second sector), on the other hand, where the primary objective is profit, the absence of a broadly-based plan in regional development can result in an uncoordinated sprawl. The third sector, which balances the strengths and weaknesses of the other two, can efficiently handle construction and lead to increased investments.

The use of the third sector was proposed in the government's New Comprehensive National Development Plan, under which such joint enterprises as Tomakomai Tōbu Development, Inc, and Mutsu Ogawara Development, Inc, were established. Some local JAPANESE NATIONAL RAILWAYS lines scheduled to be abolished have also been converted to private railways with the help of the third sector. One example is the Sanriku Line, now the Sanriku Railway.

KURAHASHI Tōru

three-generation house

(sansedai jūtaku). A type of house designed to accommodate a three-generation family. In the years immediately after World War II, there was a move away from the traditional patriarchal Japanese domestic pattern, in which three generations often lived in the same house, as more and more adult children chose to live separately from their parents in nuclear, or two-generation, families. However, in the 1980s, with the Japanese population aging rapidly and with housing and land becoming increasingly expensive, the old arrangement of the three-generation family was coming back into favor. According to the 1983 census, 36 percent of all married couples were living with the parents of either the husband or the wife. This percentage was seven percent higher than it had been in 1973. To help people deal with the problems of tight housing and the need to care for aging parents, the government established low-interest housing loans for people who want to build three-generation houses. Newly-built three-generation houses sometimes have 1 1/2 or 2 bathrooms and two kitchens to accommodate the older and younger generations of the family. Some of these houses are prefabricated structures.

NISHIMATA Souhei

Tōkai Earthquake predictions

Japan lies on the Pacific Rim, where strong earthquakes occur frequently. In the mid-1980s seismologists were predicting that a major earthquake would occur in the near future in the Pacific Ocean off the Tōkai region (Shizuoka and Aichi prefectures) of central Japan. They believed that this so-called Tōkai Earthquake, should it occur, could be of giant proportions. According to the global tectonic theory, the northern tip of the Philippine Sea Plate, off the Tōkai coast, is subducting beneath Honshū, the main island of Japan. The subduction boundary is called the Suruga Trough. The bending of the Philippine Sea Plate associated with subduction produces geological stress along this trough. Seismologists were confident that such stresses had been accumulating to such an extent that they were ready to be released. The next Tōkai earthquake, should it occur, was estimated as likely to have a magnitude of about 8.0 on the Richter scale, with seismic hazards that could be catastrophic. Therefore, the Tōkai region was of special interest for earthquake prediction in Japan. In 1979 the region was designated as an "area under intensified measures against earthquake disaster" under the Large-scale Earthquake Countermeasures Law of 1978. An extremely dense observation network with seismological, geophysical, and geochemical instruments was constructed in and around the Tōkai region in order to detect any precursors of a large earthquake. The Japan Meteorological Agency was responsible for the continuous monitoring of data from the Tōkai network. An advisory organization of the Geographic Survey Institute, composed of six eminent seismologists, was to judge the probability of a large earthquake as soon as anomalous changes in the monitored data were detected.

NISHIMATA Souhei

Tōkyō Bay Bridge and Tunnel

The construction of a bridge and tunnel across Tōkyō Bay was scheduled to begin in fiscal year 1986 as part of a project designed to provide ring roads around Tōkyō Bay that had been under study by the Ministry of Construction since 1962. The Tōkyō Bay Bridge and Tunnel project, designed to connect the city of Kawasaki (in Kanagawa Prefecture) with the city of Kisarazu (in Chiba Prefecture) across the central part of Tōkyō Bay, a distance of about 15 kilometers (9.3 mi), had been under detailed study by the ministry since 1976, and the basic study was nearing completion in 1986. The JAPAN HIGHWAY PUBLIC CORPORATION had also been conducting studies on the project since 1976. The construction was to be carried out with a combination of public and private funds.

KURAHASHI Tōru

Tōkyō Disneyland

An amusement complex opened in cooperation with the American Disneyland in April 1983. Located in the city of Urayasu, Chiba Prefecture. An exact replica of the American Disneyland in terms of attractions, services, and operation. Operated by the Oriental Land Co, Ltd. About half of the total area of 82.6 hectares (204 acres) is occupied by the five theme parks with their 33 attractions: Adventureland, Westernland (Frontierland in the US Disneyland),

Tōkyō Disneyland——Cinderella Castle

Fantasyland, Tomorrowland, and World Bazaar (Main Street U.S.A. in the United States). The remainder is devoted to parking and service areas. The complex has been extremely popular since its opening, attracting visitors not only from Japan but also from Southeast Asia.

Tōkyō Stock Exchange membership

Only members of the Tōkyō Stock Exchange are entitled to buy and sell stocks, bonds, and other securities on the exchange. According to the SECURITIES EXCHANGE LAW of 1948, membership on the exchange is limited to a set number of securities companies that is determined by the Tōkyō Stock Exchange's constitution. In 1983 the fact that membership was limited to Japanese firms became one of the issues of the so-called economic friction between Japan and the United States. Finally, in October 1985, the number of members allowed on the exchange was increased (for the first time in 17 years) from 83 to 93, and six foreign securities companies (Merrill Lynch; Goldman, Sachs & Co; Morgan Stanley & Co; Vickers da Costa Ltd; Jardine Flemings [Securities] Ltd; and S.G. Warburg & Co) were granted membership to the Tōkyō Stock Exchange, effective February 1986.   IKEDA Minoru

Tonegawa Susumu (1939–   )

Molecular biologist. Born in Aichi Prefecture. Graduated from Kyōto University. After receiving his doctorate at the University of California at San Diego, Tonegawa became a researcher at the Basel Institute of Immunology in Switzerland in 1971. In 1981 he became professor of biology and researcher in the Center for Cancer Research at the Massachusetts Institute of Technology. He discovered that the structure of DNA, a basic material in the chromosomes of the cell nucleus, which had been thought to be immutable, changes as needed to produce appropriate antibodies. He was awarded the Order of Culture in 1984.

transportation in the 1980s

Changing patterns in transportation. Changes in the structure of Japanese domestic transportation in the first half of the 1980s were more notable in freight transportation than in passenger transportation. Japan's industrial structure was moving from the emphasis on mass production centering on the heavy and chemical industries that had characterized the nation's period of high economic growth in the 1960s and 1970s toward an emphasis on assembly industries featuring lower-volume, mixed-model production with a high value added. Domestic freight transportation reflected these changes with an increasingly stronger emphasis on motor carriers, a trend that was aided by rapid development of the nation's system of superhighways. The freight volume of the JAPANESE NATIONAL RAILWAYS (JNR) dropped markedly. In 1984 it was 16.1 percent less than it had been the year before. Total Japanese domestic freight volume was 439.1 billion metric ton–kilometers in 1980 and 434.6 metric ton–kilometers in 1984. The share of this total volume carried by each of the major forms of surface freight transportation in 1980 was 8.6 percent for railroads (the JNR and private railroads), 40.7 percent for motor carriers, and 50.6 percent for coastal shipping. The cor-

responding figures for 1984 were 5.3 percent, 46.2 percent, and 48.3 percent. One of the reasons for the increased volume handled by motor carriers was the aggressive development of such services new to Japan as truck parcel delivery services and trucking firms specializing in household moving. As for trends in passenger transportation, Japan's total passenger transport volume was 782 billion passenger-kilometers in 1980 and 832.3 passenger-kilometers in 1984. The breakdown by type of transportation for 1980 was 55.2 percent for motor carriers, 40.2 percent for railroads, and 3.8 percent for airlines. The corresponding figures for 1984 were 56.3 percent, 39 percent, and 4 percent.

Reorganization of the Japanese National Railways. The deficits under which the Japanese National Railways was operating continued to mount, and on 26 July 1985 the Japanese National Railways Reform Commission submitted a report to Prime Minister NAKASONE YASUHIRO (b 1918) calling for the breakup of the JNR's passenger division into six regional railroads, which were to be placed under private management, effective 1 April 1987. Representatives of the government, members of the LIBERAL DEMOCRATIC PARTY, and the JNR began drawing up specific proposals for a bill intended to implement these recommendations.

The Shinkansen system. A new 26.7 kilometer (16.6 mi) section of track for the Tōhoku and Jōetsu lines of the high-speed SHINKANSEN went into operation in March 1985, linking Ōmiya in Saitama Prefecture with Ueno Station in Tōkyō. Passenger volume had increased steadily since the inauguration of service in June 1982 from Ōmiya to Morioka, Iwate Prefecture, on the Tōhoku Shinkansen and to Niigata, Niigata Prefecture, on the Jōetsu Shinkansen. With the addition of service from Ueno, the number of trains was increased by 50 percent, and the top speed was increased from 210 kilometers (130.4 mi) per hour to 240 kilometers (149 mi) per hour. Travel time from Ueno to Morioka was reduced from 3 hours and 57 minutes to 2 hours and 45 minutes, and that from Ueno to Niigata was reduced from 2 hours and 32 minutes to 1 hour and 53 minutes. Speed was also scheduled to be increased on the Tōkaidō and San'yō sections of the Shinkansen system from 210 kilometers (130.4 mi) per hour to 220 kilometers (136.6 mi) per hour, beginning in November 1986. This would reduce the travel time from Tōkyō to Hakata, Fukuoka Prefecture to 5 hours and 57 minutes, a reduction of 29 minutes.

Air transportation. The heavy use of Japan's three existing international airports, the New Tōkyō International Airport, the Tōkyō International Airport, and the Ōsaka International Airport, was beginning to approach the limits of their capacity, and three major projects for the construction of additional facilities were being speeded up. Construction was scheduled to begin on the Kansai International Airport (a new airport for the Kyōto-Ōsaka area), two new runways were to be added to the New Tōkyō International Airport, and the Tōkyō International Airport was to be enlarged.

In order to further stimulate the growth of the Japanese air transportation industry, the so-called airline constitution was abolished in December 1985. This so-called constitution, which actually consisted of an informal cabinet agreement of 1970 combined with a 1972 memorandum of the minister of transport, had imposed a rigid division of rights and territories among Japan's airline companies. JAPAN AIR LINES CO, LTD (JAL) had been given overseas routes and major domestic routes, ALL NIPPON AIRWAYS CO, LTD (ANA) had been given major and local domestic routes and short-distance overseas charter flights, and TŌA DOMESTIC AIRLINES CO, LTD, had been given local domestic routes. With the removal of these restrictions, All Nippon Airways began Tōkyō-Guam flights in March 1986 and Tōkyō-Washington and Tōkyō-Los Angeles flights in July of the same year.   KURAHASHI Tōru

TRISTAN

An electron-positron collision accelerator under construction since 1981 by the Ministry of Education's National Laboratory for High Energy Physics (KEK) in Tsukuba Academic New Town (Ibaraki Prefecture). (TRISTAN is an acronym for Transposable Ring Intersecting Storage Accelerator in Nippon.) This accelerator was scheduled to be completed in the fall of 1986 and to begin full-time collision experiments in the fall of 1987. Once the accelerator was operational, electrons and positrons accelerated to 30 billion electron volts would be rotated in opposite directions at a rate almost equal to the speed of light and collide head-on in a ring about 1 kilometer (3,280 ft) in diameter and about 3 kilometers (9,840 ft) in circumference. The colliding positrons and electrons would then disappear, and various new elementary particles would be produced. The purpose of the accelerator was to investigate the basic nature of matter by examining the properties of these particles.

NISHIMATA Souhei

Tsuda Kyōsuke (1907–   )

Organic chemist. Born in Saitama Prefecture. Tsuda graduated from Tōkyō University. After teaching at Kyūshū University, he became a professor at the Institute of Applied Microbiology at Tōkyō University in 1955. He served as director of the institute from 1965 until he reached mandatory retirement age in 1967. He was president of the Kyōritsu College of Pharmacy from 1967 to 1984 and also served as chairman of the Central Pharmaceutical Affairs Council from 1975 to 1980. Tsuda determined the chemical structure of GLOBEFISH poison in 1964 and later succeeded in producing it in pure crystalline form. He received the Japan Academy Prize in 1966 and was awarded the Order of Culture in 1982.

Tsukamoto Saburō (1927–   )

Politician. Born in Aichi Prefecture. Tsukamoto carried on the family furniture manufacturing and wholesale business while studying law at Chūō University. He graduated in 1952 and the same year, at the age of 25, he was an unsuccessful candidate in the election for the House of Representatives from Aichi Prefecture. On his fourth attempt, in 1958, he was elected to the House of Representatives as a candidate of the Japan Socialist Party. When the Democratic Socialist Party was formed in 1960 as the result of a split within the Japan Socialist Party, Tsukamoto joined the new party and became chairman of its Youth Committee. He became secretary-general of the party in 1974, and in April 1985 he succeeded SASAKI RYŌSAKU (b 1915) as chairman.

Tsukamyōjin tomb

A tomb mound in the Sada district of the town of Takatori, Nara Prefecture. The tomb mound is presently round in shape, measuring 18 meters (59.04 ft) in diameter and 3 meters (9.84 ft) in height; however, judging from research conducted from December 1985 to January 1986, it seems highly likely that it was originally octagonal, measuring 30 meters (98.4 ft) on the diagonal. A horizontal-hole stone chamber constructed of 400 pieces of hewn stone was discovered in 1984. The funerary articles had been taken by grave robbers. It is known that there was originally a lacquered wooden coffin because of fragments of black lacquer, nails, and a gilt-bronze coffin ornament found on the floor of the chamber. The ornament measures 5.8 centimeters (2.29 in) in diameter. A number of the teeth of the buried person were also found. Experts estimated that the teeth were those of a person 20 to 30 years of age. The size and construction of the chamber are such that the tomb is thought to have been that of a person of high rank. There had been a tradition that this was the tomb of Prince Kusakabe (662–689), the son of Emperor TEMMU (?–686). That tradition was discounted in the 1860s when another tomb was advanced as that of Prince Kusakabe; however, the estimated age of the teeth found here provides some support for the theory that it was indeed the prince who was buried in the present tomb.

Tsukuba Expo '85

World's Fair held in TSUKUBA ACADEMIC NEW TOWN in Ibaraki Prefecture from 17 March to 16 September 1985. Officially called the International Science and Technology Exposition, Tsukuba, Japan, 1985. The theme of the fair was "Dwellings and Surroundings— Science and Technology for Man at Home." This was the third international exposition to be held in Japan. (The first was held in Ōsaka in 1970 and the second was the Okinawa International Ocean Expo '75.) In addition to 48 countries and 37 international organizations, such as the International Court of Justice (ICJ), the World Health Organization (WHO), and the European Community (EC), 27 domestic enterprises and business groups and one Japanese prefecture (Ibaraki) participated. These participants vied with one another in attempting to display the most advanced state-of-the-art technology directed toward the 21st century. Exhibits included mammoth high fidelity screens, stereographic images, and robots with advanced "brains," which played the piano, painted visitors'

portraits, and performed other feats. The exposition drew over 20.3 million visitors.

Uemura Shōko (1902–   )

Japanese-style (NIHONGA) painter. Known for his elegant paintings of flowers and birds. Real name Uemura Shintarō. Born in Kyōto, the son of the painter UEMURA SHŌEN (1875–1949). Graduated from the Kyōto Municipal School of Fine Arts and Crafts (now the Kyōto City University of Arts). While still at the school Uemura became a student of NISHIYAMA SUISHŌ (1879–1958). His painting Kantei geishū (Welcoming Autumn in a Quiet Garden) was selected for exhibition at the Teiten (Exhibition of the Imperial Fine Arts Academy) in 1921. In 1948 Uemura took part in the organization of the group called Sōzō Bijutsu (Creative Arts). Afterwards he belonged to the Shin Seisaku Kyōkai (New Creative Association) and participated in the founding of the Sōgakai (Creative Painting Association) in 1974. He taught at his alma mater from 1930, becoming a professor emeritus in 1968. He became a member of the Japan Art Academy in 1981 and received the Order of Culture in 1984. His best-known works include Hoshi goi (1958, Night Herons), Oshidori (1965, Mandarin Ducks), and Juka yūkin (1966, Birds under the Trees; winner of the Japan Art Academy Prize in 1967).

ultra-high-rise buildings

Japan's frequent earthquakes long deterred builders from erecting ultra-high-rise buildings in the country. However, after World War II, remarkable progress was made in new construction technology especially developed to withstand earthquakes, and it became possible to construct extremely tall buildings in Japan. Amendments to the ARCHITECTURAL STANDARDS LAW in 1963 eased restrictions on building height, giving birth to a new generation of ultra-high-rise buildings. The first such building, the Kasumigaseki Building, completed in 1968, has 36 stories and a height of 147 meters (482 ft).

Buildings less than 60 meters (197 ft) high must conform to the seismic codes of the Architectural Standards Law. Plans for buildings higher than 60 meters must be approved by the Building Center of Japan, an auxiliary of the Ministry of Construction, to ensure their ability to withstand the twisting, shifting, and swaying that might result from a major earthquake or typhoon.

There is no clear definition in Japan of an ultra-high-rise (chōkōsō), although high-rises taller than 100 meters (328 ft) are generally classified as ultra-high-rises. These must be approved as described above. By 1985 there were 53 such buildings scattered throughout Japan, the majority of them concentrated in the Tōkyō metropolitan area. The Shinjuku district of Tōkyō is noted for its modern urban skyline, bristling with ultra-high-rise buildings. As of 1986 the tallest high-rise in Japan was the 60-story Ikebukuro Sunshine Building, completed in 1978, which reached a height of 240 meters (787 ft).

NISHIMATA Souhei

Ushijima Noriyuki (1900–   )

Western-style painter known for his poetic landscapes combining soft colors and simple compositions. Born in Kumamoto Prefecture. Graduated from the Tōkyō Bijutsu Gakkō (now Tōkyō University of Fine Arts and Music) in 1927. In the same year his painting Shibai (Stage Play) was selected for exhibition at the Teiten (Exhibition of the Imperial Fine Arts Academy). In 1942 he joined the group called the Sōgenkai. He resigned from this group in 1949 to participate in the organization of the group called the Ryūkikai. He taught at the Tōkyō University of Fine Arts and Music from 1954 to 1968. He became a member of the Japan Art Academy in 1981 and received the Order of Culture in 1983. His best-known works include Sōko (1958, Warehouses) and Yūzuki (1975, Evening Moon).

Ushiku

City in southern Ibaraki Prefecture. Ushiku, which became a city in 1986, originated as a post-station town on the highway Rikuzen Hama Kaidō. In 1896 a station on the Jōban line of the Japanese National Railways was built here. The area is predominantly an agricultural one, producing peanuts as well as spinach and other vegetables; however, in the 1960s Ushiku became a commuter suburb of Tōkyō, and the population grew rapidly. Japan's first winery, the Ushiku Chateau, was built in the Kamiya district in 1903.

The former winery now houses a restaurant and museum. Pop: 51,926.

value-added network

(VAN). General name used in Japan for the type of high-volume, on-line business-information network whose primary customers are banks, stockbrokers, freight and travel companies, and other large enterprises. This type of system was developed in the United States in the mid-1970s and was introduced to Japan shortly thereafter. (The term value-added network, which was originally used in the United States to distinguish a more expensive type of service, came to be used in Japan to refer to such services as a whole.) A VAN is a computerized telecommunications network consisting of customers and information providers. Customers can retrieve necessary business information such as inventories, distribution records, or accounting records from the database and can exchange business information with other firms in the network. In Japan, telecommunications circuits were decontrolled in 1985 when the Nippon Telegraph and Telephone Public Corporation became part of the private sector, an event which made it possible for private firms to enter the VAN business. As of 1985, more than 200 VAN companies had been established in Japan.   NISHIMATA Souhei

very-large-scale integrated circuits

The first very-large-scale integrated circuit (VLSI) was launched in the Japanese market in 1980. (Integrated circuits—commonly called ICs or chips—are complex electronic circuits built into the surface of a section of silicon wafer. VLSIs are ICs that contain more than 100,000 transistors on a section of silicon with a width of half a centimeter, or 0.2 in.) The first VLSI was a 64K dynamic RAM (random access memory) that contained 150,000 transistors. The 64K dynamic RAM is used for the memories of computers and consumer electronic products. Total Japanese production of 64K dynamic RAMs in 1985 was between 300 million and 500 million. The second VLSI, a 256K dynamic RAM, entered the Japanese market in 1983. This chip integrated 600,000 transistors. Total Japanese production of 256K dynamic RAMs in 1985 was between 150 million and 200 million.

As a result of radical breakthroughs in microelectronic technology, efforts have been made to integrate microcomputer devices into one chip to produce a one-chip microprocessor. Together with the one-chip memory, the one-chip microprocessor and the one-chip microcomputer are the major applications of VLSIs. In the mid-1980s a 1M dynamic RAM was developed by the Tōshiba Corporation. The Japanese electronics industry has established a comprehensive and advanced technology for IC and VLSI production that has made Japan the leading manufacturer in this product area. In 1986, the worldwide demand for chips exceeded one billion, and Japan supplied the world with 70 percent of those chips.   NISHIMATA Souhei

video discs

Japanese manufacturers of video discs (discs on which audio and video signals are recorded for playback on television screens) are separated into two groups that compete intensely for sales. There are two video-disc formats, optical-laser and VHD (video high-density), which offer different advantages and drawbacks in quality and convenience. Optical-laser discs pick up signals by reflecting laser light from the disc, while VHD discs use needle tracings on the disc. Since the two disc formats are not compatible with each other, buyers must choose between them. Producers of optical-laser (laser vision) discs include the Sony Corporation, Hitachi, Ltd, and the Pioneer Electronic Corporation. Matsushita Electric Industrial Co, Ltd, the Victor Co of Japan, Ltd, and the Sharp Corporation are among the manufacturers of VHD discs. About 500,000 video disc players were manufactured in Japan in 1985, and production was expected to increase steeply.   NISHIMATA Souhei

video games

The rapid spread in Japan during the early 1980s of home computers (referred to in Japan as *famikon*, short for *famirī kompyūtā* or family computers) led to a boom in sales of video or television games aimed at Japanese young people. These games were essentially the same as the computer or television games that were enjoying such a great popularity in other advanced nations of the world. As in other nations, improvements in game software made possible a shift in emphasis from early games such as the well-known "Space Invaders," which demanded little more than manual dexterity and quick reflexes, to more sophisticated games that called for true game sense and strategic ability. And, as in other nations, books that promised to help in winning the games became best sellers. Video games were first introduced in the United States in the mid-1970s, but Japanese manufacturers added hardware improvements that made possible greater speed and vastly improved picture quality and color. In addition to the usual cartridges and tape cassettes, laser disks as a medium for video game software were introduced in the mid-1980s, and by 1986 Japanese manufacturers were using only the latter. The leading Japanese manufacturer of game computers was the Nintendō Co, which had a 90-percent share of the domestic market in 1986. Sales had doubled annually since the company began selling game computers in 1983 under the Family Computer brand name, and in 1985 it sold 3.7 million sets. The company began exporting to the United States in 1986.

videotex

In 1979 the Ministry of Posts and Telecommunications and the Nippon Telegraph and Telephone Public Corporation took the lead in providing experimental videotex service in Japan under the name of CAPTAIN (Character and Pattern Telephone Access Information Network System). Videotex is the generic name for a type of electronic home information delivery service in which home computers or television sets are connected to an information provider's control computers by means of telephone lines. Videotex is an interactive service, allowing the user to communicate directly with the provider by means of a computer keyboard, and it can thus be used for such activities as shopping or banking from the home. A commercial service named Videotex Communication Service was started in Tōkyō and in the Keihanshin (Kyōto-Ōsaka-Kōbe) region in 1984. Service was later extended to Nagoya and other areas. A communication charge of ¥30 (US $0.15) for 3 minutes was uniform throughout Japan.   NISHIMATA Souhei

voluntary export restrictions

(VER). Voluntary restriction of exports by means of informal government pressure on exporters is sometimes practiced when a particular product floods the market and threatens prices. This kind of restriction had been practiced by Japan in the past with regard to exports of such products as steel and television sets. However, the term came into special prominence in March 1981, when Japan began practicing voluntary restrictions on exports of automobiles to the United States in response to overt pressure from the US government. Although Article 11 of the General Agreement on Tariffs and Trade (GATT) prohibited import quotas, such voluntary restrictions of exports fell into a grey area where legality could not be judged by the stated provisions of GATT. The voluntary restrictions were adopted under pressure from one of Japan's trade partners, and they were politically important in helping to avoid what is referred to in Japan as "trade friction." There was some concern, however, that they might be counter to Japan's ANTI-MONOPOLY LAW and the trade regulations of some countries. In March 1985 Japan decided to continue voluntary restrictions on exports of automobiles to the United States while increasing the annual export volume from 1.85 million automobiles to 2.3 million. In October 1985 a formal agreement was reached with the United States with regard to steel exports whereby the share of Japanese steel in the American market would be voluntarily limited to 5.8 percent for the following five years. Japan also practiced VER in its exports of steel and VTRs to the European Community (EC), machine tools to the United States and the EC, and television sets and fibers to the United States.   NISHIKAWA Masao

Wadachi Kiyoo (1902–   )

Geophysicist. Authority on deep-focus earthquakes (earthquakes with deep points of origin). Born in Aichi Prefecture. Graduated from Tōkyō University. In his second year at the university, Wadachi survived the TŌKYŌ EARTHQUAKE OF 1923 and resolved to make the study of earthquakes his career. Upon graduation he entered the Central Meteorological Observatory to specialize in the measurement and investigation of earthquakes as well as related forms of research. He became the director of the Central Meteorological Observatory in 1947, and when it became the Meteorological Agency in 1956 he continued as its chief until 1963. He served as head of the National Research Center for Disaster Prevention from 1963 to 1966, as president of Saitama University from 1966 to 1972, and as director of the Japan Academy from 1974 to 1980. An internationally known scientist, he was made an honorary member of the American Seismological Society. He was awarded the Order of Culture in 1985.

weather forecasting

In the face of a changeable climate and in response to a strong public demand, the Japan Meteorological Agency (JMA) made notable achievements in the 1980s in improving the accuracy of weather forecasts. The JMA's weather observation network was composed of 1,300 surface robot observation stations throughout the country. In addition, 22 meteorological radars and a geostationary meteorological satellite named *Himawari-2* (Sunflower-2) were playing important roles in collecting weather information. Observational data were automatically input to the AMEDAS (Automated Meteorological Data Acquisition System) for instant analysis. This up-to-date computerized system made weather prediction based on statistical analysis possible, and the probability of precipitation had been stated in percentages three times a day since 1980.

NISHIMATA Souhei

whaling, abandonment of

During the first years of the 1980s, the influence of American and European environmentalist groups calling for the protection of whales grew stronger year by year, and Japan was finally driven to a gradual abandonment of the practice of commercial whaling. In 1982 a general meeting of the International Whaling Commission, for the sake of preservation of natural resources, declared a moratorium on factory-ship whaling effective October 1985 and on coastal whaling effective April 1986. Four whaling nations, Japan, Norway, Peru, and the USSR, responded to this decision by filing statements of dissent. The United States pressed Japan to retract its statement of dissent, informing Japan that if it continued the practice of whaling beyond 1985 the Japanese fishing quota within the 200-mile fishing zone along US coasts would be reduced to zero within two years of that date. In an agreement between Japan and the United States reached in November 1984, the United States announced that it would recognize the continuation of whaling until March 1988 on the condition that Japan retract its statement of dissent. Japan was fearful of losing its fishing rights within the US 200-mile zone, and therefore the decision was made, in a cabinet meeting in April 1985, to retract the statement of dissent. As a result of this decision, Japanese factory whaling was scheduled to be discontinued by March 1987, at the latest, and coastal whaling by March 1988. Within the United States the validity of this United States–Japan agreement was challenged in court on the basis that it was counter to the IWC decision.

women's movement in the 1980s

In Japan as in other nations, 1975, the first year of the United Nations Decade for Women brought a new determination to elevate the status of women. Attention focused particularly on the upcoming World Conference for Women of 1980, which was to mark the midpoint of the decade. In 1975 the Liaison Group for the Implementation of Resolutions of the International Women's Year Conference of Japan was organized, with ICHIKAWA FUSAE (1893–1981) as its chairperson. The Liaison Group was a federation of approximately 50 groups, including the Japan League of Women Voters and several of the other nongovernmental organizations (NGO) registered with the United Nations, nationwide women's groups of all sizes, and the women's sections of national labor federations such as Sōhyō (General Council of Trade Unions of Japan) and Dōmei (Japanese Confederation of Labor). The Liaison Group presented to the Japanese government a number of demands that had been decided on at the Japan International Women's Year Conference in 1975, including the demand for an end to discrimination against women. Additional activities were conducted independently by the member groups. Some of the more radical feminist groups that had been formed in the early 1970s joined forces

with the Liaison Group; others declined to participate, choosing to pursue more radical activities independently under the banner of women's liberation. At the same time, there was both internal and external criticism of the Liaison Group on the grounds that its large size led to its being used by the government.

Japanese activities connected with the UN Decade for Women during the years from 1980 to 1985, which centered mainly in the Liaison Group, were many and various; they included public gatherings, protests, demands, consciousness-raising activities, involvement in international feminist activities, and the pursuit of closer relationships with foreign feminists visiting Japan. A number of the Liaison Group's member groups organized a sit-in in front of the prime minister's office in May 1980, demanding that Japanese government delegates sign the International Convention for Eliminating All Forms of Discrimination against Women, which had been instituted at the World Conference of the UN Decade for Women in Copenhagen in 1980. Due in large part to the force of such activities, the government agreed to sign the convention and sent Takahashi Nobuko (b 1916) to Denmark as Japan's first woman ambassador to sign it. By signing the convention, the government imposed on itself the task of amending Japanese laws to correspond with it. At the same time, the activities of the activist groups came to focus on such issues as amendment of the Nationality Law, reconsideration of the policy of requiring home economics courses exclusively for girls, and passage of the Equal Employment Opportunity Law for Men and Women.

Other important developments in the lives of Japanese women during the first half of the 1980s included the following. Hundreds of Japanese women, both individually and in groups, participated in seminars at the NGO forums held in 1980 in Copenhagen and in 1985 in Nairobi. When a movement arose in the Diet in 1983 to eliminate economic necessity from the conditions under which an ABORTION may be performed according to the EUGENIC PROTECTION LAW, protests were organized throughout the nation to stop discussion of the bill in the Diet. There were demands from within the more radical feminist groups for legislation abolishing the Eugenic Protection Law and legalizing abortion at the request of the woman concerned. There were also protests against the emphasis on sexual stereotypes in the mass media and opposition to proposals to ease the LABOR STANDARDS LAW's restrictions on overtime, holiday, and late-night work by women in conjunction with the Equal Employment Opportunity Law.

One result of the various women's-movement activities of the decade starting in 1975 was that Japanese local governments began to sponsor lectures about women's liberation and equality. In addition, many women's education groups came into being, and the consciousness of the average Japanese woman was raised markedly. Research geared to the development of a new world order combining the philosophies of feminism, Marxism, and ecology was being carried out by feminist scholars, critics, and activists. A systematic combination of feminist ideology and activism and further participation in the movement by the average woman were likely to be the next developments in the lives of Japanese women in the latter half of the 1980s.

KOMANO Yōko

work away from family

(*tanshin funin*; literally, "proceeding to a new post alone"). In the 1970s and 1980s increasing numbers of Japanese business and government employees who were transferred to distant cities within Japan or abroad left their families behind indefinitely and proceeded to their new posts alone. Because of its disruptive effect on large numbers of families, this phenomenon was assuming the dimensions of a serious social problem.

Despite the hardships involved (there were increasing numbers of reports of husbands whose health was affected and wives and children suffering mental disorders), Japanese employees accepted such transfers as a matter of course. Acceptance was commonly understood as a passport to advancement, and the Japanese practice of lifetime employment kept resignation from being a viable alternative to accepting transfers, for it made midcareer jobs hard to obtain.

There were strong pressures on the families of the transferred employees to remain behind in their existing homes. The most important factor was Japan's highly competitive high-school and college entrance-examination system, which made transferring from one school to another difficult or inadvisable, particularly for middle-school and high-school students. Another factor, for home-owning families, was the heavy financial investment made in home ownership and the difficulty of buying a home in the first place. Such families were reluctant to sell their homes and start over elsewhere, and they were equally unwilling to rent their homes to others.

According to estimates by the Ministry of Labor, in the mid-1980s as many as 134,000 employees a year from firms employing 1,000 or more people were accepting transfers that made it necessary to leave their families behind. Of these employees, 30 percent were men in their forties and 40 percent men in their fifties. Three out of four companies provided special expense allowances to help with the costs of maintaining separate households. Nevertheless, there remained severe emotional hardships for all members of the families concerned as a result of having to live apart. Increasing numbers of companies were recognizing these hardships by offering their employees the alternative of refusing to accept such transfers in exchange for limitations on their chances for future advancement.

IWADARE Hiroshi

Yaguchi Kōichi (1920–)

Eleventh chief justice of the Japanese Supreme Court. Born in Kyōto Prefecture. Yaguchi graduated from the Faculty of Law at Kyōto University. He served as chief judge on the Urawa District Court and the Tōkyō Family Court, as secretary-general of the Supreme Court, and as chief judge on the Tōkyō High Court. He became an associate justice on the Supreme Court in 1984 and chief justice in 1985. He was an able bureaucrat, having worked at the general secretariat of the Supreme Court for 24 years.

Yamaguchi Kayō (1899–1984)

Japanese-style (NIHONGA) painter. Real name Yamaguchi Yonejirō. Known for his paintings of birds and flowers and of animals. Born in Kyōto, Yamaguchi graduated from the Kyōto Municipal School of Fine Arts and Crafts (now Kyōto City University of Arts). In 1916, the year he enrolled in the school, his painting *Nichigo* (Noon) was selected for exhibition at the BUNTEN (Ministry of Education Fine Arts Exhibition). After graduating he studied with TAKEUCHI SEIHŌ (1864–1942). He taught at his alma mater from 1926 to 1949. He became a member of the Japan Art Academy in 1971 and received the Order of Culture in 1981. His best-known paintings include *Yōkenzu* (1937, Western Dogs), *Kurohyō* (1954, Black Leopards), and *Kouma* (1955, Colts; winner of the Japan Art Academy Prize in 1956).

Yamashita Yasuhiro (1957–)

Jūdō expert (*jūdōka*). Born in Kumamoto Prefecture. Graduated from Tōkai University. Yamashita was an open category gold medalist in *jūdō* at the 1984 Los Angeles Olympics. In 1985 he established a record by winning the All-Japan Jūdō Championship for the ninth time in succession. The same year he retired from active competition to devote himself to teaching at Tōkai University. Yamashita began learning *jūdō* while in the fourth grade of elementary school. As a freshman in high school he won the All-Japan High-School Championship. In 1977, at the age of 19, he became the youngest contestant ever to win the All-Japan Jūdō Championship. His special techniques include *newaza*, *ōsotogari*, and *hidari uchimata*. He received the government's People's Honor Award in 1984.

yambaru tenaga kogane

(*yambaru* long-armed scarab beetle). *Cheirotonus jambar* Y. Kurosawa. Japan's largest native beetle, first recorded in 1984 in the northern part of the island of Okinawa. The male ranges from 47 to 62 millimeters (1.85 to 2.44 in) in length, the female from 46 to 57 millimeters (1.81 to 2.25 in). The head and pronotum are a gold green or bronze green, and the elytra is black with a greenish tinge, leaving a few dull brownish or yellowish patches along the suture and margin. The larvae are found among flakes of decaying wood that have accumulated in the hollows of old oak trees. It takes an estimated three to four years for the eggs to develop into mature insects. *Yambaru*, the name of the beetle, is an Okinawan dialect word for the terrace-like hills in the northern part of the island.

Yasukuni Shrine official visit controversy

YASUKUNI SHRINE, which is dedicated to the spirits of Japan's war dead, was used by the government during World War II to promote nationalism. Since article 20, paragraph 3, of Japan's postwar constitution prohibits the state from engaging in any religious activity, and since article 89 prohibits state support of any religious institution, postwar prime ministers and cabinet ministers had refrained from making visits to the shrine in their official capacity as ministers of state. In a statement issued in November 1980 the government had still taken the position that official visits "in the capacity of prime minister or minister of state" would be avoided because of undeniable doubts as to their constitutionality. However, in 1985, the Council on the Issue of Visits by Cabinet Ministers to Yasukuni Shrine, a private advisory body to Prime Minister NAKASONE YASUHIRO (b 1918), issued a report claiming that official visits to the shrine were constitutional. On the basis of this report, Prime Minister Nakasone paid the first official visit by a prime minister to Yasukuni Shrine since World War II on 15 August 1985, the anniversary of the end of the war. Instead of the usual private donation of money for the offering of a sacred branch (*tamagushi*), he donated approximately ¥30,000 (US $126) of public funds as "flower-offering money," and registered as "Nakasone Yasuhiro, Prime Minister." The issue of official visits to the shrine became part of a growing domestic and international debate on the possible remilitarization of Japan, another issue in which was a proposed abrogation of the limit on defense spending to one percent of Japan's gross national product. In China demonstrations were held to protest the official visit to the shrine.

NAKAMURA Kiichi

Yoshiki Masao (1908–)

Naval architect. Born in Hyōgo Prefecture. Graduated from Tōkyō University. Yoshiki taught at Tōkyō University from 1930, becoming professor emeritus in 1968. He became president of the Science University of Tōkyō in 1982. Yoshiki is internationally known for his research on the strengths and optimal positioning of oil tanker bulkheads in order to develop lighter and larger ships and to make large ships more economical. The range of his research is wide, including such fields as the strength of materials, destructive forces, welding, and ship engineering. He received the Japan Academy Prize in 1966 and the Order of Culture in 1982.

Yotsukaidō

City in northern Chiba Prefecture. A former town, Yotsukaidō assumed city status in 1981. Yotsukaidō became an important transportation point in the EDO PERIOD (1600–1868). Its name (literally, "four roads") derives from the fact that it was situated at the intersection of two highways—the Sakura Kaidō and Narita Kaidō. An army training camp was established nearby in the early part of the Meiji period (1868–1912), and Yotsukaidō afterwards developed as an army-base town. Housing projects (*danchi*) were constructed here in the 1970s, and an industrial complex was completed in 1982, both contributing to a rapid growth in population. Peanuts and pears are grown here, though the number of farmers is declining year by year. The expressway to the New Tōkyō International Airport passes through the city. Pop: 67,007.

Yuri-2a

A broadcasting satellite launched by the National Space Development Agency of Japan (NASDA) on 23 January 1984. The satellite transmits television signals from space to 420,000 Japanese homes in areas with restricted video and audio reception, including remote islands such as the Ogasawara Islands and mountainous regions, and also to the six million urban homes which experience reception disturbances because of the proximity of high-rise buildings. The *Yuri-2a* had been scheduled to relay two-channel satellite broadcasting by the Japan Broadcasting Corporation (NHK); however, transponder failure resulted in only one channel's being available, and another broadcasting satellite, the *Yuri-2b*, was launched on 12 February 1986.

NISHIMATA Souhei

INDEX

All cross references in this supplement (words printed in SMALL CAPITALS) refer to articles in the 9-volume edition of the *Encyclopedia of Japan*, not to other articles in the supplement.

updated biographical imformation

A number of people listed in the Kodansha Encyclopedia of Japan have died since the original nine volumes were prepared. To keep the encyclopedia's information as current as possible, those people, along with their years of birth and death, are listed below in alphabetical order.

Amino Kiku (1900–1978)
Arakawa Toyozō (1894–1985)
Ariyoshi Sawako (1931–1984)
Ayukawa Nobuo (1920–1986)
Crawford, Sir John Grenfell (1910–1984)
Fujiyama Aiichirō (1897–1985)
Fukumoto Kazuo (1894–1983)
Genji Keita (1912–1985)
Gotō Ryūnosuke (1889–1984)
Hara Yasusaburō (1884–1982)
Hasegawa Kazuo (1908–1984)
Hori Ryūjo (1897–1984)
Ishikawa Tatsuzō (1905–1985)
Ishizaka Yōjirō (1900–1986)
Katō Tōkurō (1898–1985)
Kawaguchi Matsutarō (1899–1985)
Kawasaki Chōtarō (1901–1985)
Kihara Hitoshi (1893–1986)
Kodama Yoshio (1911–1984)
Koga Issaku (1899–1982)
Kon Hidemi (1903–1984)
Kōno Kenzō (1901–1983)
Kuwada Yoshinari (1882–1981)
Liao Chengzhi (Liao Ch'eng-chih) (1908–1983)
Maeda Yoshinori (1906–1983)
Maekawa Kunio (1905–1986)
Minobe Ryōkichi (1904–1984)
Mizushima San'ichirō (1899–1983)
Morito Tatsuo (1888–1984)
Murano Tōgo (1891–1984)
Nagano Shigeo (1900–1984)
Nagata Masaichi (1906–1985)
Nakamura Kusatao (1901–1983)
Nakano Shigeharu (1902–1979)
Nakanoshima Kin'ichi (1904–1984)
Nakano Yoshio (1903–1985)
Nitta Isamu (1899–1984)
Nogami Yaeko (1885–1985)
Noma Shōichi (1911–1984)
Okabe Kinjirō (1896–1984)
Ono Seiichirō (1891–1986)
Pridi Phanomyong (1900–1983)
Sakisaka Itsurō (1897–1985)
Sakurada Ichirō (1904–1986)
Sakurada Takeshi (1904–1985)
Sasaki Kōzō (1900–1985)
Serizawa Keisuke (1895–1984)
Setō Shōji (1891–1977)
Shibuya Tengai (1906–1983)
Shimmei Masamichi (1898–1984)
Shirai Seiichi (1905–1983)
Takii Kōsaku (1894–1984)
Tamiya Hiroshi (1903–1984)
Tamura Taijirō (1911–1983)
Taniguchi Masaharu (1893–1985)
Tashiro Shigeki (1890–1981)
Uemura Naomi (1941–1984)
Uemura Tamaki (1890–1982)
Umehara Ryūzaburō (1888–1981)
Watanabe Tetsuzō (1885–1980)
Yamagata Masao (1898–1981)
Yamamoto Satsuo (1910–1983)
Yamate Kiichirō (1899–1978)
Yoshida Seiichi (1908–1984)

Contributors

Asai Kiyoshi	Professor, Department of Letters and Education, Ochanomizu University, Tōkyō, Japan
Fukushima Yasuto	Dean for Security Affairs, National Defense College, Tōkyō, Japan
Furuno Masami	Editor, The Kyōdō News Service, Tōkyō, Japan
Hayashi Hikaru	Research Director, Hakuhōdō Institute of Life & Living Inc, Tōkyō, Japan
Hosoya Chihiro	Vice-President, International University of Japan, Niigata Prefecture, Japan
Ikeda Minoru	Senior Research Officer, Economic Planning Agency, Tōkyō, Japan
Iwadare Hiroshi	Staff Writer, *Asahi shimbun*, Tōkyō, Japan
Komano Yōko	Commentator
Konaka Yōtarō	Writer
Kunimasa Takeshige	Staff Writer, *Asahi shimbun*, Tōkyō, Japan
Kurahashi Tōru	Research Officer, Economic Planning Agency, Tōkyō, Japan
Matsumoto Katsumi	Director, New Media Center, The Kyōdō News Service, Tōkyō, Japan
Matsuo Hikaru	Teacher, Kanagawa Gakuen, Kanagawa Prefecture, Japan
Nakamura Kiichi	Professor, Department of Sociology, Tsukuba University, Ibaraki Prefecture, Japan
Ninomiya Masato	Attorney, São Paulo, Brazil
Nishikawa Masao	Research Officer, Economic Planning Agency, Tōkyō, Japan
Nishimata Souhei	Science Editor, The Kyōdō News Service, Tōkyō, Japan
Nomura Jirō	Staff Writer, *Asahi shimbun*, Tōkyō, Japan
Nose Takayuki	Professor, Department of Public Health, School of Medicine, Tottori University, Tottori Prefecture, Japan
Ōmori Takashi	First Secretary, Japanese Delegation to the OECD, Paris, France
Senda Akihiko	Drama Critic
Shiina Kazuo	Head of Japanese Studies Department, The Japan Foundation, Tōkyō, Japan
Tanaka Tsutomu	Deputy Director-General, Economic Planning Agency, Tōkyō, Japan
Uchihashi Katsuto	Commentator
Yamagishi Shunsuke	Writer, *Asahi shimbun*, Tōkyō, Japan
Yasuhara Norikazu	Deputy Director, Economic Planning Agency, Tōkyō, Japan
Yoshikawa Kaoru	Expert in Improvement of National Accounts, National Economic Development Board, Bangkok, Thailand

Hakuhōdō Institute of Life & Living Inc, Tōkyō, Japan

Japan Association of Museums, Tōkyō, Japan

Photographs

Chiba Katsusuke
FANUC, LTD
Japanese National Railways
Kabukiza
Matsuyama Ballet Company
National Aerospace Laboratory
Sankaijuku

Editorial Staff

Administrative Director
Fujita Minoru
Executive Editor
Alan Campbell
Managing Editors
Takekawa Toshio (Tōkyō Office)
Okazaki Noriyuki (New York Office)
Senior Editor
Suzuki Setsuko
Assistant Editor
Patricia Galloway
Editorial Assistant
Osaku Taiko
Researcher
Toshiko M. Dahlby
Editorial Consultant
Kokubo Takeshi

Art and Design
Sugiura Kōhei

Kodansha Encyclopedia of Japan (Supplement)

英文日本大百科事典(補遺)

定価——3,000円

昭和61年11月27日　第1刷発行

監　修————————エドウィン・O・ライシャワー, 都留重人 他
発行者————————野間惟道
発行所————————株式会社　講談社
　　　　　　　　　　東京都文京区音羽2-12-21(〒112)
　　　　　　　　　　電話　東京 (03)945-1111(大代表)

組　版————————大日本印刷株式会社
印刷所————————大日本印刷株式会社
製本所————————和田製本工業株式会社
表紙箔押————————株式会社　金栄堂
本文用紙————————北越製紙株式会社

N.D.C 033 64p 29cm
落丁本・乱丁本は，小社書籍製作部宛にお送りください。
送料小社負担にてお取替えいたします。
ⒸKODANSHA 1986 Printed in Japan
ISBN4-06-144540-5 (0)